EDUCATION AND HUMAN RESOURCE DEVELOPMENT

EDUCATION AND HUMAN RESOURCE DEVELOPMENT

Edited by

VIJAYA KUMARI KAUSHIK
S.R. SHARMA

S.D. INSTITUTE OF RURAL TECHNOLOGY AND CULTURE, NEW DELHI

&

ANMOL PUBLICATIONS PVT. LTD.
NEW DELHI - 110 002 (INDIA)

ANMOL PUBLICATIONS PVT. LTD.
4374/4B, Ansari Road, Daryaganj
New Delhi - 110 002
Ph.: 23261597, 23278000
Visit us at: www.anmolpublications.com

Education and Human Resource Development

ISBN 81-7488-519-6

PRINTED IN INDIA

Published by J.L. Kumar for Anmol Publications Pvt. Ltd., New Delhi - 110 002 and Printed at Mehra Offset Press, Delhi.

Contents

1

What is Educational Development

Development is a euphemism for fund raising. But it also connotes that, contrary to some popular beliefs, success in fund raising is not merely due to the activities of a charismatic president or a championship football team and requires a great deal of thought, organization and development.

It is also big business. In 1975–76, when voluntary support of American colleges and universities rose by 11% (the largest annual increase in a decade), more than $2.4 billion were received from business, foundations, and individuals. Among the major recipients were Harvard University, $59,025,806; University of California, $57,480,517; Stanford University, $41,759,938; Yale University, $37,724,243; University of Rochester, $33,577,123; University of Pennsylvania, $31,676,698; Columbia University, $30,122,556; University of Minnesota, $127,105,899; Case-Western Reserve University, $26,637,746; and University of Chicago, #26,614,127. Recalling the discussion on the diminishing difference between public and private or independent institutions in the section on Financing Higher Education, it is interesting to note that among these leading recipients are one quasi-public and two clearly public institutions.

There are, in fact, at least three major kinds of fund raising campaigns that take place at an institution, each of them quite distinct. There is the major campaign, the ongoing annual givers campaign, and the efforts to obtain funding from federal and private foundation sources. All should be part of a carefully orchestrated plan and the activities associated with them made known to all of those who are concerned with the governance of the institution.

THE CAPITAL CAMPAIGN

The major capital campaign can produce a very substantial influx of funds within a relatively short time frame (capital campaigns can be initially planned to extend over several years and will, at times, be subsequently extended beyond the time initially contemplated because of failure to meet campaign goals). The capital campaign is usually, but not necessarily, related to a specific objective or set of objectives and, in many instances, may coincide with some special event that tends to enhance its appeal and give focus to the campaign. Its major thrust is a targeted sum of money to be obtained largely through one-time major gifts. It can be anticipated that a small fraction of the donors-will produce in excess of 60% of the total dollars, and most of this will come, or be pledged, in the first six months of the campaign.

The launching of a capital campaign is not to be taken lightly. It demands a very intensive activity and extensive commitments from many people. To some extent, it conflicts with the ongoing givers campaign, although, when used properly, it can be a source for identifying staunch regular donors.

A major capital campaign should be preceded by a market analysis that seeks to determine an appropriate campaign goal, as well as whether the campaign is likely to succeed or not. The answer might be negative simply because the timing (e.g., the current status of the economy) may not be right. In this connection it is also not unusual for institutions to defer the formal announcement of a campaign until they have secured sufficient pledges to serve both as a stimulus to the campaign and to insure its likely success.

In some instances, institutions engage consulting firms that specialize in this kind of market analysis to assist them in making an advance assessment before launching a campaign. Among the considerations involved in determining whether to use such assistance are the size of the campaign and the nature and availability of university resources. The general guidelines outlined in the discussion on the use of consultants are equally applicable here.

However, the use of consulting assistance in the development area is sufficiently widespread to warrant a few additional words. In this area, perhaps more than in most others, it is imperative to determine before hiring a consultant, what it is that the consultant is to do. What they cannot do is reasonably clear. Consultants should not be expected to identify specific prospects, nor should they be expected to raise funds. In fact, internal development staff does not truly raise funds, but instead facilitates the process by which the President and other key figures who personify the institutions raise funds.

Some institutions need counsel to help them develop new approaches to fund raising. Others need an objective, comprehensive and systematic analysis of their potential and the identification of new sources of support. A facet of this takes the form of individualized prospect research or the preparation of campaign promotional and communication materials. Consultants can assist an institution to establish a properly functioning development organization (including recruitment and training of key personnel), or they can accelerate the learning process of existing staff members. Finally, consultants frequently play a significant role in the management of a major capital campaign or in the management of a significant fund raising event associated either with a capital campaign or with an ongoing program.

ANNUAL GIVERS CAMPAIGN

The ongoing annual givers program is frequently thought of as an alumni plan. While, undoubtedly, alumni constitute a natural and primary source of repetitive giving, there are many other "friends" of the institution that can be regarded a potential repetitive donors. Statistics suggest that any donor who makes a substantial gift (substantial should be defined for these purposes in relation to the donor's means), can be counted upon to make repeat donations as many as six to eight times. But these are not automatic.

An annual givers program is not normally conducted with the same degree of intensity as a major capital campaign, but requires an equally high degree of organization. Both require a high degree of familiarity with tax and estate law, particularly if the institution is to make full utilization of deferred giving programs.

There are a variety of deferred giving techniques. Among them, the charitable remainder UNTRUST has considerable appeal to donors and to the done institution. In general, the characteristics of these trusts are that:

- The donor irrevocably transfers money, property, or both to the trustee (either the institution itself or some other entity, frequently a bank), who invests and reinvests the assets as a separate fund;
- Donor (and/or other designated beneficiary) receives an amount each year determined by multiplying a fixed percent, say five percent, by the fair market value of the trust assets, valued each year. Any income not paid out is added to principal. If income is insufficient to pay the required amount, capital gains or principal make up the deficit;
- On the donor's death, death of other designated beneficiary, or expiration of the term of the trust, payment terminate and the then assets of the UNITRUST are the absolute property of the designated charitable remainderman.

Clearly, this type of giving enables the donor to continue to enjoy the benefits of the income from an amount he plans ultimately to donate, either for himself or a designated beneficiary. At the same time, he secures immediate tax advantages, relinquishes the burden and the risk of investing the funds in question, prevents the dissipation of the principal by family members who may be incapable of managing funds, and protects against the creditors of the donor and beneficiary. For the institution, this form of deferred giving provides certainty as to the gift and, in some instances, may provide an immediate income, over the above the return committed to the donor or beneficiary during the life of the trust.

However, institutions should be conscious of the administrative requirements associated with this type of program. They should also be aware that agreements governing this type of trust should not be entered into without benefit of legal advice, and those acting for the institution must be fully current on applicable state and federal law. Trustees, in particular, must be conscious of the fact that these trust agreements impose special fiduciary responsibilities.

FEDERAL AND PRIVATE SOURCE OF FUNDING

Pursuit of federal and private foundation sources of funding is frequently relegated to the research administration function because these sources are normally drawn upon most frequently to support faculty research. (See discussion on sponsored activity in Chapter Six.) Professional "grants-men" may be found, both in full-time positions on many campuses, or in the ranks of outside consultants. Such individuals, can, in some instances, play an important role. The art of proposal writing can be overstated and its needs can normally be readily accommodated within the institution; i.e., it is not difficult to find assistance within the institution if the preparation of an articulate grant proposal is truly a difficult chore for a faculty member. Normally, however, the difficulty in articulation is symptomatic of a faulty conceptualization of the project to be undertaken. The special value of "grantsmanship" assistance lies in connection with those funding sources, particularly private foundations, where the priorities and interests that will govern the award process are not fully discernible from published materials.

GENERAL OBSERVATION

There are a number of general observations that are applicable in varying degrees to all three of the types of fund raising activities touched on above. First, mission evaluation, in addition to being essential to the survival of the institution in the marketplace, is extremely relevant to fund raising. While some donors will undoubtedly support the institution because of sentimental association with it as an entity, support will come predominantly from those who identify with the institution's mission, or some aspect of it. This does not mean that an institution should gear its activities to the interests of potential donors. Quite to the contrary, it should be wary of undertaking commitments that are essentially incompatible with the nature and long-range goals of the institution simply because funding support for those commitments is available.

On the other hand, the self-evaluation that should be an ongoing process with any institution should, necessarily, include questions that are pertinent to fund raising. To what interests are we appealing when we ask donors for support? Which are our special attributes as an institution that can persuade prospective donors that we merit their support? Can we define the types of donor to whom our mission and programs would be most appealing? Have we done an adequate job of articulating for ourselves and for our prospective donors what our institution is all about?

An information system is essential to any effective and comprehensive fund raising program. At a minimum, such a system should: assist in monitoring payments against pledges; trigger congratulatory notes or cards to major donors on appropriate occasions and trigger repeat requests to past donors at appropriate intervals. In addition, a cataloging of donor interests that can be accessed on a timely basis can facilitate an intelligently targeted approach in the annual program. For example, donors who have an identified interest in a particular subject area can be viewed as potential supporters of an academic chair in that discipline area. A means of courting such donors is to invite their attendance at special lectures or colloquia related to the subject matter of their interest.

Developing sources for potentially significant or major donors requires extensive research beyond the review of alumni lists. Some very basic resources include:

- Who's Who in America
- Regional *Who's Who* and also local and national professional directories (for doctors, engineers, lawyers, et al.)
- *Poor's Directory and the Directory of Directors*
- *Dun and Bradstreet's Directory of Corporate Executives*

Social registers, where available
City and state directories of business and professional firms
The Foundation Directory

Other useful publications include *The Wall Street Journal, The New York Times, Business Week* and others. The aggressive and informed development staff will probably subscribe to a clipping service to maintain current information relative to its major donors, present and prospective.

Because donors have special interests, they will tend to condition their gifts in many ways. They will frequently designate a specific purpose for the gift. Or they may restrict the gift to the maintenance of the principal and the use of interest income only. Institutional representatives must be imaginative, forceful and persuasive to seek to minimize the conditions imposed by donors, because unrestricted funds quite obviously have the most utility for the institution. Since, as noted above, appeals for support must frequently, be made on the basis of special interests, it is frequently not possible to obtain a completely unconditional donation. Under those circumstances a second desirable alternative is for the institution to seek donations in those areas which relieve the institution of current operating costs (or more precisely, provide income to support such costs). Scholarships support is one of the more obtainable forms of support and generates tuition income. Support for an academic chair provides in important relief in the faculty salary area.

Development is one of three major funding sources (Endowment Fund Management, and Student Recruitment being the other two) in higher education management that require particular focus in today's difficult financial climate. This is especially true of the smaller institutions, many of which are struggling for survival and many of which handle the three areas of activity cited in a less than fully effective way.

The smaller institutions generally cannot afford the investment for the highly skilled management required in these areas and paradoxically they are most in need of such skills. On the other hand, some small institutions have a proportionately large staff investment in these activities, relative to their overall resources. But it is an investment that is frequently not producing an adequate return.

Reporting relationships is a key element in determining the effectiveness of the development operation. Does the development officer report directly to the President? The President is frequently the chief fund raiser for the institution but rarely has the time to exercise meaningful supervision over the development office. Or does he report to someone who can assess his performance and guide him in the application of his specialized skills in the most productive manner?

Participation is another key ingredient to the effectiveness of a development officer and the programs he establishes. This has two facets.

First is the participation of the development officer. Is he afforded sufficient participation in the mainstream of the institutions activities to enable him to acquire the degree of familiarity and understanding that permits him to speak of the institution with conviction and persuasiveness? Although development officers are in a very real sense engaged in "selling" the institutions to prospective donors, some development officers have little or no understanding of the product they are selling; i.e., they do not know the qualities that make the institutions unique and give it its special identity. Relating back to the discussion on donor restriction, development officers are frequently not given a sufficient understanding of the various programs and the nuances of financing them to deal effectively with funding sources to secure funds in the way they can be used best.

Another facet of participation relates to those who participate in the development activity. Such participation should not be, but frequently is, confined largely to the development officer and the president. The president, as the principal, most prestigious, and often the most articulate spokesman for the institution, will necessarily be involved in fund raising activities, particularly in relation to major sources of funding. But Presidents tend to be overused, particularly when the development officer is lazy or unimaginative or the president has a particular predilection for fund raising.

Trustees should have a key role in the development activity. This does not mean that they should be selected on the basis of their donations (although such a practice is by no means unheard of). But it is not unreasonable to expect them to contribute in accordance with their means as a reflection of their interest in the institution. In the absence of this kind of example, support from donors more removed from the institution is much more difficult to obtain.

It is important to recognize that the trustees constitute the key link to the business community from which a major portion of the institution's contributions will be derived. With their wide and influential circle of contracts, trustees can be highly successful fund raisers for the institution, if stimulated to play this role and provided with sufficient information as to institutional needs.

It is in part for this reason that institutions frequently establish a trustee's subcommittee on development. Such a subcommittee will work closely with the development officer, will receive periodic reports on the various aspects of development activity, including collection of pledges, and will have a role in the formulation of development campaigns.

Generally, the faculty constitutes a major untapped source for participation in fund raising activity. Even in the area of seeking research support, an area most directly of interest to faculty members, many institutions lack a systematic program for stimulating faculty participation. This is even more true of other aspects of fund raising.

Yet, faculty have the motivation or can be motivated, to raise funds, if not for the general use of the institution, then for their specific departments. This is recognized at those institutions that employ the budgeting concept of "every tub on its own bottom" (see discussion on Budgeting in Chapter 8) where each department is encouraged to generate its own funds as a means of initiating new programs or sustaining program initiatives.

Faculty members also have the ability to be highly persuasive fund raisers, since they will be the most articulate spokesmen for the programs in which they are involved and because they are apt to have made lasting impression on some former students who are now highly successful and may be viewed as sources for direct contributions and contract to other potential donors. It should be noted in this connection that assistance in fund raising need not be confined to alumni. One institution (in fact a public institution) has been very successful in establishing a national network of "friends," none of them alumni, who are active and effective fund raisers for the institution.

In summary, the development activity is vital to the private institution and of growing important to the publics. The competition for support among a wide range of eleemosynary institutions has become more keen, placing a high premium on effective fund raising. At least four key ingredients to effective fund raising are information, organization, participation, and mission evaluation.

2

Theory of Human Development

Attribution theory is the term given to the various theories concerned with the study of how people in everyday life figure out what causes their own behaviours and that of others, and what causes events. Social psychologists have typically conceptualized the attribution process as one in which a naive person first observes a behaviour or an event and then on the basis of past experience, available information, and/on motivational tendency forms a cognition called attribution about why an event or a behaviour occurred. Attributions are considered to be necessary for the understanding, organization and formation of meaningful perspectives about myriad events which people observe every day. Furthermore, the main tenet of attribution theory is that individuals' emotional, cognitive, and behavioural reactions are based on their causal explanations of why people behave the way they do. This assumptions implies that attribution theorists believe that individuals react in accordance to a way they perceive and understand their world.

Attribution theory grew out of the area of person perception. But, whereas person perception deals with the description of the stimulus person, attribution theory focuses on the loci of causality of the person's behaviour. Nevertheless, both areas assume that the outcome of perception or attribution is subjective. The contributions to attribution theory have focused on four major issues: (a) What are the antecedents of an attribution? (b) What are the contents of the attributions process? (c) What are the processes through which people make attributions? and (d) What are the consequences of the attributions? During the 1970s the study of attribution became one of the central areas of investigation in social psychology. This growing up occurred since the process of attribution has been related to a wide range of psychological functioning—from interpretation of internal states including perception of emotion, freedom, psychological arousal, and attitudes to strategic choices in interpersonal conflict setting and evaluation of help giving. Moreover, principles of attribution theory have been utilized to analyze different psychological phenomena such as aggression, attraction, moral judgment, learned helplessness, or close relationships (see Harvey et al. 1976, 1977, 1981).

At present, attribution theory consists mostly of a series of fragmented sets of explanations or descriptions pertaining to specific cases of attribution (Kelley and Michele 1980). In this respect the term "attribution theory" may be misleading, since a general inclusive theory has yet to appear. The pioneering work by Heider (1958) and the later works by Jones and his colleagues (Jones and Davis 1965, Jones and McGillis 1976) and by Kelley (1967, 1972a, 1972b) are considered among the most influential contributions to the study of attributions.

NAIVE PSYCHOLOGY OF HEIDER

Fritz Heider is considered to be the father of attribution theory. He was born in 1896 in Vienna, Austria. He studied with several of the major Gestalt psychologists in Germany, and this Gestalt influence is evident in his work. He came to the United States in 1930 and spent many years arguing in vain against the prevailing behavioural perspective within American psychology. First in a paper on phenomenological causality in 1944 and then in an extensive discussion on the phenomenology of social perception published in a book (1958), Heider laid the foundations for many of the basic concepts in attribution theory. His analysis is phrased in commonsense language, and Heider calls his psychology naive psychology of attribution (Schneider et al. 1979). The first is that an adequate understanding of a person's behaviour is contingent on the description of how this person perceives and describes his or her social world. Second, Heider assumes that people desire to predict and control their environment. People want to be able to anticipate the effects that their own and others' behaviour will have on other people, on the environment, and on themselves. This goal can be achieved if people are able to interpret and infer the casual antecedents of behaviours. Third, Heider believes that there are some basic similarities between object and person perception. Predictability in the social world is achieved by the same processes that are involved in perception of the physical world. For both cases, people look for enduring or dispositional properties in others to explain particular behaviour.

Central to Heider's theoretical position is the proposition that people perceive events as being caused and that the causal locus can be either in the actor or in the environment. In Heider's analysis, an action outcome or effect is perceived to be an additive function of the effective environmental force and the effective personal force. Personal force is seen as a multiplicative function of the actor's power and motivation. According to Heider, power is determined primarily by ability, although other characteristics may affect a person's power. The motivational factor refers to a person's intention (what they are trying to do) and exertion (how hard they are trying to do something). One of the most important decisions the perceiver makes is an estimate of the extent to which the internal rather than the environmental force was responsible for the effect of a person's actions. But Heider further suggests that individuals go beyond the person-environment discrimination to differentiate between personal and impersonal causality. Personal causality refers to those instances of internal causality when a person intentionally produces an outcome. Impersonal causality refers to externally caused effects and to effects that are caused by a person unintentionally. The intentions of the person are important aspects of the perceiver's attribution.

In his theorizing, Heider assumed that lay persons can rationally analyze the causes of their own and other's behaviours. However, he pointed out that sometimes people make attributions that are based on insufficient information or on inadequate analysis of information, or they reflect the person's own psychological needs and motivations as opposed to an objective and logical assessment of available information. The contribution by Heider represents a profound set of observations based on brilliant armchair insights about commonsense attributional behaviour. Though it has not served as a basis for much empirical work, it had immense influence on more systematic theorizing on attribution by Jones and his colleagues, Kelley, Bem, Weiner, and others whose works have provided bases for specific predictions regarding attributional reactions.

THEORY OF CORRESPONDENT INFERENCES

Jones and Davis (1965) entered their attributional ideas into the realm of person perception: how the perceiver tries to infer what effect the actor intended to produce with his or her acts and how those inferred intentions are used to infer dispositional properties of the actor. In making these inferences, individuals tend to identify different action alternatives that the actor did not choose and compare their possible effects with the effects of the chosen action. The perceiver sorts through those effects of the chosen action which would not have occurred if the actor had chosen any other alternative action. The perceiver assumed that, on the one hand, the actor wanted to avoid the negative noncommon effects of the unchosen alternatives, but on the other hand, the actor especially wanted to achieve the positive noncommon effects of the chosen action. The negative noncommon effects of the unchosen alternatives plus the positive noncommon effects of the chosen action provide much information which serve as a basis for attributing dispositions. In this case, the observer can be to a large extent certain that the actor's behaviour reflected an underlying disposition, that is, there is correspondence of inference. To illustrate the process described above, it is possible to consider the case of the teacher inferring why the very good high-school senior has applied to a mediocre college in the vicinity. The teacher may decide that the student could apply to the best colleges in the country which will require much effort in comparison to the selected college. In addition, the selected college enables the student to be close to his or her home. Since mediocre colleges are in other parts of the country as well, the teacher may infer that the student is very attached to his or her family and, therefore, wanted to choose a college close to home. Two factors increase an individual's tendency to make dispositional attributions: (a) hedonic relevance, which refers to the extent to which a person's actions are rewarding or costly to the perceived; and (b) personalism, which refers to the perceived intentionality of a person's actions to the perceiver.

In a more recent theoretical paper, Jones and McGillis (1976) have made some additions to correspondent inference theory. They stress that correspondence will be increased to the extent that behaviour departs from what the perceiver expects the stimulus person to do. According to Jones and McGillis, there are two general sources of expectations about others. Category-based expectancies are based on an individual's knowledge about what particular kinds of people are like, similar to the process of stereotyping. Target-based expectancies are gained from knowledge about a particular actor.

Covariation Model and Causal Schemata Model

Two particularly influential models were suggested by Kelley (1967, 1972a, 1972b). While the first model, the covariation model, deals with cases in which the perceiver has information regarding the event, or behaviour, the second model, the causal schemata model, deals with cases of a single observation with little information.

The first model (Kelley 1967) uses the principle of covariation which states that the effect is attributed to a cause which is present when the effect occurs and is absent when the effect does not occur. The principle implies temporal contiguity. The notion of covariation was used to examine variations in effect with respect to entities, persons, time, and modalities of interaction with the entity. Presenting his covariation model, Kelley argued that people often make causal attributions as if they were analyzing data patterns by means of analysis of variance, a statistical technique of examining the effect of an independent variable on a dependent variable. On the basis of this technique, kelley theorized the conditions under which individuals attribute the causes of an event to the person or to the environment. Specifically, he suggested that people assess causality for a particular behaviour by using four criteria more or less automatically and simultaneously. They check (a) distinctiveness across entitles (was the response made uniquely to this entity and not to others?); (b) consensus (was the response made uniquely by this person, or did others respond similarly?); (c) consistency over time (was the response made consistently over time?), and (d) consistency over modality (was the response made consistently across different modalities of interaction with the entity?). Kelley hypothesized that attribution to the environment rather than to the person requires that the actor respond differentially for different entities, that the actor respond consistently over time and modalities, and that the person's response be in agreement with other people's response to this entity.

This analysis suggests that individuals act like scientists examining the various possible causes for a given effect. They look for a systematic pattern of relation and infer cause and effect relationship from those patterns. However, while the analysis of variance is appropriate for certain cases in which the person conducts a complete causal analysis on a basis of multiple observations, individuals do not always make attributions in this way. Often the individuals have a small of data and incomplete data patterns from a single observation. Under these circumstances individuals use more simplistic principles in their attribution process. Kelley (1972a) suggested that in these situations individuals use their causal schemata to infer causality.

A casual schema is a conception of the manner in which two or more causes relate to a particular kind of effect. A casual scheme is learned, stored in the memory, and then activated by environmental cues. It answers the attributor's need for economical and fast attributional analysis under situations offering limited information. Causal schemata allow causal sense to be made of the world, and they provide stability and organization to the perceived world. Examples of causal schemata are the multiple-sufficient scheme and the multiple-necessary scheme. The first one indicates that the presence of two or more causes are sufficient for the occurrence of the effect, and the second one implies that several causes are necessary for the effect to occur. Some of the schemas can be formalized in two principles. The discounting principle implies that if an individual perceives several possible causes for the actor's act and all of them are plausible, then he or she is less confident about which cause produced the effect (multiple-sufficient scheme). The augmentation principle implies that if there exists an inhibitory cause which prevents the effect from occurring, then the facilitative cause is perceived as very effective, if the effect occurs despite the inhibitory cause (compensatory schema).

SELF-PERCEPTION THEORY

Bem (1972) has suggested that a person's internal states, such as attitudes, beliefs, or emotions are not directly experienced, but may be arrived at via an attribution process similar in kind whereby the individual infers the internal states of another person. Calling this process self-perception, Bem posited that in situation in which internal cues are weak, ambiguous, or uninterpretable, individuals are in the same position as an outside observer and, therefore, have to rely on external cues to infer own internal states. This theory is in startling contradiction to the usual practice in psychology of assuming that behaviour is a consequence of awareness as reflected in attitudes, cognitions, or emotions. In this conception, people are strictly information processors without any motivational drives in their examination of their behaviour.

BIASES AND ERRORS

Although attribution theorists have compared individuals to naive scientists who, for the most part, make systematic use of available information in their attempts to explain their own or another person's behaviour, they have also acknowledged a possibility of biases and errors. In recent years empirical research has shown that attributions are often affected by systematic biases and errors. This line of research is based on assumptions that there exist known criteria of valid attributional inference and that there exist psychological factors that bias human attributional inference from such criteria.

It has been suggested that the various biases of attributional inference be classified as either motivational or cognitive in origin. Motivational biases are characterized by a tendency to form and hold beliefs that serve the individual's needs and desires. Individuals are said to avoid drawing inferences they find threatening, unpleasant, or incongruent and to prefer inferences that are satisfying, pleasing, or need congruent. Depending on the momentary salience of different needs, such motivational influences could presumably yield judgmental biases and errors. A number of motivational biases have been indicated. For example, investigators have argued that individuals are motivated to enhance and protect their egos. Thus, in situations of success they readily attribute it to themselves, but they tend to externalize failure. Also, it has been suggested that individuals are motivated to organize the perceived social events in a predictable and controllable manner. Thus, they tend to overestimate their control over events and to underestimate the role of uncontrollable factors.

Cognitive biases originate in human limitations to process information. These limitations are reflected in the strategies which direct people's attention to some types of information and hypotheses rather than to other types. As a result, individuals underestimate or disregard information relevant to this judgment in question. An example of cognitive bias occurs when individuals rely on information that is salient or available to them at the time they make their judgments. Thus, people may use information that is not representative of the population as a whole, tend to ignore consensus information of how other people act in the same situation, or tend to overestimate the importance of dispositional characteristics in others' behaviour. With regard to the latter bias, a theory by Jones and Nisbet (1972) is of special interest. They pointed out that people tend to attribute their own actions to the constraints of the situation but attribute the behaviour of others to their personalities. Two main reasons were identified for this bias. One reason is that actors have different information available than to observe. Actors know about their own past history and therefore have more consistency and distinctiveness data available to them, whereas observers typically have only consensus data. Another reason refers to differences in the salience of the various forms of information. The actors view their behaviour in the context of their past behaviour, so their variations in response to different situations are highly salient, making the possible environmental cause more salient. In contrast, observers view the behaviour of any particular actor in the context of how his or her behaviour differs from the behaviour of other people in that same situation. Therefore, the idiosyncratic factors in the actor are highly salient in explaining this behaviour.

A THEORY OF LAY EPISTEMOLOGY

Of special interest for attribution theory is a theory of lay epistemology by Kruglanski (1980). In this theory Kruglanski has attempted to formulate a general framework that allows the various attributional models to be considered in common theoretical terms. According to lay epistemology, attribution making is knowledge-seeking behaviour which follows a particular sequence, referred to as the epistemic process. Specifically, Kruglanski suggests that the epistemic process consists of two phases: problem formulation and problem resolution. In the phase of problem formulation the individual is motivated to gain knowledge regarding a specific question, for example, a question about cause. In the phase of problem resolution the individual deduces his or her inferences from certain premises in which he or she already happens to believe. This phase is governed by the principle of logical consistency. The epistemic process may be affected by different needs and/or desires of the individual as well as by the availability of hypotheses and/or information.

Attribution theory constitutes a special case of the epistemic question. A causal inference is render exactly in the same way as any other inference, by the principle of logical consistency. According to lay epistemology theory, various attributional models focus on specific cases of causal inferences without extracting a general principle.

DEVELOPMENT OF ATTRIBUTION INFERENCE

The study of causal thinking is not new in developmental psychology. Piaget (1930) devoted considerable effort to understanding children's causal thinking. But it was the appearance of attribution theorizing which provided the impetus for empirical research regarding the development of causal perception. It seems obvious that from the first years of life, children infer causality. their learning about cause-effect comes from two sources. First, agents of socialization communicate cause-effect relationships to children. Second, children themselves observe repeated reoccurrence of events from which they infer cause-effect relationship. But, in spite of the early use of attributions only in the late childhood do children become capable of comprehending the use of various principles of attribution.

Research has shown that young children are able to attribute an effect on a basis of a single observation. They attribute causality to those factors that are temporally contiguous, spatially proximal, physically similar, and antecedent to the effect. Studies have indicated that from as early an age as 3 years, children can identify causes on the basis of temporal order (covariation principle) as long as the task is simple, familiar, and does not require advanced verbal skills. The use of temporal order precedes the use of spatial contiguity as a basis for causal inference. Specifically, the use of the covariance principle deteriorates in the following situations: (a) when children observe a sequence of events that contains more than one cause-effect instance, (b) when the information is presented in a simple summary form, and (c) when a temporal delay between the cause and effect occurs. Also, they are willing to accept imperfect cause-effect covariation. In addition, it has been found that young children can combine multiple causes when predicting an effect and have less difficulty using an augmenting principle than in using a discounting principle. It is only during the first five years in school that the described difficulties seem to disappear and older children begin to apply various attributional principles with greater reliability and across a large set of task conditions (Sedlak and Kurtz 1981).

On the basis of empirical studies, three levels of development of attribution making have been identified. It has been found that at a very early age children behave as if they comprehend various principles before they can make appropriate judgments using self-report techniques. At the next level, children make schema displaying consistent causal judgment before they can explain the attributional logic underlying these responses. Finally, at the age of 10 or 11, children become able to articulate the underlying attributional principles (Kassin 1981).

APPLICATION OF ATTRIBUTION THEORY TO EDUCATION

Because the attribution process is believed to be an integral part of many of the most significant aspects of people's lives, its principles have been applied to the analysis of various real-life situations, ranging from a jury deliberating about whether to attribute the crime to circumstances or to the defendant's disposition to a teacher puzzling about whether the student failed because of lack of ability or lack of trying (e.g., Frieze et al. 1979, Antaki and Breisin 1982). Two attributional modes applied to education have instigated much empirical research. The first model deals with the relationship between attribution and achievement-related behaviour; the second model focuses on the development of intrinsic motivation by students.

Attributional Model of Achievement-related Behaviour

A model which has a direct implication for education is Weiner's attributional model of achievement-related behaviour (Weiner et al 1972, Weiner 1974). A classroom is a place where student's achievements are constantly evaluated and, therefore, the causal explanation of why students have failed or succeeded is an important question. The answer determines to a large extent the behaviour of students as well as of teachers. According to Weiner, causal perceptions of success and failure mediate between the antecedent conditions and achievement-related behaviour (Weiner 1974, Weiner et al. 1972).

Specifically, in his most recent formulation, Weiner (1979) has suggested that individuals use a variety of causes to explain their success or failure on achievement task. These causes can be classified along three dimensions. One dimension, locus of causality, differentiates the causes in terms of their internality/externality. while some causes,such as ability, effort, or mood, might be considered internal because they might be believed to originate within the person, other causes, such as luck, home conditions, or task difficulty, might be considered external because they might be believed to originate outside the person. The second dimension differentiates causes in terms of their stability over time. while some causes, such as mood, effort, or luck, may be considered unstable because they may be believed to fluctuate over time, other causes, such as ability, task difficulty, or home conditions may be considered as stable since they may be believed not to change over time. The third dimension differentiates causes in terms of their controllability. while some causes, such as effort, attention, or other's help, may be believed to be under the volitional control of the person, other causes, such as mood, luck, or ability, may be believed not to be under the volitional control of the person.

The above described dimensions have important consequences. They are related to individuals' cognitive reactions or expectations regarding future outcomes, affective reactions related to self- esteem, and behavioural reactions of achievement-related behaviour. Weiner (1974, 1979) has postulated that expectancy for future success is determined by the stability of the causes. Ascription of an outcome to unstable causes produces greater shifts in expectancy of achievement to the desired outcome than does ascription to stable causes. Failure at an achievement task attributed to unstable causes may result in expectations for eventual success, since unstable causes might change. Failure due to stable causes is expected to continue, since these causes are believed to remain. similarly, if success was attributed to stable causes, continued success would be expected.

The locus of causality dimension is an important determinant of affective reactions. Individuals who attribute their success to internal causes experience affects of price, competence, confidence, and satisfaction, while individuals who attribute failure to internal causes experience feelings of guilt and resignation.

Of special interest is the link between causal perception of success or failure and achievement-related behaviour. There is a substantial amount of evidence indicating that causal perception of success and failure influences the individual's persistence, intensity, and choice behaviour of achievement tasks. Individuals who tend to attribute their failure to unstable-controllable causes, such as effort, tend to persist long in failure situations. This attribution of a failure enables them to believe that there is a possibility of modifying the outcome in the future. Attribution of a failure to stable-uncontrollable causes does not leave the possibility of changing the outcome in the future and, therefore, there is no reason to persist. The belief in unstable-controllable causes, such as effort, causes the person to assume that the outcome depends on will. Therefore, these individuals perform with great intensity on achievement tasks. On the other hand, the belief is table or uncontrollable causes, such as ability or mood, does not motivate the person to perform with intensity, since there is belief in having control over the causes of success of failure. finally, it was found that individuals tend to prefer to perform task that are compatible with their causal perception. For example, students who generally attribute their achievement outcome to ability are likely to choose tasks in which competence is requisite to outcome. Conversely, students who tend to attribute their success to luck prefer tasks which depend on chance and avoid tasks requiring competence.

Finally, on the basis of Weiner's model (Weiner 1974) it was suggested that two general categories of antecedents influence causal perception of individuals: personal dispositions and available information. The personal dispositions category consists of three subcategories: (a) personality tendencies; (b) demographic influences; and (c) causal schemata. The available information consists of four subcategories: (a) own performance; (b) others' performance; (c) constraints and nature of the achievement task; (d) other's influence.

Recently, Bar-Tal (1979) extended Weiner's model to explain interpersonal interactions in the classroom. According to Bar-Tal, teachers as well as students make attributions regarding the successes and failures of their students. Thus, in the same way that student's causal perception of their own successes or failures is related to their achievement-related behaviour, the teacher's causal perception of their students' successes or failures is related to their behaviour towards their student through expectations regarding students' future achievements. Furthermore, the model suggests that teachers' behaviour greatly influences students' causal perception of their academic achievement, whereas students' achievement-related behaviours influence teachers' causal perception of students' academic outcomes.

An Attributional Model of Intrinsic Motivation

Lepper and Defoe (1979) applied the attributional model of intrinsic motivation to the classroom setting. This model has been based on Bem's (1972) self-perception theory. According to Lepper and and Defoe, students in the classroom make attributions regarding reasons for engaging in various activities. If a student who is engaged in an activity perceives his or her actions to be controlled by salient and powerful extrinsic contingencies such as a promise of tangible reward or the teacher's surveillance, he or she will be likely to attribute his or her behaviour to those extrinsic factors. But if such extrinsic constraints are not salient or are insufficient to explain this engagement in the activity, the student will attribute his or her behaviour to intrinsic factors. This conception implies that inappropriate use of tangible rewards in the classroom may have detrimental effects of performance and subsequent interest in the task. Offers of rewards in such situations may decrease students' intrinsic motivation to engage in this activity.

3

Creativity and Human Development

Although there may be agreement on what constitutes an act of creation as in the case of $E = mc^2$, the *David, the Eroica,* or for that matter even lesser works, there is disagreement regarding almost every aspect of its nature and development. Definitions vary; modes of identification vary; theories vary; research methods and results vary. Agreed upon only is that creative thinking is the highest of mental functions and creative production the peak of human achievement.

There is no universally accepted definition of creativity any more than there is of intelligence (Getzels and Dillon 1973, Barron and Harrington 1981). The most widely applied definitions may be classified according to the emphasis placed on the product, the process, or the experience of creativity. Some definitions are formulated in terms of a manifest product: it is novel and useful. The criterion here is a statistically infrequent tangible response or idea that is adaptive and sustained to fruition. Other definitions are formulated in terms of an underlying process; it is divergent yet productive. The focus is on the course of change and development in the psychic life of the creator leading to useful invention. Still other definitions are formulated in terms of a subjective experience: it is inspired and immanent. Creativity is defined by the flash of insight, the transcendent sensation itself, without reference to whether it will result in anything tangible. Definitions have also centred on the quality of the problem rather than the solution, the significant element in creation being the envisagement of the imaginative problem, for it is the fruitful question to which the novel solution is the response.

None of the existing definitions of creativity is immune from the objection that each omits some component vital to the others. A suggested omnibus definition of creative thinking is: the product has no novelty and value for the thinker or the culture; the thinking is unconventional, highly motivated, and persistent, or of great intensity; the task involves a clear formulation of an initially vague and undefined problem (Newell et al. 1962).

IDENTIFICATION

The indices or measures of creativity are as varied as the definitions (Getzels and Dillon 1973). In general,the numerous modes of identification may be classified into a half- dozen categories: tangible achievement, ratings, intelligence, personality, biographical characteristics, observation of performance, and psychometric assessment.

The most common mode of identification is by achievement. Deeds and thoughts which reflect manifestly superior accomplishments may be determined, especially in the form of prizes, awards, or other marks of public recognition. Under the assumption that an observer can provide a valid judgment of another person's inventiveness and originality, rating have been used as an index of creative ability. since creativity is presumably a function of intellect and the intelligence test is the best available measure of intellectual functioning, a super IQ has been used as an indication of creative potential. An empirically derived profile of the creative personality is formulated, and the closeness of fit of traits of personality is used as a model of identification. the distinctive biographical characteristics of persons known to be creative are compiled and then used to predict the future creative performance of other persons by matching the biographical characteristics. Task requiring creative ability such as writing a story or formulating a fruitful problem are assigned and the observed performance judged for originality. Finally, just as there are intelligence tests, there are creativity tests like the Remote Associate Test, AC Test of Creative Ability, Torrance Tests of Creative Thinking, and other such psychometric instruments.

THEORY

The predominant conceptions of creative thinking derive from sources as diverse as classical learning theory, psychometric models of intellect, and psychoanalysis, which do not, of course, exhaust the variety of views.

For associationists, thought is a chain of stimulus-response connections. A problem initiates a succession of previously learned responses to try out in a new situation. There is no fundamental difference between the higher and lower mental functions, between trial-and-error, logical, or creative thought. The creative thinking process consists simply of the forming of associative elements into new combinations that are in some way useful; the more mutually remote the combinatory elements, the more creative the process of solution (Mednick 1976).

For Gestalt theorists, thought does not proceed through trial-and-error associations. It proceeds through cognitive reorganization of a problem situation where there is a structural gap into a solution situation where the gap is closed and the structural trouble disappears. In creative thinking, the unstable structure of the problem situation produces tensions which the creator reduces through a solution that meets these conditions: it does justice to the facts, it fits the personalized view of the creator, it presents the simplest possible structure for the complex set of problematic conditions (Arnheim 1966).

The disagreements among psychometric conceptions of thought and creativity are equally sharp. Terman founded his *Genetic Studies of Genius* (1925, 1926, 1930, 1947, 1959) on the assumption that the source of giftedness is in superior intellect, and since the general intelligence test is the most valid measure of intellect, a high IQ is the most valid index of giftedness.

According to this concept, ability to solve the kinds of problems presented by the intelligence test is the principal ingredient of creative thinking, and intelligence as represented by the IQ metric is the primary determinant of creativity and even of genius.

For factor analysts like Guilford (1950), the aspect of intellect represented by the IQ metric is only one of numerous factors, and not necessarily even the most important one. He disaggregated the factors of intellect, distinguishing especially between convergent and divergent thinking. Convergent thinking is the generation of new information maximally dependent on known information as in most intelligence test problems where the only acceptable solution is a single already-known solution. Divergent thinking is the generation of new information minimally dependent on known information, and the acceptable response to a given problem may be a variety of emergent solutions characterized by fluency, flexibility, originality, and elaboration, which are said to be the principal components of creativity.

Despite Freud's (1961) admonition that before the enigmas of creativity even psychoanalysis must lay down its arms, a steady flow of psychoanalytic studies has provided a distinctive and influential conception of creative thinking. There is a psychic cleavage in thought between unconscious nonrational primary processes and ego-controlled rational secondary processes. The source of creativity is in the unconscious primary processes. When these are not repressed but are sublimated and become ego- syntonic, the conditions exist for acts of creation or "special perfection" (Freud 1959 p. 127). The psychic function of the creation for the creator is the discharge of pent-up tension until a tolerable level of equilibrium is reached.

There are disagreements in psychoanalysis too, neopsychoanalysts shifting the orthodox emphasis on the unconscious processes (Rothenberg and Hausman 1976 pp. 127–61). It is said that when conscious processes predominate, thinking is rigid since the conscious symbolic functions are anchored in the literal relationships of reality; and when unconscious processes predominate, thinking is even more rigid since anchorage is to an unreality not open to the corrective influence of introspection or experience. Creativity depends on the extent to which preconscious processes can function between the oppressive conscious and unconscious processes (Kubie 1958). In this conception, the unconscious is not the source of creativity but a cause of rigidity.

PARADOX IN CREATIVE THOUGHT

The variety of definitions, modes of identification, and theoretical formulations reflect a key paradox of creative thinking (Getzels 1964). Despite the self-evident need of conscious effort and rationality and the development of reality orientation and logic with age, creative thinking entails at least in part child-like playfulness, fantasy, and the nonrationality of primary-process thought. A pertinent and illuminating distinction has been made between the *cogito* and *intelligo* components of creative thought, the one meaning originally to "shake together" and the other to "select among" (Hadamard 1954). Cogitation and intelligence: on the one hand, to let one's memorie, conjectures, fantasies rise freely; on the other, to choose rationally from the emerging combinations the patterns having significance in reality. The several theories seem to focus on one or the other of these components, artificially separating processes which in actually are inextricably united.

The accounts given by creative thinkers of their thought processes are compelling in this respect. Poincaré tells how he struggled with a mathematical problem to no conclusion and finally turned away from it to go on to a geologic expedition. One day, while engaged on other matters, the solution "appeared" in his mind. He writes of this and other similar experiences. "Most striking at first is this appearance of sudden illumination, a manifest sign of long, unconscious prior work. The role of this unconscious work in mathematical invention appears to me incontestable" (Hadamard 1954 p. 14). A. E. Housman (1955) writes of this poetic creation, "There would flow into my mind, with sudden and unaccountable emotion, sometimes a line or two or verse, sometimes a whole stanza at once, accompanied, not preceded, by a vague notion of the poem which they were destined to form a part of" (p. 91).

Two features of these any many other such accounts are notable. One is the similarity of the descriptions in the arts and sciences. The second is the insistence upon the union of spontaneous, almost involuntary imagination with conscious rational effort. Sometimes the process begins with the conscious effort as in the case of Poincaré, which is then followed by a "sudden illumination"; sometimes the process seems to begin with a sudden illumination as in the case of Housman, which is then worked out by conscious effort. But always there is the alternation and combination of elements from the nonconscious sphere, or what Galton called the "antechamber" of thought, and the conscious sphere, or what Galton called the "presence" chamber of thought (Hadmard 1954 p. 25). When communication between the spheres is cut off, there is one hand the futility of fantasy out of touch with purpose, or on the other, the sterility of mimetic product untouched by imagination.

PROBLEM FINDING, PROBLEM SOLVING, AND CREATIVITY

Underlying the prevailing conceptions of creative thinking, despite their apparent disagreement, is a common paradigm of human action that has dominated psychology and education. Implicitly or explicitly, all the conceptions are founded on the homeostatic model of self-maintenance and the drive-or tension-reduction principle of behaviour.

The organism's natural state is said to be equilibrium, and the organism always acts so as to avoid the tension of conflicts or problems or, if they are unavoidable, to solve them in order to return to the optimum state of rest and equilibrium. Just as hunger is a problem, generating tensions which motivate the organism to seek a solution in food, so do other problems, including intellectual ones, with which the human being is confronted generate tensions which motivate him or her to seek solutions, which may eventuate in acts of creativity. The motive for thinking is the reduction of tensions generated by problems with which one is confronted; the creator is a person especially adept at solving in novel ways the problems with which he or she is confronted.

Herein lies a critical anomaly. The prevailing conceptions of creativity obscure what artists and scientists themselves say is the distinctive mark of their creative work, namely, that it is as much a process of problem finding or forming as of problem solving. Albert Einstein (Einstein and Infeld 1938) goes further and argues that finding and formulating the problem may be more important than attaining the solution. In his words, "The formulation of a problem may be more important than its solution, which may be merely a matter of mathematical or experimental skill. To raise new questions, new possibilities, to regard old questions from a new angle, requires creative imagination and marks real advance in science" (p.92). This is true not only in science but in art and in all activities calling for creative thought.

Despite the testimony of scientist and artists regarding the importance of formulating the right problem, the assumption seems to have been both in research and in education that fruitful problems are just there. They need not be sought or their formulation given serious attention. Only answers and solutions need be sought and only their attainment deserves consideration and instruction. Although there are numerous theories, instruments, investigations, and educational programmes in problem solving, there is no comparable work in problem finding. The prevailing conceptions of thinking and creativity have focused on the problem of the solution and neglected the problem of the problem (Getzels 1979).

It has not seemed sensible to raise any questions about the meaning or nature of problems. A problem is a problem, an obstacle, a difficulty, and it seemed unnecessary to say anything else. Yet closer examination revealed that different and even contrary phenomena are often subsumed under the single term problem. At one extreme, a problem may refer to an undesirable situation the individual wishes to avoid or mitigate; at the other, it may refer to a desirable situation the individual strives to find or create. It is no contradiction when a doctoral student at the dissertation phase of his or work says that his or her problem is to find a problem.

Three general types of problem situations may be identified: presented, discovered, and created. In a presented problem situation, a problem exists and it is propounded to the problem solver. A teacher teaches that the area of a rectangle is side *a* time sies *b*, and the pupil is required to solve the problem: what is the area when *a* is 3 and *b* is 4? The problem is a given, and in the particular instance, it has a known formulation known method of solution, and known solution. All the problem solver has to do is plug the number into the formula to attain the solution that matches the already known solution. there is no need or opportunity for imagination or originality. This is the typical problem situation in the school setting.

Finally, there is the created problem situation. Here the problem does not exist until someone invents or creates it. A psychometrician invents a series of problems to test problem-solving abilities; the scientist conceives of the problem; what is the nature and speed of light?; the artist creates a still-life problem where no such problem existed before. It makes no sense to think of these situations as merely obstacles one encounters through accident, ill-fortune, ignorance, or ineptitude.

Quite the contrary; these are situations people strive to find and formulate. Indeed, a well-formulated problem is at once a result of knowledge, a stimulus to more knowledge, and, most important, is itself knowledge (Henle 1971). It is the created problem situation that scientists and artists describe as at the foundation of their creative work. Yet it is this type of problem that is hardly ever met within the school setting.

RESEARCH

In his presidential address to the American Psychological Association in 1950, Guilford (1950) called attention to the circumstance that up to that time only 186 out of 121,000 entries in *Psychological Abstracts* dealt with creativity. Within a decade following the address, several hundred publications were appearing yearly and were increasing at almost a geometric rate. It is obviously impossible here to do more than touch on several of the major issues from the massive, variegated, and controversial literature, namely, the relations between creativity and intelligence, creativity and educational performance, and the development and characteristics of creative persons.

Creativity and Intelligence

Even before the advent of the intelligence test, studies reported that some persons of "intellectual type" and "logical power" performed poorly on indices of imagination (Getzels and Jackson 1962). With the greater precision provided by the IQ metric, Terman's study showed that a fourth of the gifted children with IQs of 170 or above had only fair to poor achievement, and Hollingworth (1942) reported that some of her children with the highest possible IQ seemed entirely uncreative.

Creative individuals unquestionably perform better than the average on intelligence tests, but the correlation between the intelligence and the creativity tends to be low. As one illustration (MacKinnon 1964), the correlation between the rated creativity of 60 eminent architects and their scores on an adult intelligence scale was –0.08. Since it is not possible to identify the creativity achievement of children, research with them has most often dealt with the relation between performance on divergent-thinking tests and on intelligence tests. Although the hundreds of reported correlations vary from 0 to +0.7 depending on the divergent-thinking tests, the heterogeneity of the sample, and the nature of the testing situation, a recent review of the work (Barron and Harrington 1981) gives +0.3 as a "reasonable estimate" of the central tendency.

Creativity and Performance in School

The expected observation by Getzels and Jackson (1962) that despite a 23-point difference in IQ, their high-creativity and high-IQ groups performed equally well on standard measures of achievement gave rise to a number of studies with similar and discrepant results. Explanations for the diversity of results called attention to the possible effects of relative rigidity and permissiveness in the learning conditions of the schools, and systematic interactions between convergent and divergent teachers and convergent and divergent pupils.

Three other observations regarding the relation between creativity and school performance are worthy of note. Students with high divergent-thinking scores seem to do better as they progress up the academic ladder; at age 15, the diverger is less academically successful than the converger but by college entrance the balance has tended to redress itself (Hudson 1968). British students in the humanities were found to be relatively weaker in IQ and better in divergent-thinking tests, while those in science were the reverse (Hudson 1966). Although here as elsewhere, there are contrary observations, the preponderance of observations shows that teachers tend to prefer the high-IQ over the high-creative student (Torrance 1962a).

The experience of the creative student in the educational setting is complicated in the extreme. Presumably school is where creative talent should be recognized and nurtured. Yet in practice, educational institutions at all levels may so focus on academic performance to the exclusion of all else that they not only obscure potential creative talent but act as an incubus to its expression.

The experience of some American novelists in instructive (Hattam 1968). James Fenimore Cooper was expelled from Yale. Herman Melville left school before he was 15 years old. Hawthorne, who graduated from Bowdoin, wrote that he was "an idle student, negligent of college rules, rather choosing to nurse my own fancies." Stephen Crane attended Lafayette College but did not graduate. Mark Twain and Sherwood Anderson went to work at the beginning of their teens. William Faulkner's education was irregular after the fifth grade, and he did not graduate from high school. Ernest Hemingway graduated from high school but did not go to college. F. Scott Fitzgerald failed a third of his courses at Princeton and maintained a D average in the rest. After publishing *This Side of Paradise,* he wrote the president, "It was a book written with the bitterness of my discovery that I had spent several years trying to fit in with a curriculum that is after all made for the average student."

Had school achievement alone been used as the criterion of creativity these individuals would surely have been counted among the uncreative, as not doubt students with talent in other fields have also been. To cite the classic case, Albert Einstein's headmaster told his father that Albert would "never make a success at anything," and Albert was expelled from high school with the admonition, "Your presence in the class is disruptive and effects the other students" (Clark 1971).

Development and Characteristics of Creative Persons

In creativity as in other aspects of human development, the heredity-environment issue is not yet amenable to fruitful investigation. Studies have instead revolved around such problems as the influence of age, family background, and child-rearing practices. Although one of the result is unequivocal, some generalizations may be ventured if it is understood that there are the inevitable exceptions to what seems to be the rule.

Adult creativity tends to mature early and reach its highest point in the 30s, but there are significant variations by field of endeavour, achievement in mathematics being earlier than in, say, philosophy (Lehman 1953). Since no criteria of creative accomplishment for children are available, their creative development has typically been studies through performance on divergent-thinking tests. Observations in the United States have revealed the following: an increase in divergent-thinking abilities from age 3 to 4 1/2; a drop upon entry to kindergarten; a rise and then a sharp drop at about the fourth grade; and relatively steady rise, albeit with some gender and test variation, through grade 11. This pattern varies in different cultures and for black American children (Torrance 1962b).

Most of the research has focused on family influences and child-rearing practices (Getzels and Dillon 1973). Significant birth-order effects have appeared with substantial consistency, first-born males being more creative than later-born siblings. Mothers of more creative children were less restrictive and more self-assumed. They preferred change, valued autonomy, and were less sociable, conscientious, and inhibited. They were less concerned with making a favourable impression and less nurturant or obliging toward others. These are traits suggesting that the mothers of creative children may themselves be more creative than the general population and foster creativity in their children through the force of their own unstereotyped behaviour.

Although studies of single characteristics of creative persons often produced inconsistent observations, certain patterns of characteristics appears quite systematically. Creative persons in a variety of fields exhibited the same pattern of values and interpersonal relations, including high theoretical and aesthetic values, high self-sufficiency, introversion, greater concern with ideas than with people, and uninterest in social activities. They also exhibited a common pattern of perception and cognition, including preference for complexity, independent judgment, resistant to group pressures, and willingness to take risks. Children who were judged creative were humorous in their free association and aspired to unconventional rather than conventional careers. Although there is a long tradition that creative performance is related to neuroticism, a number of studies with a variety of children found no relation between measures of creativity and measures of emotional disorder.

With rare exceptions (Torrance and Wu 1981), studies of the development and characteristics of creative persons are retrospective, carried out after the artist or scientist had become worthy of biographical notice. A unique developmental study (Getzels and Csikzentmihalyi 1976) took a different approach; it was prospective, that is, it was longitudinal investigation of would-be male artists from the time they undertook serious study at one of the leading museum-connected art schools in the United States to the time they became or failed to become professional artists. This permitted the observations not only of those who undertook to become artists and succeeded but also those who, with apparently equal graphic talent, failed, allowing developmental comparison not ordinarily possible.

Instead of the typical retrospective account of art as a calling that attracted the graphically talented person with the finality of divine order, the prospective investigation revealed an intricate web of actions and reactions which led to a career that was often not so much engineered as fortuitous. The first attempts at drawing were cartoons and copies of comic book figures, which were not substantially superior than those of other children. But their drawings were noticed and praised, and became ways by which the future artists gained attention and demonstrated competence just as other children did through athletics, school achievement, or good looks.

Elementary and secondary school were bleak experiences. Sports, the main way of gaining recognition for most boys, were usually alien and threatening for the future artists. They turned ever more to drawing, which progressively became not merely a demonstration of competence but a means of self-expression and self-affirmation. Even, so, the decision to become an artist did not come easily. Many tried other activities before enrolling in art school. The most important determinant of whether to apply one's graphic talent to fine art, art education, advertising, or industrial art was the values that were held. Although all the art students held significantly higher aesthetic and theoretical and lower social and economic values than the norms, those with the highest aesthetic values chose fine art, those with the highest social values chose art education, and those with the highest economic values chose advertising or industrial art.

A number of personal, school, and family characteristics, including lack of concern for social approval, high ratings in originality and artistic potential by their instructors, and family affluence were related to the success of the former art students in becoming successful fine artists after graduation from art school. There was a strong unanticipated and inexplicable effect of sibling position.

Eldest sons accounted for 81 percent of the successful artists as against only 33 percent of the unsuccessful ones; 53 percent of the unsuccessful artists and none of the successful ones were middle sons. Perhaps the most intriguing and pedagogically relevant observation pertained to the role of problem finding in creative achievement. Not only was superiority in problem finding related to the originality of a drawing produced at the art school but the ratings in problem finding while in art school were related to success professional fine artists 5 to 6 years after the graduation from the school.

EDUCATIONAL ISSUES

It is evident that no single set of educational principles can be drawn from the extant work on creativity. The definitions, modes of identification, theoretical formulations, and research results are all too diverse to permit unequivocal conclusions. It is, however, possible to raise a number of illustrative issues for further consideration by teachers and investigators.

First, with respect to the kinds of problems dealt with in the classroom, a distinction can be made among presented, discovered, and created problems differing in the opportunity they provide for creative thinking. What is effect of quantitatively different representation of those problems in the classroom on the students' modes of thinking and learning?

Second, although such broad categories as convergent and divergent thinking do not exhaust the possibilities, they do suggest the possible existence of different styles of both learning and teaching, the one style focusing rather more on the acquisition of skills and established knowledge, the other on the cultivation of imagination and creativity. what is the effect of the interaction of those different styles among students and teachers?

Third, there is a paradox in teaching for creative thinking. On the one hand, solving problems requires conscious effort, possession of already-known facts, application of well-honed skills, rationality of attack, that is, aspects of so-called secondary-process thought. On the other, creative thinking seems to entail, at least in some degree, regressive childlike playfulness, acceptance of fantasy, toleration of nonrational impulse, that is, aspects of so-called primary-process thought. How can instruction proceed in developing secondary-process thought without thereby irrevocably cutting the person off from all aspects of primary-process thought, and conversely of course, how can encouragement of the acceptance of primary-process thought proceed without thereby derogating the indispensability of secondary process thought?

Finally, from the inception of interest in fostering creativity in the classroom, two lines of instructional strategy have been proposed. One line bids to foster creative thinking through revising the curriculum material and teaching methods in the specific subjects taught, the other through instituting course of instruction in creative thinking as such. It would be comforting to be able to say with assurance that the one is superior to the other, or under these conditions this strategy is superior and under those the other. That is not yet possible in any systematic way. The strategies raise once more the age-old unsettled educational issue of learning sets and transfer. Can a set for creative thinking be taught, and if it can, is such a set most effectively taught as a specific skill in a given subject or as a general attitude or talent transferable across the entire gamut of school subjects and beyond?

4

Resource Management in Education

The purpose of this chapter is to outline the elements involved in resource management in schools and to apply them to current practice. Initially, the changing context and framework of resource management in the 1990s will be considered. Following this a theoretical review will examine the central feature of resource management, the budgetary process, and then move on to consider two main approaches to budgeting. This will then provide an analytical background against which to review a school-focused case study.

RESOURCE MANAGEMENT IN THE 1990s

The growth in the number of delegated schemes for school finance during the 1980s, culminating in the introduction of local management of schools (LMS) in the 1988 Education Reform Act, is reading to revolution in resource management practice in schools.

The 1990s is an era in which schools operate with considerable financial autonomy. The polarisation of power to the centre (government) and periphery (schools) at the expense of the local education authority (LEA) will mean that schools have to adopt sophisticated resource management skills and approaches.

LMS delegates to schools control over the major part of their budgets. An analogy that is worth considering is that of a landlord and tenant relationship. The LEA acts as the landlord responsible for capital expenditure, as represented by the school building and major structural work, while the school is responsible as the tenant for everything that goes on inside. The school, therefore, has in its budget funds for teachers' salaries and other staffing costs, equipment and books, heating and lighting, rates, examination fees and all internal maintenance associated with normal 'wear and tear'. Unlike the previous financing system the school does not receive an allocation for each of these items but is allocated a lump sum and has the choice of how much to spend on each category. The amount which the schools are allocated is determined by a formula in which at least 75 per cent is based on pupil numbers 'weighted' by the age of those pupils.

The key areas of LMS as they effect resource management planning can be summarised as:

1. Financial delegation
2. Formula funding
3. Open enrolments
4. Staffing delegation
5. Performance indicators

The dynamic effect of these five factors is considerable. If parents perceive that the quality of education offered by a school is inadequate, they will move their children to another school by exercising choice through the mechanism of *open enrolments*. As pupils move around the system the funding moves with them. Thus, schools not only have to deal with financial delegation but they have to be very aware of market forces. The way in which the school is perceived by the local community may depend not only on overt *performance indicators* such as language and numeracy skills but also on covert performance indicators such as how the pupils behave on the bus going home or smoking outside the school premises. The amount of money received under *formula funding* will vary according to the number of pupils coming to the school. As the school has *staffing* delegation it will adjust the number of staff by hiring or firing according to this movement of pupils and funding. The impact of this can be assessed by the diagram in Figure 4.1 (which assumes 100 per cent funding from pupil numbers).

In the diagram 'fixed costs' include maintenance, head teacher's salary etc., while a large proportion of the variable costs will be represented by teachers and their salaries. If extra pupils come to the school the money can be spent on the variable costs, increasing teaching numbers and providing more books and equipment. This would be represented in the diagram by moving from point A to point C. The converse is true because if a school loses pupils (represented by moving from point A to point B) it is not that the school spends any more on fixed costs but because of the reduction in pupils and hence funding, fixed costs take a larger proportion of the available budget. The amount remaining for teachers, books and equip-

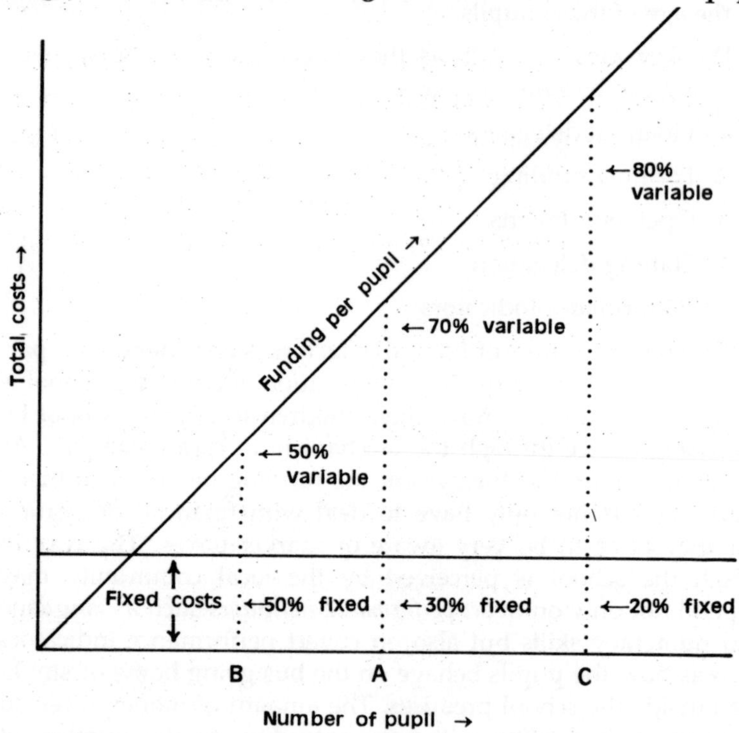

Fig. 4.1 Formula-based Funding.

ment is reduced, making the school less attractive to parents. Thus, pupils moving around the system can enhance a school's provision if it is a net gainer but cause severe problems very quickly if it is a net loser. As a result LMS rewards expanding schools and penalises contracting ones.

Financial delegation in the 1990s therefore does not only involve the school having control of its budget. It means that it has control in the context of a market-oriented environment which has a dynamic and fundamental effect on the nature of the budgetary process.

Traditional methods of school finance have resulted in the LEA having the critical management responses for resource decisions. A school has had a restricted spending function when it came to utilising the limited amount of money available to buy books and equipment under its capitation allowance. The era of local management of schools means that the traditional spending function associated with capitation has to be replaced with a whole school budgetary process and plan. The next section of this chapter looks at the theoretical aspects which underpin this budgetary process and plan.

ELEMENTS AND DIMENSIONS OF THE BUDGETARY PROCESS

What is a budget and what is the budgetary process? Schick (1972) states that 'budgeting always has been conceived as a process for systematically relating expenditure of funds to the accomplishment of planned objective'. Irvine (1975) sees a budget system as enabling management more effectively to plan, coordinate, control and evaluate the activities of an organisation. Hofstede (1968) sees the four basic functions of budgets as authorising, forecasting, planning and measuring. As can be seen, budgeting is not just a mechanical or technical exercise, a point developed by Irvine (1975):

> A budget, as a formal set of figures written on a piece of paper, is in itself merely a quantified plan for future activities. However, when budgets are used for control, planning and motivation, they become instruments which cause functional and dysfunctional

consequences both manifest and latent which determine how successful the tool will be.

Simkins and Lancaster (1987) summarise the functions of budgets in Figure 4.2.

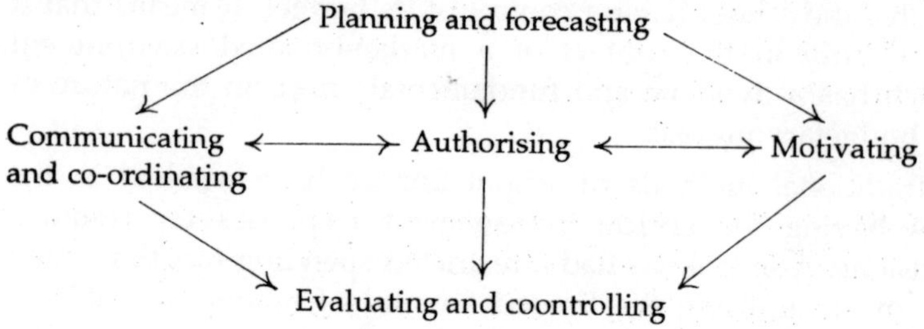

Fig. 4.2 Functions of Budgets.

A useful broad classification is provided by Schick (1972) who builds on Anthony's (1965) three-fold classification of management processes: (a) strategic planning; (b) management control; and (c) operational control; and states that 'every budget system, even rudimentary ones, comprises planning, management and control processes'. A useful analysis of the way in which different levels of management may be involved in the functions of budgeting is provided by Davies (1984) who uses Anthony's three levels of management and relates them to people in Figure 4.3.

Davies further suggests that these different levels of management may concentrate on different budgetary functions as represented in the matrix in Figure 4.4.

An alternative grouping of the functions of budgets is provided by Simkins and Lancaster (1983). They divide these functions between operational and strategic activities, although a better categorisation could be functional and managerial activities.

The essential functional activities would be firstly, the *acquisition* or resources which involves the identification and securing of resource and then, secondly, the *allocation* of resources. This involves determination of the appropriate amount of resources to be distributed to different parts of the organisation. The third

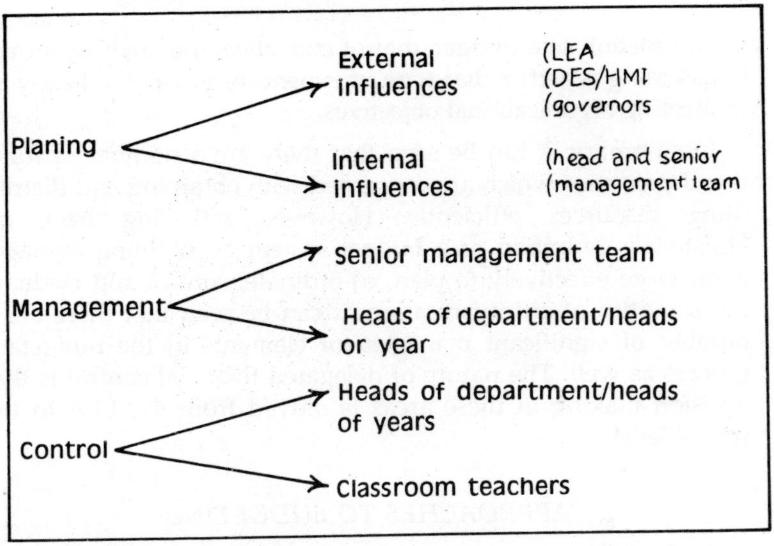

Fig. 4.3 Levels of Budgetary Management (Davies 1984).

Resource:	Generation	Allocation	Utilisation	Replenishment	Evaluation
Planing	x	x		x	x
Management		x	x	x	x
Control			x		x

Fig. 4.4 Functions and Levels of Budgetary Management.

functional activity is that of *spending* when decisions are translated into action where, for example, goods are actually purchased. The fourth functional activity is that of *control* are allocated as originally planned and authorised. While these activities are fundamental to ensure that the mechanics of the budgetary process work, it is also necessary to consider the management activities which should take place. Firstly, a budget should be a *planning* document in that an organisation should clarify its goals and priorities in a forward looking way and relate them to available resources. Secondly, the budget is an important part of the *choice* process. It should provide the basis for costing alternative courses of action so that the resource implications of decisions can be assessed. In the final management function of a budget, that of *evaluation*, the analysis moves to assessing whether that type of expenditure was the best way of meeting organisational objectives.

In summary, it can be seen that there are a number of functional processes which are concerned with obtaining and distributing resources efficiently. However, reflecting back on Hofstede's definition of a budget system as enabling management more effectively to plan, co-ordinate, control and evaluate the activities of an organisation, it can be seen that there are a number of significant management elements in the budgetary process as well. The nature of delegated financial control is that decision making in these areas is moved from the LEA to the school level.

APPROACHES TO BUDGETING

Having assessed the central elements in a budgetary process, consideration will now be given to two broad frameworks into which differing budgetary processes can be categorised. The two broad categories could be considered as national approaches, often called rational/economic approaches, and political approaches.

Rational/Economic Approaches

Rational approaches are based on the assumption that organisations have clear objectives and resource allocation is organised in a systematic way to facilitate the achievement of those objectives.

In essence, after assessing the alternative expenditure options, spending patterns should reflect rational choices in order to maximise the achievement of the organisation's objectives. In evaluating this approach, it is possible to isolate key elements which underpin a rational budgetary approach.

The first of these elements is that budgets should be *objective* in that they relate directly to fulfilling the objectives of the organisation. Expenditure patterns should relate to outputs rather than being characterised by a list of resource inputs. The latter would be called a subjective budget and would list items in headings such as buildings, staff, rent, rates, capitation, in terms of the total spent in each category, rather than show how part of each category related to a particular programme. Hence, objective budgets are often called *output* or *programme* budgets. By using this approach it is claimed that important management processes are facilitated. These are firstly, the formulation of clear objectives and, secondly, planning, as resources must be clearly related in advance to objectives. Thirdly, the approach requires that choices are made, as assessing and opting between alternatives is necessary. Finally, evaluation takes place as criteria in the form of objectives provide a 'bench mark' against which to assess performance.

The second key element in a rational approach to budgeting is the *base* on which the range of choices is to be set. The traditional incremental approach is one in which last year's expenditure provides a base from which to make minor adjustments (disjointed incrementalism). This approach is criticised by Wildavsky:

> ... traditional budgeting also has the defects of its virtues... comparing this year with last year may not mean much if the past was a mistake and the future is likely to be a bigger one. Quick calculation may be worse than none if it is grossly in error. There is an incremental road to disaster as well as faster roads to perdition; simplicity may become simple-mindedness.

The alternative to incrementalism provided by the rational perspective is zero-based review. With this approach there is a need to justify all expenditure and not just that expenditure at the margin or additional expenditure. As Wildavsky (1978) states:

> ...the past, as reflected in the budgetary base...is explicitly rejected. There is no yesterday. Nothing is taken for granted, everything at every period is subjected to searching scrutiny.

As a facilitator of management activities this imposes an opportunity—cost framework in that it encourages the reappraising of how differing expenditure patterns can best make a contribution to achieving organisational objectives. It also encourages evaluation because if choice is to be made between alternatives then evaluation of past and future spending in the alternative areas has to be assessed.

The third and final key element in a rational approach concerns the time-scale of the budget. Traditional budgets have been on an annual *time-scale*. The weakness of this is that it fails to view the implications of the spending when it makes its impact but only when the spending actually takes place. If the planning and choice possibilities are to be fully utilised then a time-scale that allows them to be fully understood has to be in operation. Therefore a multi-year time horizon budget needs to be implemented.

The rational approach has led to the development of PPBS (Planning-programming-budgeting systems) and ZBB (zero-based budgeting) systems. However, despite early adoption there have been considerable doubts as to the effectiveness of such rational approaches. These doubts centre on three points. First is the difficulty in agreeing on objectives for education and translating them into programme goals. Second, the information requirements are considerable and the time taken assembling data may work against the efficiency that the organisation is trying to achieve. Finally, constant review and justification of budgets may deny managers a stable and predictable environment in which to operate effectively.

Brackett, Chambers and Parrish (1983) state:

> Another lesson implied in the budget reform literature is the importance of simplicity and comprehensibility of the innovation. Aaron Wildavsky argued that while PPBS had many shortcomings, the fundamental reason for its demise was that no-one knew how to do programme budgeting.
>
> ...While the same accusation was nc explicitly levelled against ZBB, the complexity of the procedures, the esoteric nature of the terminology, the potential for overwhelming paperwork and the inapplicable nature of several of the key concepts oppose acceptability.

POLITICAL APPROACHES

Because of the criticisms of rational approaches discussed above, political budgetary approaches show a remarkable capacity to persist Wildavsky (1974) makes the point that 'the largest determining factor of the size and content of this year's budget is last year's budget'. Why should this be so and the rational processes just described not take prominence? There are three key factors that influence the persistence of traditional budgeting processes. These can be seen as the process of incrementalism, the influence of micro-political forces and the tendency of organisations to satisfies rather than optimise goals.

The major factor in the incremental process is that the previous year's budget and level of expenditure is not challenged—there is general acceptance that it is valid. Attention is given to minor adjustments in the spending pattern or the justification of additional spending. There is no significant attempt to assess the validity of existing spending patterns. This approach provides a predictable and stable organisational climate. It also necessitates very little in terms of information and time requirements compared with zero-based approaches.

The micro-political dimension of budgeting is based on the view that budgetary decisions are not necessarily made on rational-economic grounds but that the deciding factors may be other influences such as the power base of individuals or groups and their value systems. Two useful statements which illustrate this are provided firstly by Pettigrew (1973).

> Political behaviour is defined as behaviour by individuals, or, in collective terms, by sub-units, within an organisation that makes a claim against the resources sharing system of an organisation.

and secondly, by Wildavsky (1968):

> If politics is regarded as conflict over whose preferences are to prevail in the determination of policy, then the budget records the outcomes of this struggle.

Therefore, gaining resources may not depend on the logic of the case but on a number of other factors. Greenwood *et. al.* (1980) express this as:

> A department's share of scarce resources depends upon the skill of its advocates in the use of essentially political tactics such as knowing how much to bid for, how far to pad estimates, how far to over/underspend, how to 'read' the political climate, how to generate and utilise public support.

The way in which the budgetary process is managed by the people involved may be as important as what is being managed as far as outcomes are concerned. Therefore, asking questions about objectives, planning, choice and evaluation may not be as important as asking questions about political forces at work if resource patterns are to be understood. Simkins and Lancaster (1983), for example, list seven questions for consideration:

1. Which are the key groups that compete for resources in the budget any process?
2. What differences in values and interests exist among them and how are these expressed in budgetary terms?
3. What sources of power can groups and key individuals bring to bear on the budgetary process?
4. Who controls the budgetary process itself and what means do they use to do so?
5. What political strategies and tactics are used to influence budget allocations?
6. What kind of coalitions are formed and bargains struck?
7. Who gains and who loses from the budgetary process?

These dimensions should be considered when assessing resource patterns from a political perspective.

A third concept used in understanding political approaches is the organisational process approach. In a commercial or industrial setting it is often assumed that organisations try to maximise profits as their main goal. However, the risks involved in profit maximisation may be unacceptable to managers who may prefer to safeguard their position by reducing competition through takeovers instead of maximising profits by competition.

They may also aim to produce satisfactory levels of profit to keep shareholders happy and grant over-generous wage rises to avoid labour conflicts. The aim is to provide a series of acceptable solutions which meet the needs of the various constituencies that make up the organisation. Thus, the concept of an acceptable solution which satisfied the different goals and objectives in an organisation may be preferred to the most efficient one on rational grounds. In a school setting this would mean that differing objectives may be met and individual teachers supported, which would lead to overall harmony but not necessarily maximise purely educational outcomes. This satisficing element together with political and incremental forces form the key elements in political approaches to budgeting. The way in which these concepts relate to the rational perspective in resource management in practice will be analysed in the next section.

A FRAMEWORK FOR ANALYSING BUDGETARY PRACTICE

It is proposed to take the seven functions of budgets on pages 49/50 as the first dimension of a matrix structure to which either the rational economic or a political model can be applied in order to form the second dimension.

Earlier in this chapter the three key elements of rational approaches were identified as: relating expenditure of funds to fulfilling organisational objectives, a zero-based approach to choice and decision making and a multi-year time horizon for budgetary decision making. Putting by Bush (1986), it is proposed to use the following factors as an indicator of the existence of a rational economic decision-making process:

1. A clear perception of the choice opportunity.
2. Analysis of the choice opportunity to include data collection and evaluation of alternatives.
3. A zero-based approach to assessing alternatives.
4. Choice of expenditure alternatives to meet organisational objectives.

5. Budgetary time scale to encourage planning over a multi-year time horizon.
6. Monitoring and evaluation of the efficiency and effectiveness differing strategies.

If these then represent key factors of the rational approach, the political approach can also draw on the perception of Bush (1986) for indicators of the political model.

The key elements of the political approach identified earlier in the chapter, those of incremental budgetary approaches, micropolitical factors and satisficing behaviour of groups, can be set in the following framework to provide factors that can be used as indicators of the existence of political decision-making process:

1. Group activity and interest groups are the focus rather than the institution as an entity.
2. There is an incremental approach to the budgetary process.
3. Goals are seen as unstable, ambiguous and contested.
4. Decisions emerge after a complex process of bargaining and negotiation.
5. Decision-making is likely to be determined, ultimately, according to the relative power of the participant individual and groups and may involve conflict between the various parties.
6. There is evidence of satisficing behaviour.

Looking at the elements in the rational and political models of resource decision making, a list of six key factors of indications of behaviours emerges for both approaches. These key factors combine with the seven functions of budgets to produce the framework shown in Figure 4.5.

In each of the seven categories the rational and political model indicators provide a framework for analysing the budgetary approach that is being used in a particular school. This analytical framework is used to assess practice in the following case study of a secondary school where the distribution of capitation allowances is a microcosm of resource behaviour.

	Rational model indication	*Political model indicators*
Acquisition Allocation Spending Control Planning Choice Evaluation		

Fig. 4.5 A Framework for Analysing Resource Management Practice in Schools.

CASE STUDY: SCHOOL CAPITATION AND ITS DISTRIBUTION

This case study by Davies and Ellison (1987) is based on a survey of all the secondary schools in Cheshire to elicit comments on their practice of capitation distribution. The aim of the survey was not to produce a set of quantified results from a pre-set questionnaire but, rather, to isolate key management issues which would prove instructive for schools establishing a formula-based scheme or modifying one and in particular in establishing a formula-based system at Alsager Comprehensive School (the case study school).

The senior management in all the survey schools were concerned with the central problem described by one school as 'any distribution of monies to departments is fraught with difficulties—each department is aware of its own pressing needs and yet the overall sum available is insufficient to meet the needs of all'. This problem is best approached by a distribution of money to departments which reflects their needs within the framework of meeting the overall school aims. Obviously, equity in the distribution of money cannot mean equal shares for all. Some subjects, for a variety of reasons, are more expensive than others. How to allow adequately for this difference presents a complicated problem. Traditionally, an approach has been used where adjustments in previous allocations have been made after qualitative assessments of changed circumstances by the senior management of the school. There are a number of weaknesses in this approach:

1. The original base figure which is adjusted annually may bear no relation to the true needs of the department. Some departments may 'cope' and be seriously underfunded! At the same time others may, through overfunding, be absorbing an unfair amount of scarce resources.

2. A situation develops in which department heads gain extra resources or prevent cuts in their allocation because of their micro-political skills, rather than because of their departmental needs.

3. Schools which operate option choices in years four and five and the sixth form may experience a considerable fluctuation in demand between courses which may not be reflected in pre-set department allocations.

4. It overlooks the need to assess and reassess the needs and changing demands made on department funds.

5. It may have a dysfunctional effect on staff motivation if figures for capitation 'appear from on high' rather than from a more open assessment of needs and available resources.

The Experience of Some Cheshire Schools

The survey schools which have, for a variety of reasons, decided to operate a formula-based approach all took a number of points into consideration when devising their own particular scheme. While it is recognised that each school may put a differing stress on the varying components in a formula system to match the school's own needs and educational philosophy, the following points seem central to developing a successful formula distribution scheme.

1. A basic acceptance that there are certain expenses common to all subjects dependent on (a) the number of pupils taught and (b) the number of periods taught.

2. A method of recognising that some age groups are more expensive to teach, for example, those at examination level which require specific books and materials.

3. A means of measuring the differing costs inherent in different subjects, such as classroom-based and workshop-based subjects.
4. Recognition that there are areas to be catered for which lie outside the subject departments and need to be kept outside the distribution mechanism, for example, administration, library, orchestra etc.
5. Provision must be made for emergencies and a degree of flexibility maintained to allow for changing circumstances, such as the introduction of a new subject or course.
6. Full and open discussion by all the participants in the scheme.
7. A review process so that 'weightings' developed for differing subjects do not become 'binding precedents' but can be changed and adjusted as experience or circumstances dictate.

The way in which these points are developed into a practical scheme can be seen by the case study school, Alsagar Comprehensive School. This is how one school has used a formula-based system as a management response to a resource distribution problem.

THE INTEREST IN CAPITATION ALLOWANCES AT ALSAGER COMPREHENSIVE SCHOOL

Alsager Comprehensive is an 11-18 school of 1,400 pupils. It is organised in year groups and faculties and has been part of the Cheshire 'Cost Centre' scheme since 1976.

Previously funds were distributed by the head after he had asked faculty heads to submit their 'bids' on behalf of the departments in their faculty and these bids had been discussed at faculty heads' meetings. While some staff felt that this system was successful, others believed it to be unfair, especially in times of contracting resources. Criticisms of the system could be summarised as:

(i) the lack of knowledge and understanding about the basis for allocation;

(ii) the perceived lack of rationality when making cuts;

(iii) the lack of relationship between funding and pupil numbers in a subject.

(iv) the fact that an allocation could be related to the influence of individual faculty heads.

The deputy head (curriculum) proposed that a formula approach be considered by faculty heads and most were in favour of developing such a system. It was quite easy to decide on age weighting and a factor to take account of pupil numbers. During several formal and informal meetings much of the discussion centred on the following:

(a) The percentage allocated to a discretionary fund (for curriculum development, library, careers, etc.). Several felt that this figure could determine their acceptance or rejection of the whole scheme. If the figure was too high, many future decisions could still be influenced by powerful personalities. On the other hand, faculty heads were worried that a how curriculum development fund would make it difficult to cope with future changes, especially GCSE.

(b) Subject weighting—it was agreed that Mathematics should form a base of one and figures were suggested for other subjects in order to start the discussion. Several of the proposals were accepted but, in other cases, subject staff put forward arguments for a higher weighting. This discussion gave faculty heads a chance to learn about the requirements of their colleagues and to justify their own weightings. It was agreed to incorporate most of the alterations, except that a compromise was reached on the Craft subjects. The Mathematics department felt that their allocation was being eroded as other weightings increased, so they were finally given a weighting of 1.2.

The system which was adopted is based on the chart shown in Figure 4.6.

The senior management of the school had made two broad policy decisions regarding the distribution of resources. Firstly, based on past experience, they split the cost centre monies 56 per cent to capitation and 44 per cent to other expenditure headings which operate under the Cheshire 'Cost Centre' scheme.

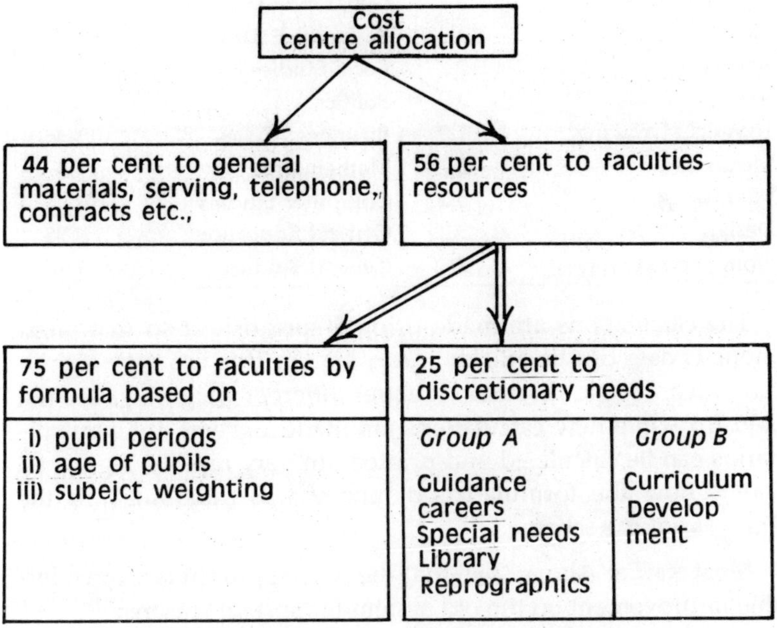

Fig. 4.6 The Division of Cost Centre Funds.

Secondly, they retained 25 per cent of capitation monies outside the formula system for discretionary allocations. As such it can be seen that this is not a zero-based allocation system or a total formula-based system. The school is operating a formula-based system within fairly rigid parameters.

Age and Subject Weightings

The age and subject weightings agreed at Alsager were:

Age weightings:

Years 1–3	1
Years 4 and 5	1.5
'A'/'S' level	2

Subject weightings

English/Drama	1.2	Humanities	1.4
Music	1.5	History	1.4

Languages	1.2	Geography	1.4
PE	1	Religious Education	1.4
Science	2	Local Studies	1.4
Art	2	Politics	1.4
Technical Drawing	1.5	Business Studies	1.4
Metalwork	3.2	Mathematics	1.2
Woodwork	3.2	Computer Studies	1
Design	3.2	General Education	0.75
Home Economics	2	General Studies	1

The calculations are made using a spreadsheet so that alterations is data can be quickly incorporated. This is a very significant advantage as discussions about different weightings are not held up while new calculations are made. Several different scenarios can be calculated and printed out very rapidly. Figure 4.7 shows how the formula-based money was distributed in the first year of the scheme.

Most staff at Alsager feel that the new approach is a considerable improvement on the old system for several reasons:

(i) it is more open—staff can understand the basis on which allocations are made.

(ii) It has been developed to meet the particular needs of the school.

(iii) It is more rational, relating to departmental needs by taking account of demographic factors and expense.

(iv) It can be adapted as circumstances change.

This case study suggests that by moving to a more open formula system rather than the previous 'bidding' system, the school is adopting a more rational approach. Certainly the opening up of knowledge about finance does enable all heads of faculty to have an organisation-wide view rather than bidding behind closed doors. However, the weightings adopted may reflect individual bargaining power as well as more rational assessment of need.

Table 4.1

Formula-based Distribution of Capitation Allowance at Alsager Comprehensive School

1	2	3	4	5	6	7	8	9	10	11	12	13	14
Subject	*Subject weighting*	*Number of pupil-periods taught, years 1–3*	*Age weighting, years 1–3*	*Total number of pupil-periods, years 1–3, weighted by age and subject*	*Number of pupil-periods taught, years 4, 5 and 6, 'O' level*	*Age weighting for years 4, 5 and 6 'O' level*	*Total number of pupil-periods, weighted by age and subject, years 4, 5 and 6, 'O' level*	*Number of pupil-periods, 'A' and 'S' level*	*Age weighting for 'A' and 'S' level*	*Total number of pupil-periods, 'A' and 'S' level, weighted by age and subject*	*Total number of weighted pupil-periods*	*Total finance (£27,365) divided by total number of weighted periods, i.e. 53p per unit*	*Capitation distribution to departments (£)*
English/Drama	1.2	2167	1	2602	1556	1.5	2801	181	2	435	5837	0.53	3093
Music	1.5	616	1	923	30	1.5	68	37	2	111	1102	0.53	584
Language	1.2	2259	1	2711	740	1.5	1332	220	2	528	4571	0.53	2423
PE	1.0	1446	1	1446	770	1.5	1155	0	2	0	2601	0.53	1379
Science	2.0	2265	1	4350	1720	1.5	5160	404	2	1616	11306	0.53	5992
Art	2.0	644	1	1288	332	1.5	996	48	2	192	2476	0.53	1312
Technical Drawing	1.5	223	1	335	128	1.5	288	0	2	0	623	0.53	330

1	2	3	4	5	6	7	8	9	10	11	12	13	14
Metalwork	3.2	406	1	1299	222	1.5	1066	0	2	0	2365	0.53	1253
Woodwork	3.2	399	1	1277	38	1.5	183	0	2	0	1460	0.53	774
Design	3.2	0	1	0	140	1.5	672	28	2	179	851	0.53	451
Home Economics	2.0	383	1	766	456	1.5	1368	44	2	176	2310	0.53	1224
Humanities	1.4	1428	1	1999	0	1.5	0	0	2	0	1999	0.53	1060
History	1.4	279	1	391	580	1.5	1218	152	2	426	2035	0.53	1278
Geography	1.4	279	1	391	542	1.5	1138	172	2	481	2010	0.53	1066
Religious Education	1.4	279	1	391	76	1.5	160	0	2	0	551	0.53	292
Local Studies	1.4	0	1	0	44	1.5	92	0	2	0	92	0.53	49
Politics	1.4	0	1	0	0	1.5	0	120	2	336	336	0.53	178
Business Studies	1.4	0	1	0	608	1.5	1277	264	2	739	2016	0.53	1068
Mathematics	1.2	2032	1	2438	1542	1.5	2776	222	2	533	5747	0.53	3046
Computer Studies	1.0	0	1	0	274	1.5	411	36	2	72	483	0.53	256
General Education	0.75	0	1	0	506	1.5	569	0	2	0	569	0.53	302
General Studies	1.0	0	1	0	87	1.5	131	81	2	162	293	0.53	55
Total		15105		22286	10391		22861	2009		5986	51633		27365

THEORY AND PRACTICE COMBINED

The case study demonstrates that resource management is a complex managerial activity. It should not consist merely of spending money, in terms of the framework established earlier. It should be seen as seven functional stages of the budgetary process which take place in a political or rational context.

In the case study, the movement to a formula-based capitation system has had a profound managerial effect. It is not only concerned with a different method of allocation. *Planning* and *choosing* between alternative systems and evaluating them takes place thus encouraging a more open approach. This, in itself, can develop a framework of trust within the school. However, it is difficult to say that it is a rational approach. The formula framework promise a rational approach but, in fact, the contrary may be the case. The initial distribution between capitation and other expenditure followed an incremental approach as it was based on previous patterns of expenditure. There is no evidence of examining outputs and relating expenditure to them. Instead it is merely an input distribution system. The weightings are based on agreement between the faculty heads and this may be a function of their power and past spending allocations rather than an objective assessment of need. The system does not take a zero-based view of needs but has an incremental approach as the formula is replicated from year to year. Therefore, it can be seen that the application of the rational and political framework is a valuable way of identifying the underlying approach to budgeting in a school. The way that schools handle this relatively small amount of the total budget can be an indicator of their management approach in the larger framework of LMS.

Schools have always been involved in issues of resource management such as the allocation of capitation allowances. They have also allocated staffing once the level had been determined by the local education authority. What LMS does is radically expand the area of school responsibility. Do schools take their small-scale budgetary approaches, built up over the years by dealing with capitation, or do they reappraise their resource management on two fronts. Firstly, it is important to look at the stages of budgeting and move from the functional processes of acquisition, allocation, spending and control to the more strategic resource activities of planning, choice and evaluation. Secondly, the opportunity exists to reassess the rational or political approaches to resource management practice. By not addressing these issues school management would be failing to seize the opportunity of LMS and would merely be extending the previous resource practice into the new era.

It is hoped that the reader will use these perspectives to reassess practice in his/her school to meet the challenge of the 1990s.

5

Human Resource Management in Schools

There is a need to consider the range of possible models of human resource management (HRM) drawn from outside education. The models are used here to develop principles which inform staff management in schools. These principles are identified as leadership, team management, performance management and organisational design. The potential of each perspective is considered and the chapter concludes with a summary of the factors needed for the successful implementation of human resource management in schools.

The principles, processes and skills of HRM are among the most neglected and misunderstood aspects of education management. The effective management of teaching staff has either been non-existent, regarded as a low priority or actively denied. There has been little understanding or recognition of the rights of teachers as employees let alone as adults with needs, expectations and aspirations. In essence the principles of pastoral care for children have not been extended to adults.

This raises two issues. Firstly, who cares for the careers? The demands upon teachers, reflected in concerns about stress, morale and motivation, are indicative of the lack of a supportive infrastructure and appropriate management processes and skills. Secondly, the integrity of pastoral systems and management processes is contingent upon their being reflected in all aspects of school management.

This situation is explained by a variety of factors:

1. 'No Time for Management'

Schools have 'no time for management' (Handy 1984). The technical and professional activities of teaching staff are perceived to be so important that the task predominates to the subordination or exclusion of the process. This is reinforced by Handy's view that schools have a multiplicity of purposes and these are not discriminated between or prioritised, nor do they include any reference to the management of adults.

2. Professional States

The aspiration to professional status is a major constraint upon effective management. The historical and social claim to professional autonomy is counterproductive in an environment where pedagogic autonomy is increasingly inhibited, entry to teaching is controlled by DES policy and not be a professional body, conditions of employment are nationally prescribed and major management initiatives, such as staff development, appraisal, recruitment and promotion, are increasingly subject to DES guidelines.

3. Diffuse Structures

The management structures of schools generally bear little relationship to the principles of effective staff management. Structures have been used to implement pay scales rather than principles of organisational design. This is reflected in the artificially tall pyramids found in management structures in secondary schools and the often ambiguous roles of deputy heads in primary schools. Similarly, the pastoral-academic split in secondary schools reinforces the notion that, in education, from does not follow function.

4. Organisational Schizophrenia

Handy's (1984) phrase encapsulates a major problem in the management of teaching staff. The evolution of the role of teachers and the view of the social purpose of schools have led to a multiplicity of demands on teachers which are not necessarily compatible and may be contradictory, if not actually mutually exclusive. This is best exemplified in the ambiguous, or sometimes non-existent, aims and objectives of schools. There are three issues associated with institutional aims and objectives: (i) the extent to which they are aims and objectives rather than social platitudes and/or moral aspirations; (ii) the extent to which objectives are differentiated from aims and are capable of implementation; and (iii) the extent to which they refer to teaching and non-teaching staff as well as children.

5. Limited Management Perspective

Personnel management in general has been a 'poor relation' in all organisations but particularly in education. The increasing recognition of the importance of human resource management in the industrial and commercial sectors is only now being reflected in schools. This is indicated, for example, in the absence of management training in initial teacher training, problems in responding to the demands made by Circular 6/86 and the uncertainty surrounding the introduction of teacher appraisal. The problem is further exemplified in the limited reference to staff management issues in the preparation of teachers for middle and senior management roles.

6. Political Control

Effective staff management in education is highly problematic because of the fragmented and diversified centres of control. Few organisations have to cope with the range of different inputs at national, LEA and institutional level. Nationally imposed conditions of employment and salary scales have to be managed at LEA level and then implemented at school level. Policy at national and LEA level is politically motivated and does not always reflect principles of effective management.

7. Children

There is an implicit expectation by teachers that the needs and right of children are paramount—if necessary to the exclusion of their own. This is reflected in high levels of commitment and professionalism which may result in stress and burn-out.

The practical outcomes of these factors are illustrated in the research of Torrington and Weightman (1989). They characterise the management of secondary schools as having a number of features—many of which may be attributed to the absence of effective staff management policies. Teaching and non-teaching staff in schools are a seriously under-utilised resource. This is particularly true of women teachers and non-teaching staff. Senior and middle managers in schools often lack an explicit management role. This is due to a lack of clarity in role definition, lack of training and inappropriate deployment of non-teaching staff. Schools are often task-centred to the detriment of effective personal relationships, inevitably compromising decision-making procedures and perceptions of individual credibility.

The picture that emerges from this research is one of schools working very hard to stand still. Individuals often deploy enormous amounts of energy to relatively little effect because they are carrying out functions for which they have not been trained or which are inappropriate to their status. In essence, schools are often reactive and the individuals within them victims because of a lack of management skills, procedures and perspectives.

The changing context of educational management requires schools to adopt proactive staff management strategies in order to come to terms with a range of complex issues:

1. The introduction of performance management through appraisal-linked staff development.
2. The need to have staffing strategies appropriate to LMS and increased institutional autonomy.
3. The need to develop equal opportunities policies.
4. The recognition that institutional improvement and quality management have to be reflected in staffing policies and processes.
5. The recognition of an ageing cohort of teachers and the need to manage morale and motivation.

6. The recognition of good staff interpersonal relationships as fundamental to all management processes and important as a model for pupils.
7. The need to incorporate non-teaching staff into all aspects of effective institutional management.
8. The need to develop systematic succession planning linked to individual career development.
9. The need to develop management procedures which are understandable and credible to the institution's environment.
10. The need to recognise and treat adults as adults.

A MODEL FOR HRM IN EDUCATION

'Personnel Management' has been widely used for 50 to 60 years to describe a range of activities, a body of knowledge and a set of skills associated with the recruitment, administration and development of staff. The culture of personnel management was essentially subordinate to the technical activities of the organisation (witness the relative status of personnel and training departments in many industrial and commercial organisations). This led to a view of people as a cost, to be controlled and administered. Equally, the growth of the personnel function tended to minimise the responsibility of *all* managers for the effectiveness of staff management either denying the significance of skills for managing people or delegating personnel issues.

Human resource management emerged in the 1980s to compensate for these shortcomings. HRM does not invalidate the procedures and skills of personnel management but, rather, places them in a different conceptual framework. Staff become an asset in which to invest, to be developed so as to help the organisation achieve its aims and objectives. The cultural shift is, therefore, from control to enabling, to providing people with the resources, targets and opportunities to contribute to the growth of the organisation whilst enhancing themselves.

The danger in the education system is that there will be an emphasis on procedures and practices at the expense of personal growth and relationships. In Torrington and Weightman's

(1989) terms the work of managers may be defined as 'agendas, lists of things to be done' which are achieved through networks—'co-operative relationships with people who can help to get things done'. Effective management simplifies agendas, enhances and enables networks.

Effective staff management is, therefore, as much concerned with 'why' and 'how' as 'what' and 'when'; in other words, organisational processes are as significant as organisational tasks and the one should inform the other. Handy's (1984) analysis of the education system identifies a tripartite culture: in primary schools children are 'workers', in secondary schools they are 'products' and in post-compulsory institutions 'clients'. Although dominant task orientation has particularly explicit manifestations in the management of secondary schools, it is equally significant in the relationships between adults in other sectors.

Parallel with the shift in emphasis epitomised by the concept of human resource management is the growing emphasis on 'excellence' and 'quality' as the criteria for effective management. The movement for excellence is most widely known through the work of Peters and Waterman (1982). They identified a variety of factors which were found to be held in common by a number of American companies recognised as meeting the criteria for excellence.

1. **A bias for action**: Effective organisations are not inhibited by bureaucratic structures but are proactive in anticipating problems and generating solutions.

2. **Close to the customer**: Ensuring that the products and services provided are those which are actually required.

3. **Autonomy and entrepreneurship**: The culture of effective organisations recognises and rewards creativity and initiative, failure is not penalised.

4. **Productivity through people**: People are seen as the sole basis for success which is developed through respect for the individual expressed through trust. Contributions from all are expected, recognised and rewarded.

5. **Hands-on, value-driven**: Management is about the implementation of values which are explicit and form the basis for action.

6. **Stick to the knitting**: Identifying that which is done best and ensuring that every aspect of management is geared to maintaining it.

7. **Simple form, lean staff**: Effective and successful organisations have simple management structures, i.e. autonomous teams focused and co-ordinated by central management which is not disproportionately top-heavy.

There are obvious problems in applying principles derived from American commerce and industry to British schools but these criteria do provide a basis for analysis.

Total quality management (TQM) is an approach to management based largely on the works of Crosby (1979) and Deming (1982). The principles were first applied in Japanese industry but are now finding increasing acceptance in the UK. The essence of TQM is the process of reducing costs by improving quality, so enhancing customer satisfaction. A crucial contribution of TQM theory is the redefinition of the concept of the customer. Although, traditionally, customers are perceived as external to the organisation. TQM defines all working relationships in terms of customer satisfaction and quality is defined in terms of conformity to customer requirements.

The notion of quality is encapsulated in the related principles of conformance to requirements and fitness for purpose. This presupposes detailed definition by customers of their requirements and the development of processes to ensure that those requirements are met. It is these processes which provide the principles for staff management and enhance the quality of working relationships within the organisation.

Crosby (1979) proposes 14 steps to quality improvement and these are complemented by Deming's four points. Although there are some significant variations between these writers, they do identify a number of implications for staff management. Firstly, quality is the primary responsibility of senior management who must transmit quality values to all but must also build quality into managerial relationships, notably through communication, commitment, recognition and providing facilitating structures in the context of explicit objectives. Secondly, quality is achieved through effective teams where the outcomes of inter- and intra-team relationships are as significant as the technical functions of the teams.

Thirdly, quality is only possible where every component of the organisation's needs is defined and appropriate training procedures are identified and implemented in order to improve the staff selection process. Fourthly, detailed evaluation and monitoring procedures must exist which are used as the basis for managing change. Finally, there needs to be a commitment to continuous improvement through development.

Drawing on the insights identified above—combining the principles of human resource management, management of excellence and total quality management—it becomes possible to propose four principles for human resource management in education (see Table 5.1).

Table 5.1

The Components of Human Resource Management

	Principle	*Processes*	*Skills/qualities*
1.	Leadership	Appointment procedures	Assertiveness
		Appraisal systems	Conflict management
2.	Team management	Career development	Counselling
		Consultative procedures	Decision-making
		Effective communication	Delegation
		Employee services	Innovations
		Equal opportunities policies	Interpersonal skills
		Evaluation procedures	Management of change
		Health and safety	Negotiating
		Industrial relations	Planning
		Job analysis	Prioritising
3.	Performance management	Managing information	Problem solving
		Organisational development	Stress management
			Target setting
		Record keeping	Time management
		Succession planning	Vision
		Training design	
		Welfare systems	
4.	Organisational design		

1. **Leaderships:** Concerned with vision and growth rather than sustaining systems.
2. **Team management**: Concerned with task and process and the quality of personal relationships.
3. **Performance management**: Providing the means to enhance competency and stimulate development in order to achieve organisational objectives.
4. **Organisational design**: Establishing a structure where from follows function and which contributes directly to institutional purposes and processes.

It is not possible to discriminate between the components of each category. All are interdependent and each principle in turn depends upon the effective management of appropriate processes which require relevant skills and qualities.

LEADERSHIP

Leadership is central to the effective management of educational institutions. Successive HMI reports have identified the quality of leadership as the social determinant in creating an ethos which allows a school to operate to maximum effect. Leadership is axiomatic to human resource management and it is impossible to draw neat boundaries between the various principles identified in this chapter. Leadership is about vision, motivating, managing teams, creating appropriate structures and being as concerned with the people as the tasks.

The centrality of leadership has led to a significant body of literature which analyses leadership styles, the nature of power and authority and the relationship of the leader to the organisation and external bodies. At the same time there has been an uncertain analysis of the relationship between management and leadership. Classical theories of management have tended to see leadership as a sub-set or function of 'management' as an entity. The full implication of this approach will be discussed below but in the education system this has led to leadership being confused with technical competence (the headteacher as leading professional) or with implementation (the headteacher as administrator). In the context of HRM neither of these approaches is appropriate or effective.

In essence, the conceptual change involved is encapsulated in the formula that leadership provides the context in which management takes place and that leadership is about people while management is about resources. There is an inevitable tension in applying this maxim to schools—the notion of collegiality based on a community of professionals may inhibit the scope for individual leadership. In direct contradistinction to this is the legal administrative role of headteachers which, combined with the lack of time, compels a focus on routine procedures as is demonstrated in the research of Morgan, Hall and Mckay (1986) and Torrington and Weightman (1989). Both pieces of research stress how little time is spent with adults and how much time is spent either teaching or in fragmented and relatively trivial administration at the expense of creating effective personal relationships and articulating a sense of common purpose.

There is clearly no general agreement within the education system as to what the functions of the headteacher are, it therefore becomes difficult, if not impossible, to generate criteria for effectiveness. An analysis of the traditional functions of heads might produce the following list:

1. **Leading professional:** The 'expert' practitioner providing examples of good practice as teacher/academic and career.
2. **Boundary manager**: Controlling the relationships between the school and its environment, acting as focal point and figurehead.
3. **Manager**: Co-ordinating and controlling, decision-making and monitoring implementation, setting structures and deploying staff.
4. **Administrator**: Carrying out routine procedures.
5. **Policy maker and planner**: Determining values, establishing aims and objectives, prioritising and communicating them.
6. **Conflict manager**: Resolving disputes, acting as a mediator.
7. **Facilitator**: Providing guidance, i.e., facilitating motivation, stimulating effective communication and providing recognition and feedback.

The empirical work of Morgan *et al.* and Torrington and Weightman would seem to indicate a significant emphasis on 1, 2, 3 and 4 with substantially less stress on 5, 6 and 7. This goes to the heart of the issue of implementing HRM in educational institutions. An emphasis on technical activities and on what is often, essentially, administration implicitly denies that staff are an asset. Leadership in the context of HRM requires an emphasis on policy making and managing interpersonal relationships and the effective delegation of other functions.

The problem is further exacerbated by the prevailing view as to the nature and constituents of leadership in schools. There are a number of models which seek to explain the components and implications of different approaches to leadership which may actually serve to compound the problem:

- trait theories
- style theories
- contingency theories

Trait theories stress the personality of the leader above all other factors—leadership requires a range of inherited characteristics or personality traits which are given priority over the job nature and demands of the job itself. Selection for senior posts is therefore more important than training; if people who display the appropriate qualities are placed in the correct context then they will flourish.

There is no consensus view as to what constitutes the most desirable traits but qualities such as intelligence, initiative, self-confidence, enthusiasm are regularly featured in studies. There are obvious problems with this approach: there is no common definition as to the components of these qualities, there is no reliable method of identifying them and a list of qualities may well include contradictory elements. In spite of these qualifications, this approach has dominated the selection of leaders in the education system. Selection methods based on references and panel interviews, without systematic job and person specification, give preference to intuitive judgements which inevitably focus on traits. Academically the traits approach has been very largely discredited, partly because of its lack of precision and partly because it has demonstrably not worked in identifying the most effective leaders, yet it is still the most commonly used approach.

Style theories are a much more sophisticated means of analysing the implications of different types of leadership. Blake and Mouton (1978) developed a model which allows a comparison in terms of the relative significance attached to the dimensions of concern for *production* and concern for *people*. Concern with production is defined in terms of task completion while concern with people is related to the emphasis on the needs of the individual, i.e. a process orientation. By examining the two dimensions, it becomes possible to identify a range of leadership styles and their practical implications:

- The impoverished manager' has now concern for task and people, minimum effort for production and minimum involvement with staff.
- 'The authority—obedience manager' has high concern for production and minimal regard for people who are essentially means to achieve the task. Results are obtained but at the cost of personal relationships and the outcomes are not necessarily the optimum possible.
- 'The Country Club manager' has high concern for people, low concern for production. Achievement of the task is secondary to the avoidance of conflict and the maintenance of social equilibrium. However, this may generate stress by inhibiting innovation and creativity..
- 'The organisation manager' has moderate concern for both people and production: he/she is likely to stress high concern for ethos but, under pressure, is more likely to opt for a production orientation.
- 'The team manager' has high concern for both production and people and works to integrate both by helping individuals to meet their own needs through the organisation.

The team approach balances task and process, optimising both and seeing people and production as being inextricably linked—high output depends on high personal satisfaction and commitment. Blake and Mouton argue that although the team approach is an ideal it can be worked towards by a process of diagnosis and training.

Blake and Mouton's analysis is effectively complemented by the best known of the contingency models—Adair's (1983) model of action-centered leadership. Adair argues that any working situation produces three sets of needs for the people involved and therefore effective leadership is determined by the variables operating in a given situation:

1. **Task achievement**: Attaining objectives, planning the work, allocating resources and monitoring progress.
2. **Team development**: Creating a cohesive unit, enhancing morale and team consciousness, improving communication and setting and monitoring standards.
3. **Individual needs**: Giving praise and recognition, resolving conflict and facilitating individual growth and development.

Effective leadership seeks to integrate these three elements so that each is optimised and enhances the other two. As with Blake and Mouton, there is a clear emphasis on the importance of people as well as task. The components of Adair's three elements indicate the factors that are relevant to effective leadership. However, there is still a need to discriminate between the management skills appropriate to completing the task and the leadership qualities relevant to meeting individual and team needs. What is important is the relative significance to be attributed to task and process and the extent to which leadership is concerned with the minutiae of institutional administration or the vision and mission of the school.

The principles of human resource management (seeing people as an asset) and TQM (stressing the importance of integrity in all relationships) lead to a definition of leadership as a facilitating and empowering function. If leadership is linked to motivation theory and the notions of expectancy and valence accepted, then leadership becomes a creative and enabling function. The role of the leader is to facilitate motivation and, in practical terms, this means:

1. Creating and sustaining a vision that is communicated and lived.
2. Negotiating targets to help individuals to achieve organisational goals.

3. Providing resources to ensure that targets can be met.
4. Ensuring that individuals have the knowledge and skills to work effectively.
5. Providing explicit guidance on standards and levels of performance.
6. Giving recognition, feedback and reward where appropriate.

Hodgson (1987) provides a useful synthesis of this approach in distinguishing between leadership and management.

Leadership	*Management*
Doing the right things	Doing things right
Path finding	Path following
Learning from the organisation	Being taught by the organisation

The components of leadership are, therefore, seen in terms of effective skills and qualities rather than cognitive technical knowledge. The traditional approach to the training and selection of headteachers has been on the basis of technical competence reinforced by practical experience. Selection procedures have thus been largely exercises in historical data gathering, confirming the ability of candidates to do their present job rather than the one for which they have applied.

If the leadership of educational institutions is to be effective then a number of fundamental changes are needed. There must be systematic and detailed definition of the qualities appropriate to a particular post which recognise the leadership content of the role. Secondly, it is necessary to identify the leadership function which permeates all levels of the institution and thus develops a culture or creativity that discriminates between leadership and management, so enhancing both. Thirdly, appropriate training and development strategies must be established which are based on analysis and creating the capability to act; such training is thus confrontational and enabling. Within schools, structures and procedures must be created which discriminate between management and leadership and allow each to function appropriately. Fifthly, selection procedures must be introduced which are based on accurate and relevant person and job specifications and which are predictive in nature. Finally, appraisal procedures must be established which monitor and enhance the individual's ability to work to maximum effectiveness.

The practical manifestations of leadership as opposed to management in schools include:

- Communicating an explicit attainable and unique vision.
- Displaying a positive commitment to the vision, the institution and the people.
- Recruiting, reinforcing and developing talent.
- Celebrating and learning from success, establishing excellence as the basis for action.
- Delegating as much as is reasonable and appropriate, creating autonomy and responsibility.
- Building and working through teams.
- Recognising and rewarding success.
- Working through personal relationships.

TEAM MANAGEMENT

Few components of managing are as abused as the concept of the 'team'. As a label it conveys a sense of purpose and purveys an often spurious impression of coherence and integrity in working relationships. Applying the label often serves as an imprimatur of management respectability. The emergence of curriculum teams in primary schools and senior management teams in secondary schools indicates the potency of the concept.

However, the principles of effective team management are often not reflected in the practice. This is demonstrated by the research of Murgatroyd (1985) and Torrington and Weightman (1989). Amalgamating their insights produces the following factors which indicate the problematic nature of teams in schools:

1. There is too much emphasis on the tasks (agendas) of managing and not enough on the processes (networks).
2. There is insufficient emphasis on working for action and too much on the formulation and debate of principles.
3. Teams are often reactive and concerned with routine.

4. Teams are insufficiently concerned with their own social needs, i.e. they ignore their own need for development and social maturing.

The outcomes of working in such 'teams' will include: poor communication and/or high level of conflict, limited or conditional commitment, poor quality decision making with limited innovation, inhibited implementation, confused objectives and poor motivation compromising performance. These factors not only impose limitations on the ability of the team to work effectively in achieving its outcomes but detract from its credibility in its relationships with other teams. In the case of the 'task' team, its ability to complete the task effectively is constrained; for the senior management team it may lose authority and credibility, and in the case of the team-structured organisation all procedures are compromised.

There are large number of variables influencing the effectiveness of work-group and the extent to which they are effectively managed will determine how far groups, coalitions and regular meetings become teams. The crucial determinant of team effectiveness is the extent to which teams are deliberately created and managed to be the means by which the organisation functions as opposed to being purely symbolic structures. Effective teams must have a specific and real function, be an integral part of the organised structure and be proactively managed as a social entity. This approach involves:

- the deliberate selection of members of the team;
- the training and development of members of the team;
- the development of the team itself;
- managing relationships with other teams;
- relating the team to the organisation as a whole in structural terms;
- relating team objectives to organisational objectives.

Managing effective teams is thus a matter of achieving synergy between a variety of elements (s_e Figure 5.1).

In order to synergy to be achieved then three elements of team management need to be addressed: building, maintenance and review.

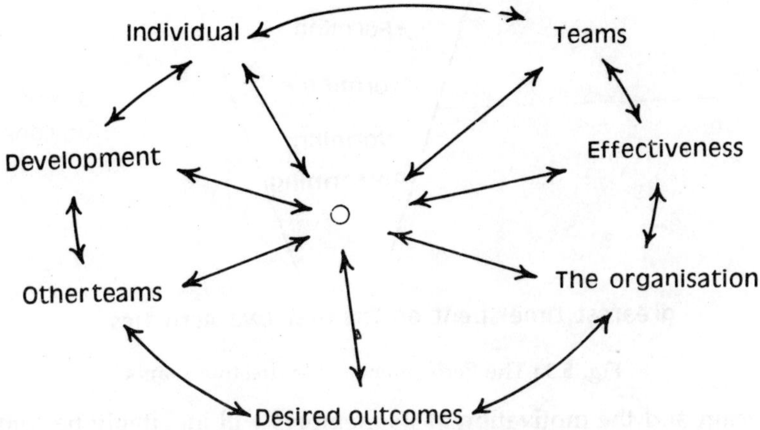

Fig. 5.1 The Components of Effective Teams.

Team Building

The composition of teams in schools is rarely the result of systematic analysis of functional needs and recruitment by logically derived criteria. The determinants are usually historical, concerned with status, the result of 'opting-in' (or 'opting-out') for a variety of motives and inappropriate delegation. The stages in the development of a team may be identified shows as in Figure 5.2)

Forming:	identification of task
Storming:	debate over procedures and outcomes
Norming:	establishment and consolidation of working principles and interpersonal processes
Performing:	effective completion of task and enhancement of personal relationships

Fig. 5.2 Stages in Team Maturity.

As Figure 5.2 illustrates, it may be derived that teams which are not effectively constituted will have difficulty moving out of the forming and norming stages and that the majority of their time will be spent in these activities (see Figure 5.3a).

The outcome for such a team will either be failure to achieve the task, or the imposition of dominant leadership, or the formation of a sub-group. Whichever outcome, the credibility of the

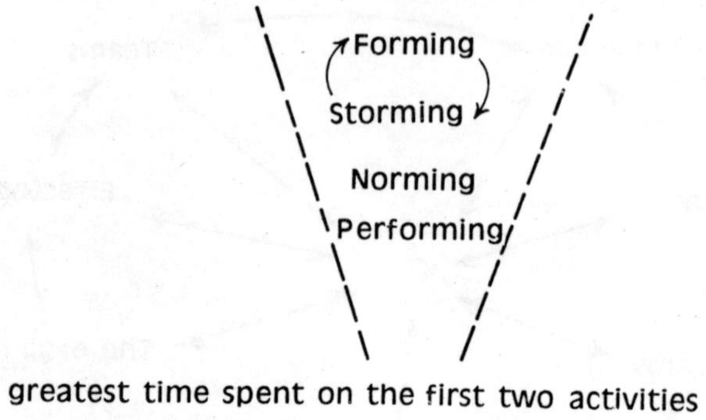

Fig. 5.3a The Performance of Ineffective Teams.

team and the motivation of its members will inevitably be compromised.

By contrast, an effectively constituted team will move through each of the stages, spending a maximum amount of time in the 'performing' stages (see Figure 5.3b).

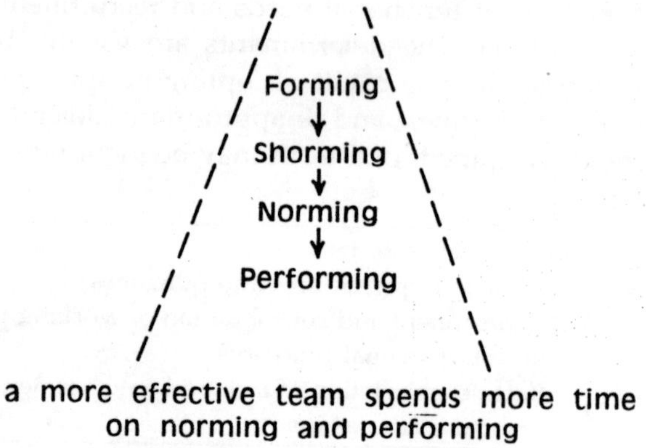

Fig. 5.3b The Performance of Effective Teams.

The determinants of effective and ineffective teams include a wide range of variables, but two which are particularly relevant in this context are the basis on which the team is constituted in terms of the definition of roles and the way in which the relationship between those roles is determined.

Belbin (1981) has found that one of the key determinants of a team's success is the nature of the interaction in terms of the qualities brought to completing the task. He argues that status, technical knowledge and experience are not necessarily the most significant determinants of an individual's contribution. In fact 'alpha' teams (composed of high achievers) may perform less successfully than those made up according to Belbin's criteria for effective task achievement. He identifies eight role types which refer to the potential contribution in terms of behaviour rather than knowledge or status. The types that Belbin identifies are:

Company Worker:	capable of converting plans into action
Chairman:	controls and makes best use of the team is able to balance contributions towards an objective; stable and dominant.
Shaper:	pushes the team towards action, sets objectives and looks for outcomes; dominant, extrovert and anxious.
Plant:	innovates, generates new ideas and approaches, problem solver; dominant, intelligent and introvert.
Resource Investigator:	the team's contact with its environment, generates ideas and resources; intelligent, stable and introvert.
Monitor Evaluator:	analyses problems and evaluates contributions; intelligent, stable and introvert.
Team Worker:	supports and rein ces, improves communications, fosters team spirit; stable, extrovert and flexible.
Completer-Finisher:	ensures attention to detail maintains schedules; anxious and introvert.

There are a number of implications which may be drawn from Belbin's approach. Use of his self-analysis inventory can help an existing team to diagnose the behavioural factors which might explain its failure or success. Failure of a team might be explained by an imbalance of team types, the absence of crucial roles or a mismatch between team role and hierarchical status.

The potential of Belbin's analysis for team management includes clarifying team needs when recruiting new members, allocation of roles, identifying training and development needs, constituting new team and serving as a basis for team review.

Although there are problems in directly transferring Belbin's analysis into educational institutions there does appear to be the basis of using it as a means of managing the issues identified at the start of this section.

Team Maintenance

Systematic approaches to team building can pre-empt many of the problems of effective team management but there is an equal need for Murgatroyd's (1985) notion of 'self-renewal'. Teams need to be developed in terms of their ability to interact and to make use of systematic approaches to problem solving.

In order to achieve this, teams have to work towards the situation where the knowledge and skills of all members are fully utilised. Just as it is necessary to ensure full involvement of members, so the time available has to be used to best advantage. However, the efficiency of team management has to be balanced by the effectiveness of working relationships so that the outcome reached is not only the 'best fit' decision but also enhances team relationships and generates full commitment.

The enhancement of team relationships can only be achieved if team maintenance is perceived as a learning process following the established models of action learning (see Figure 5.4.).

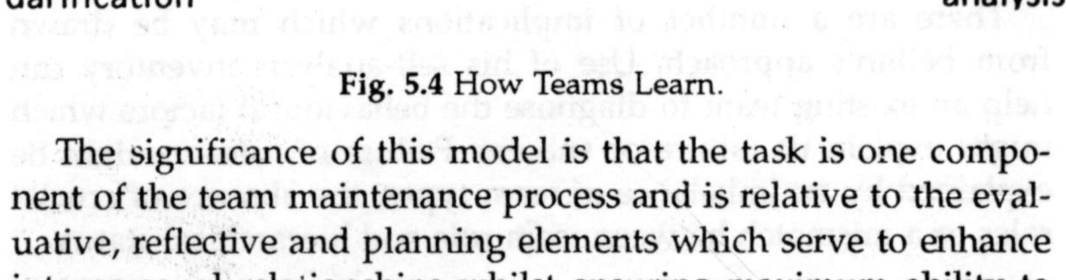

Fig. 5.4 How Teams Learn.

The significance of this model is that the task is one component of the team maintenance process and is relative to the evaluative, reflective and planning elements which serve to enhance interpersonal relationships whilst ensuring maximum ability to complete the task. The qualities which are required to maintain and enhance a team include:

- specific, understood and accepted objectives;

- open and authentic communications;
- a high level of mutual trust and reciprocated concern;
- recognition of conflicts and direct resolution of them;
- detailed understanding of the knowledge, skills and qualities of the team;
- consensus decision making;
- distributed leadership;
- respect for individuality;
- team relationships which are dynamic, growing and derived from personal and team learning.

In essence, effective teams spend as much time on the *how* as on the *what*.

Achieving this situation is not a random outcome but is the result of adopting a proactive process-based approach to all aspects of team working and the provision of appropriate training. Such listening, consensus decision making, conflict management, negotiating agreement, creative problem solving, self-appraisal and group dynamics. These skills not only facilitate the functioning of the team but the training process itself becomes a team maintenance activity.

Team Review

Review is axiomatic to the working of effective teams and is not a post *facto* activity but is implicit in every aspect of the team in terms of task and process. The place of review may be summarised as shown in Figure 5.5.

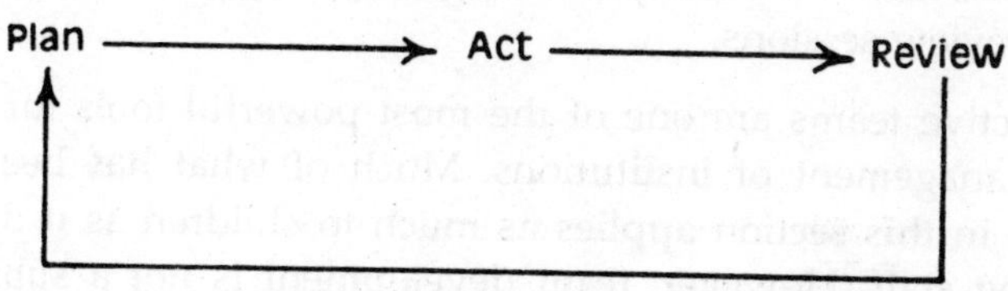

Fig. 5.5 Management of Team Processes.

In practical terms this means that any team activity has three components rather than one. Planning and reviewing should be implicit in any team meeting—as much as the actual activity. Thus the traditional formulation of an agenda needs to be changed so after a meeting starts with clarification of purpose, agreement on timing allocation of tasks and consolidation of process issues from previous meetings. The completion of the agenda then needs to be followed by a review process, either formal or informal, which analyses the factors contributing to a successful or unsuccessful activity in terms of the perceptions of all the individuals involved. The review process should result in an agreement of action to be taken at the next meeting to consolidate and celebrate strengths and to overcome weaknesses.

Such a process is essential to help a team to mature because it is only through reflection that a team can emerge from the coming and storming stages. The major inhibitions to this process are a natural reserve, the fact that people may not be used to being open about their feelings, a lack of trust caused by limited understanding and, finally, reserve brought about by the relative status of team members, personality and gender issues and a lack of training. These difficulties may be overcome in a number of ways.

1. The use of active learning, experiential training techniques so that skills are developed in a non-threatening environment.
2. The use of a facilitator to lead analytical review sessions and to provide data on team behaviour.
3. The use of an analytical inventory to provide a focus for review sessions.

Effective teams are one of the most powerful tools for effective management of institutions. Much of what has been discussed in this section applies as much to children as it does to teaching staff. However, team development is not a substitute for individual development—the team is only as effective as its individual members in terms of their qualities and skills and their ability to use these in conjunction with others.

PERFORMANCE MANAGEMENT

One of the most significant indications of the lack of importance attached to staff management in education is the low priority attached to motivation and development. A cursory study of motivation in education reveals a multitude of studies of pupil motivation but virtually none of teaching staff, let alone non-teaching staff. The concept of professional autonomy could be seen as militating against recognition of the need to manage motivation or to engage in systematic development.

There is no clear theoretical model to explain the relationship between motivation, job satisfaction and performance. A number of models exist which can help to develop a conceptual framework to explain motivation at work. All human behaviour may be characterised as being subject to drives aimed at achieving a goal in order to satisfy a need. The achievement of a goal will serve to reinforce the behaviour and so establish a causal connection between needs and goals.

Must of the rhetoric surrounding motivation is based upon a number of misapprehensions, each of which may be answered:

1. Morale and motivation are the same—motivation is an individual, unique and subjective phenomenon.
2. Managers can motivate staff—motivation is at the control of the individual, therefore management policies can only support, reinforce or enhance the individual.
3. Motivation is an 'event' in itself—motivation is made up of a number of factors of which the most important are the perceived value of the outcome to the individual and the correlation between that outcome and the effort necessary to achieve it.
4. Motivation is therefore about and performance.

For the manager the critical relationship to understand is that between the potential 'drive' of an individual and the nature of needs. There are a number of classifications of needs but three broad categories are generally adopted:

(a) Economic—pay, security and external factors.

(b) Social—relationships and involvement in the organisation.

(c) Personal—a subjective response to work and how it meets needs for growth and satisfaction.

The way in which these needs might be managed is considered in two contrasting theoretical models—content theories and process theories. Content theories are concerned with explaining those things which actually motivate people at work arising from needs, expectations and goals. If content theories are concerned with what motivates then process theories are concerned with how motivation works. They are therefore concerned with the variables which influence the initiation, direction and continuance of behaviour.

The most widely used content models are those of Maslow and Herberg. Maslow suggests that human needs operate in a hierarchy, that people are always wanting and expecting and so the satisfaction of one level of the hierarchy stimulates demand for the next level. Maslow's hierarchy has been traditionally represented as a pyramid (see Figure 5.6).

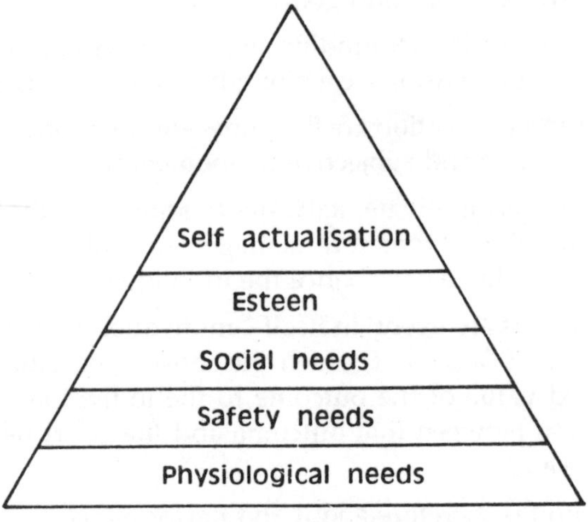

Fig. 5.6 Maslow's Hierarchy of Needs.

There is a clear distinction between what might be termed 'lower order' needs and 'higher order' needs and the strength of the model is based upon one level becoming dominant as the subordinate need is satisfied. Thus, only unsatisfied needs motivate, although the relative levels of satisfaction may be variable, Maslow's model is obviously not empirically based but, even as the basis of a conceptual framework for managing staff, it has serve limitations:

1. It ignores the possibility of altruistic behaviour which may reject subordinate levels in favour of self-actualisation.
2. For some individuals self-esteem may be more important than social needs.
3. In some instances the imperatives of lower order needs may preclude the possibility of following higher order needs.
4. Self-actualisation is too vague a concept to usefully inform managers.
5. Continued satisfaction of a need may lead to relative significance being diminished.
6. Satisfaction of higher order needs may will change the perception as to what constitutes satisfaction of lower order needs.
7. Work is only one of a potential range of sources of satisfaction.
8. It is not possible to assume a homogeneous worldforce.
9. There is no conceptual link in his model between satisfaction and performance.

Subsequent theories (notably the work of Herzberg (1974) have attempted to overcome these problems. Herzberg developed a more sophisticated analysis of the significance of higher and lower order needs. His analysis of attitudes to motivation and work developed a distinction between two elements, hygiene factors and motivators—dissatisfies and satisfiers (see Figure 5.6).

Hygiene factors	*Motivators*
Company policy and administration	Achievement
Supervision	Recognition
Salary	Nature of the work
Interpersonal relations	Responsibility
Working conditions	Advancement

Fig. 5.6a Herzberg's Two-factor Theory

Hygiene factors are essentially extrinsic and motivators are intrinsic. Hygiene factors are concerned with dissatisfaction with environmental issues so that, for example, improvement of pay or working conditions will not motivate but will only remove dissatisfaction. This is not to diminish the importance or significance of these factors; workers have a right to proper working conditions and appropriate management behaviour. This raises significant problems in the education system where, historically, responsibility for hygiene factors has been fragmented and of disputed significance.

Equally, the management of motivation in education has been problematic--for many of the reasons identified at the start of this chapter. Herzberg stresses the importance for motivation of the organisation of work, the quality of personal relationships and the potential for development. This leads to two significant practical outcomes of Herzberg's work, job design and job enrichment. Both are concerned with an explicit recognition in managing a workforce that the way in which the organisation is structured, work is delegated and responsibility apportioned have direct relevance to managing performance. However, concentration on what motivates, as in the content theories, ignores three substantial issues:

- The fact that an individual's perception of his or her needs will change over time and context.
- Management practices based on hierarchical/satisfiers/dissatisfier approaches ignore the complexity of human behaviour.
- It is not just what motives so much as what motives and how it might be achieved.

In response to these issues, process models of motivation have emerged which recognise the complexity of the relationship between the what and the how. Process or expectancy theories of motivation are based on the premise that people are motivated by the expected outcomes of their actions. Motivation is therefore a causal relationship between effort expended, the performance attained and the reward related to the performance. The potential of a factor to motivate is, therefore, contingent upon the perceived relationship between the value attributed to the outcome, the likelihood of performance leading the most effective leaders, yet it is still the most commonly used approach.

Style theories are a much more sophisticated means of analysing the implications of different types of leadership. Blake and Mouton (1978) developed a model which allows a comparison in terms of the relative significance attached to the dimensions of concern for *production* and concern for *people*. Concern with production is defined in terms of task completion while concern with people is related to the emphasis on the needs of the individual, i.e. a process orientation. By examining the two dimensions, it becomes possible to identify a range of leadership styles and their practical implications:

- The impoverished manager' has now concern for task and people, minimum effort for production and minimum involvement with staff.
- 'The authority—obedience manager' has high concern for production and minimal regard for people who are essentially means to achieve the task. Results are obtained but at the cost of personal relationships and the outcomes are not necessarily the optimum possible.
- 'The Country Club manager' has high concern for people, low concern for production. Achievement of the task is secondary to the avoidance of conflict and the maintenance of social equilibrium. However, this may generate stress by inhibiting innovation and creativity.
- 'The organisation manager' has moderate concern for both people and production: he/she is likely to stress high concern for ethos but, under pressure, is more likely to opt for a production orientation.
- 'The team manager' has high concern for both production and people and works to integrate both by helping individuals to meet their own needs through the organisation.

The team approach balances task and process, optimising both and seeing people and production as being inextricably linked—high output depends on high personal satisfaction and commitment. Blake and Mouton argue that although the team approach is an ideal it can be worked towards by a process of diagnosis and training.

IMPLICATIONS FOR MANAGERS

1. Rewards need to be appropriate to the individual, i.e. valued and possible.
2. The casual link between effort, performance and outcome has to be viewed in individual and subjective terms.
3. Outcomes have to be negotiated, not set arbitrarily.
4. Managing motivation is concerned with understanding the individual and managing the variables.
5. Managers therefore need the interpersonal skills to identify and understand individual perceptions.
6. Job design, appraisal, target-setting, feedback and review are the practical activities associated with managing motivation.

Managers cannot motivate; they have to operate procedures which allow them to identify, support and reinforce individual perception and this is best done through appraisal linked to professional and personal development.

The appraisal of staff in the context of development and motivation is concerned with managing individual perceptions and relating them to organisational needs. Appraisal is therefore not about identifying individuals for financial reward or promotion nor is it about penalising 'poor' performance—they are separate management processes. In order to improve and enhance performance, appraisal must conform to the following criteria:

- It is developmental, being the diagnostic component of a structures and systematic approach to the management of training and development.
- It is formative as it is based on qualitative judgments which are the basis for future action.
- It is negotiated, i.e. it is based on shared perceptions of performance relative to agreed criteria.
- It is continuous, since it is a long-term strategy to enhance individual performance in the context of institutional objectives.

- It is hierarchical, i.e. it is the process by which the managerial relationships of the institution are expressed and developed.
- It is internal, because it is concerned with the institution's performance and the quality of its internal relationships.

Appraisal is thus a process of negotiating individual targets in order to improve personal performance and so enhance the quality of educational provision. If appraisal meets the criteria outlined above then a number of benefits accrue: more systematic identification of agendas for staff development, improved communication, enhanced self-awareness and improved self-analysis, improved management of learning and greater opportunities for recognition and praise.

However, these outcomes are contingent upon a supportive infrastructure of values, processes and skills which integrate what the school exists to do with appropriate management strategies which are carried out by individuals with relevant skills and personal qualities.

The structure of managing performance in educational institutions can be illustrated as shown in Figure 5.7.

Such a structure requires that aims and objectives are explicit and differentiated. Many schools produce aims which are essentially vague aspirations and objectives which are unattainable as they are not translatable into actions nor can their achievement be measured. By these criteria many schools consistently 'fail' as they publish the same objectives every year.

Once initial aims and objectives are established then all other processes and outcomes are functions of, and subordinate to them. Thus the skills, knowledge and qualities of individuals appointed to the institution are formulated in such a way as to contribute to be achievement of institutional aims. Equally, training and development is based on the formulation of the current situation being diagnosed against stated outcomes and used as a vehicle to 'close the gap' in individual and organisational terms.

In order to work this process requires leadership in the terms discussed earlier in this chapter; it also requires 'open' management expressed through consultative procedures, effective delegation and a climate conducive to review, target setting,

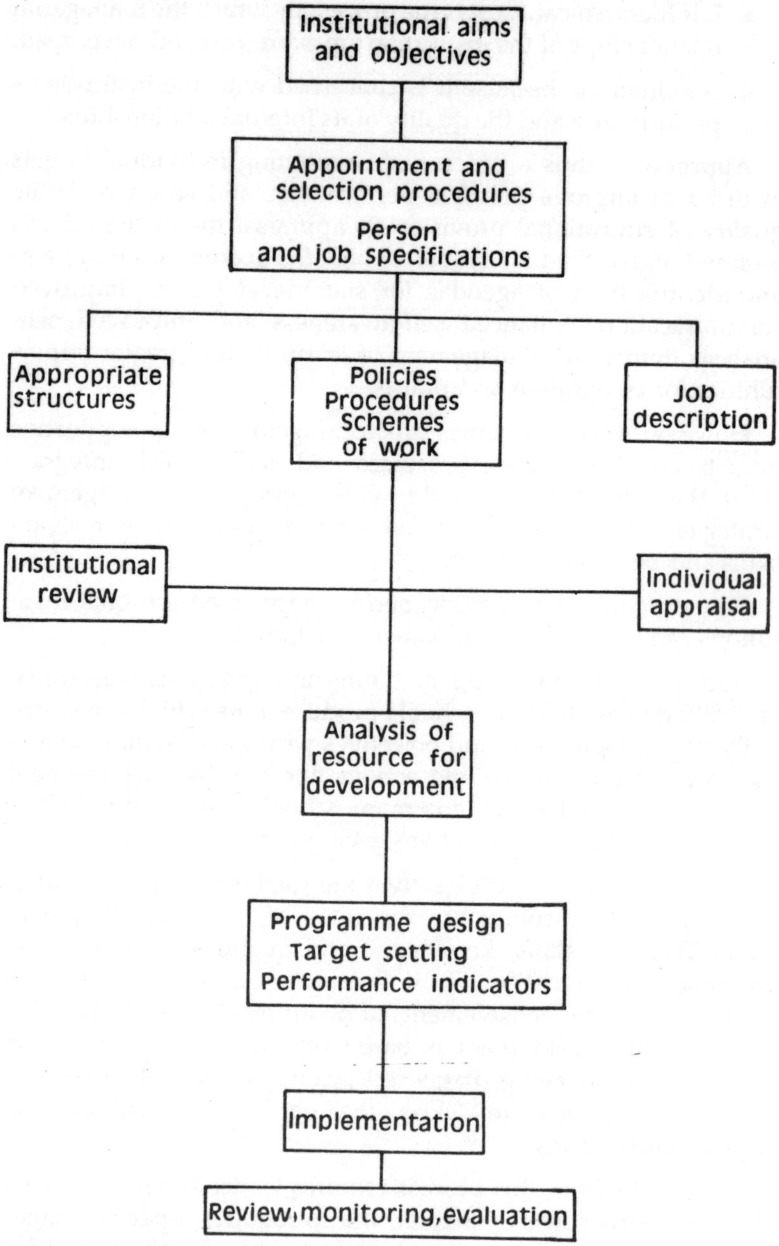

Fig. 5.7. Performance Management in schools.

monitoring and evaluation. It is also contingent upon the avoidance of the rationalistic fallacy that there is only one correct view of the institution. This implies significant negotiating skills in order to diagnose, manage and reinforce the outcomes of individual motivation.

However close the match of management behavior to the criteria described, performance management can only work in the broader context of managing change through learning.

ORGANISATIONAL DESIGN

The relationship between effective management of staff and organisational design is essentially that of form and function. No amount of leadership, motivation or team development will work unless the school is structured in such a way as to support, reinforce and facilitate the development of people. Urwick (1947) summarises this in the following terms:

> Lack of design is illogical, cruel, wasteful and inefficient.

Drucker (1968) reinforces this point even more emphatically:

> Good organization structure does not of itself produce good performance.... But a poor organization structure makes good performance impossible, however good the managers... improving organization structure will always improve performance.

An organisation that is not appropriately structured can experience the following problems:

- low motivation and morale and in extreme cases, anomie
- poor quality decision making
- ineffectual co-ordination
- potential conflict
- inability to convert principles into action
- role conflict
- inflexibility when faced with change

- inhibition of potential
- a waste of the resources of talent, money and time.

It is difficult to establish the precise rationale for the traditional hierarchical model which pervades the educational system. From the smallest primary school to the largest secondary school, the dominant model is the hierarchy expressed in terms of line management with the division of work into compartments with a clear span of control. There is a tension between this pseudo-rational structure and the notion of schools as professional communities.

The illogicality of the existing hierarchical model for educational institutions is highlighted by applying the following criteria:

1. Does from follow function? To what extent is the learning process of the classroom reflected in the working relationships within the institution as a whole, i.e. do schools practise in their structures what they preach in their aims?
2. Is there clear line management? Is it the right of individuals to know for what they are responsible and for whom and to whom they are accountable? Does the linear structure of schools reflect the reality of working relationships?
3. Do duties, authority, responsibility and relationships correlate? How real are many so-called management posts in schools, e.g. deputy heads in primary schools and middle managers in secondary schools? Is the notion of a 'teaching head' compatible with effective leadership?
4. How large are work teams? In most educational institutions teams are imbalanced; if they are too large or too small they will be dysfunctional.
5. How much authority is delegated? To what extent is delegated responsibility matched by authority and discretion?
6. Is the structure balanced? What is the ratio between those who teach and those who administer and manage?
7. How are sub-units co-ordinated? For example, is the division between academic and pastoral functions appropriate and is a departmental structure appropriate to managing

cross-curricular factors, especially when the pupil experience is not divided into compartments?

8. Are working relationships defined and public? Schools rarely have explicit aims and objectives which are translated into individual had specific job descriptions, targets and performance indicators.
9. On what basis are work teams established? Are the criteria managerial or are they historic, incremental, random and *ad-hoc?*
10. Does the structure facilitate development? To what extent is the structure capable of change, adaptation and development, allowing for individual development and sensitivity to the external environment?

In many class schools manifestly do not meet these criteria. The movement away from a tall hierarchy to a flat hierarchy, a matrix model or a team-based structure will always be artificial if the infrastructure of pay, delegation and management roles is not amended. Equally significant is the extent to which traditional structures are appropriate and relevant to the changing demands upon schools. The implementation of local management of schools, the national curriculum, appraisal and the need for marketing all impose demands upon institutions which will be impossible to meet if existing structures are retained. The challenges facing schools are considered in detail throughout this book but in essence they require a management response. The practical components of such a response are discussed below but one perspective is crucial with regard to organisational structure; it should reflect the integrity of relationships and be a vehicle for effective management. Simplistic hierarchies do not meet this criterion.

Handy (1989) has developed a model which might serve as the basis for determining the future structure of schools. The Shamrock organisation is made up of three (or possibly four) elements. The first is the professional core who are essential to the organisation and who manage its professional knowledge, giving the organisation should be contracted out to the second element which provides specialist services which increase expertise and diminish costs. The third element is the flexible labour force, part-time and temporary employees who provide expertise and skills in response to changing needs. The fourth leaf of Handy's Shamrock is the client or customer. He points out that in many areas, especially service industries, organisations have improved their efficiency and effectiveness and increased the perception of quality by getting the clients to do the work—self-service outlets are an obvious example.

Although Handy's model is essentially abstract it does assume significance when schools are placed in the context of local management of schools and the National curriculum. The Shamrock organisation offers some interesting implications for the future organisational design of schools:

1. A genuinely professional core can be created which has a specific focus: the delivery of the national curriculum.
2. It is necessary to question the extent to which such a core needs to be organised interms of hierarchies or fragmented by function.
3. Teachers should not seek to be involved in every aspect of the school—administrative/clerical, catering and many aspects of the pastoral function should be contracted out to specialist providers.
4. LMS may well increase the use of part-time contracts and these will need to be managed in such a way as to enhance and support the core.
5. The core will need to recognise that it does not have a monopoly of expertise and knowledge. The community, parents and pupils themselves have significant contributions to make. For example, a major constraint upon effective management of human resources in secondary schools is the notion that the curriculum can only be delivered by one teacher in one classroom teaching one subject to one class. The use of pupil-managed learning has profound implications for the more effective deployment of skilled resources.

CONCLUSION

This chapter offers a number of critical insights into the introduction of human resource management in schools. The movement from theory into practice raises two main-issues. The first is a recognition that much of what has been described above already exists, but needs to be made explicit and systematic; and secondly, there must be a recognition that partial attempts to change are almost inevitably doomed to fail in that they will always be compromised and administered by the history and culture of many schools.

Human resource management in schools requires a total approach which has the following components:

1. Headteachers being leaders and not teachers with 'extra jobs'.
2. Senior staff and middle managers having an explicit management role and being trained and developed to do it.
3. A vision which is translated into genuine aims and attainable objectives that inform job design, delegation, the creation of work team and operating procedures.
4. Recognising that management structures and procedures exist to facilitate action and are not ends in themselves.
5. Making time and releasing creative energy by incorporating the community and children into management processes so that they can contribute to, rather than be subjects of, school management.
6. Recognising that the integrity of the learning process applies as much to adults in schools as it does to children.

6

Psychological Environment in Schools

The classroom psychological environment is the climate or atmosphere of the class as a social group that potentially influences what students learn. Because the classroom environment, as it has been investigated, refers to the less tangible aspects of the context of teaching and learning, it is often inferred by asking students to perceive and rate the psychological characteristics of their classroom group on questionnaire items. These items typically concern the affective and social relations among the class members, the emphasis given to efficient completion of learning tasks, and the implicit and explicit system of rules and organization of the class. The purpose of this article is to (a) describe the scope of the field of research on classroom psychological environments, (b) discuss its theoretical and historical underpinnings, and (c) synthesize educational research on the measurement of empirical relationships between psychological environments and learning.

SCOPE OF RESEARCH

Since the late 1960s, educational researchers and evaluators issued or published about 200 reports concerning student perceptions of the social-psychological dimensions of their classroom group such as cohesiveness, satisfaction, goal direction, difficulty, competitiveness, and friction. Reviews of this work (for example, Randhawa and Fu 1973, Shulman and Tamir 1973, Walberg 1974, 1976, Moos 1979a, 1979c) discuss theoretical, methodological, and practical issues and conclude that such perceptions are useful as independent, mediating, and dependent variables in educational investigations in natural settings. Items measuring these dimensions require the respondent to agree or disagree with such items as "Students enjoy their work in the class" and "Most students know the goals of the lessons." Much of the research shows that social-psychological perceptual scales provide statistically reliable sensitivity to variations in curriculum, teacher training, and instructional innovations as well as to efforts to increase teamwork, cross-sex/cross-ethnic-group cooperation, and similar group properties. Other work reveals that such perceptions reflect and mediate teacher and student characteristics and that they provide diagnostically valuable profiles of class and individual morale or climate that supplement conventional testing programmes.

Educational evaluators throughout the world rely heavily and, in many cases, exclusively on conventional standardized tests of achievement and other outcomes of learning. Few responsible evaluators wish to discontinue their use, yet few claim that such tests give a complete picture of the educational process and outcomes. First, the tests themselves do not reflect such valued traits of the individual as good citizenship, ethical maturity, and creativity that educators try to foster; neither do they accurately predict, for groups with a given amount of education, indexes of adult success such as peer-rated competence, self-rated happiness, income, political participation in society, and prizes and awards. Second, even though they allow comparisons of individuals and groups with one another across time, they afford little indication by themselves of the causes of differences and changes in outcomes.

For these reasons, evaluators began several decades ago to collect data on the context and means of education to test causal explanations of how factors in the educational environment produce learning. Administrative, economic, and sociological measures (e.g., class size, expenditures per student, and social class) proved convenient enough to measure but explain little variance in learning. Counts of teaching behaviors account for a small to moderate amount of variance in learning but are time consuming and expensive to obtain.

In the late 1960s, however, three investigators and their colleagues began sustained series of programmatic investigations of educative environments of school-age children that resulted in several inexpensive and practical instruments and techniques for measuring variables that account for a considerable amount of the variance in learning outcomes. Kevin Marjoribanks, inspired by Chicago and British research and working in Toronto (Canada), Oxford (England), and Adelaide (Australia), developed parent-interview measures of the educatively stimulating qualities of the home environment. Rudolf Moos at Berkeley and Standford, California (USA), measured the social environments of hospital wards, dormitories, and college and school classes, analyzed their common characteristics, and showed how profiles of comparative information can be used by leaders and groups to improve aspects of group climate such as perceived task orientation and satisfaction. At Harvard University and the University of Illinois at Chicago (USA), Herbert Walberg and his students developed and established the validity of student-perception measures of classroom social environment to predict cognitive, affective, and behavioral learning outcomes, and Walberg carried out or served as an advisor to a large number of educational evaluation projects making use of environmental assessments. Since 1975, evaluators and researchers in Africa, Australia, Asia, Europe, the Middle East, the United States, and South America have used or translated such measures, or developed similar ones and found them useful in a wide variety of educational evaluation. Recently, the Australian Barry Fraser and his students have implemented a substantial programme of research on psychological environments in relation to curriculum and instruction; and Australia is the most active centre of educational research on this topic today.

A considerable number of review articles and collections of original studies are published. See Moos (1973) and Insel and Moos (1974) for an analytic treatment of psychological research on a variety of human settings; Campbell (1970) and

Marjoribanks (1974) for valuable but neglected collections of substantive work on learning environments carried out in Australia, Canada, England, and the United States; Khan and Weiss (1973), Randhawa and Fu (1973), Shulman and Tamir (1973), and Walberg (1971, 1974a) for substantive and methodological reviews; and Walberg (1974b) for a source book of learning environment instruments and evaluations by several research groups. A review of the psychology of learning environments, including their historical antecedents, a framework for research on classroom perceptions, and developments in research are presented by Walberg (1976).

More recently, Moos's (1979b) book presented a conceptual mold of interactions between people and their environments and reported findings based upon the administration of environment scales to nationally representative samples of 10,000 college students and over 10,000 junior and senior high-school students in more than 500 classrooms in the United States. Evidence of the impact of the teacher as a major force in educational environments is reviewed in Peterson and Walberg's (1979) volume which reports several inquiries into instruction which contribute to an understanding of how the actions of teachers influence environmental factors. Walberg (1979) edited 20 studies that provide data on the effects of environmental influences on scholastic achievement and deal with educational environments outside as well as within the classroom. The most recent works are Fraser's (1981) extensive review of learning environment research in curriculum evaluation published in *Evaluation in Education: An International Review Series*; his (1980) edited collection of studies and reflections in *Studies in Educational Evaluation*; and a meta-analysis of classroom psychological environments in relation to learning published in the *British Educational Research Journal* (Haertel *et al*. 1981).

HISTORICAL AND THEORETICAL UNDERPINNINGS

It is said that large battalions are victorious; but, as Leibenstein (1976) notes, Leo Tolstoy in *War and Peace* maintained that, in military affairs, the strength of an army is the product of its mass and some unknown X, or the spirit of the army. The task of science, according to Tolstoy, is to discover the nature of X. Simply knowing the observable inputs such as number of guns, men, and the commands of the generals is not enough; the group spirit or effort is crucial in determining outcomes. Beginning in the Second World War, psychologists began quantitative and qualitative documentation of teamwork in the military, business, and industry for outcomes and productivity.

Economists also have recognized that productivity depends not only on the factors that can be purchased (traditionally, capital, land, labour, and technology) but also on "X- efficiency", for example, effort and morale. In *Beyond Economic Man,* Leibenstein cites extensive evidence that output can be raised greatly by improved organizational arrangements, consultancies, and other efforts to improve industrial relations. Frequently, the ratio of best to worst output per worker is 4:1 and can rise as high as 30:1. Since it is difficult for managers to write completely detailed contracts for work to be performed even in simple jobs, general rather than close supervision, effective psychological incentives, and the encouragement of group and individual motivation often serve as keys to increased output.

Research on the sociopsychological environment of the classroom emphasizes perceptions and judgments of such morale factors. Investigators of learning environments often ask students to judge the suitability of their own classroom's often ask students to judge the suitability of their own classroom's psychological environment. As the primary consumers of educational efforts, students are at a good vantage point for making such judgments. Compared with a short-term observer, students can weigh in their judgments, not only the class as it presently is, but also how it has been since the beginning of the year. Students are able to compare from the student-client point of view their class with those in past grades, with other they are presently taking, or even with other social groups of which they are members. Students form a group of 10 to 40 sensitive, well-informed judges of the class; an outside observer is a single judge who has far less data and, though highly trained and systematic, may be insensitive to what is important for psychological incentives in a particular class.

Investigators of learning environments have tended to use general ratings of the environment, rather than counts of specific teacher or student acts. These subjective ratings of perceived behavior are referred to as "high-inference" measures. "Low-inference" measures, on the other hand, involve specific teacher or student behaviours.

Thus one way to find out about, say, the suitability of the learning environment is to ask the students, teachers, and trained observers to report their perceptions. Students, however, stand at a superior vantage point; what they take in makes the difference in learning. By the age of 10 they have encountered a variety of educational environments; they are with their teacher for many hours during the year; they are sophisticated judges with plenty of information to weigh. Their perceptions, as partakers of classroom social transaction, are of great value, and it is easy enough (and incrementally valid) to ask for them. Fiedler's (1975) study of classroom transaction showed that students' perceptions of their own influences on the class, but not observer estimates of the same, predict academic gains.

This is not to say that "objective" tests, counts of teacher behaviour, and the like must be put aside, but only that by themselves they may be a narrow approach to understanding. Behavioral efforts to link classroom treatment with learning are numerous, expensive, and difficult. Investigating the links of perception with behavioural treatments and learning may yield more revealing clues to the puzzle of optimizing classroom learning.

MEASUREMENT AND VALIDITY

The most commonly used instrument for research on classroom psychological environments is the Learning Environment Inventory (LEI). Sample items and reliabilities of the 15 scales are shown in Table 6.1.

Table 6.1

Sample Items, Reliabilities, and Consistencies of 15 Subscales from The Learning Environment Inventory

Subscale	*Sample Item*	*Class Relia-bility*	*Percent Positive Corre-lations Learning*[a]
Cohesiveness	All students know each other very well	0.84	86
Satisfaction	The students enjoy their class work	0.79	100
—Friction[b]	Certain students are responsible for petty quarrels	0.80	0
Apathy	Students don't care what the class does	0.77	14
—Cliqueness	Some students refuse to mix with the rest of the class	0.74	6
Democracy	Students have about equal influence on the class	0.61	85
Competitiveness	There is much competition in the class	0.56	67
—Diversity	Interests vary greatly within the group	0.36	30
—Favoritism	Certain students are favoured more than the rest	0.65	10
Goal direction	Each student knows the goals of the course	0.73	73
Material environment	The room is bright and comfortable	0.79	86
Formality	The class has rules to guide its activities	0.87	65
Difficulties	Students find the course work hard to do	0.81	87
Speed	The course material is covered quickly	0.76	54
—Disorganization	The class is inefficient and not organized	0.87	6

[a]The learning criteria include cognitive, affective, and behavioural measures including higher mental processes and self-concept

[b]Subscales preceded by a minus sign measure aspects of the sociopsychological environment which are negatively related to learning outcomes

The LEI has been used to obtain scores not only for individual students but for entire classes as well. For classroom-level assessments, scores of all students are averaged for each scale. To establish there liability of the LEI for each of these two applications, two types of reliability coefficients are required. At the individual level, the traditional alpha reliability coefficient is appropriate but, at the class level, intra-class correlations are more informative. Both of these indices have been computed for all the LEI scales. For the 15 scales, alpha measurements of internal consistency range from 0.54 to 0.85, with values above 0.70 for nine of the scales. Intraclass correlations range from 0.31 to 0.92 with values from 0.70 for 12 of the scales.

The 105 items on the LEI can be administered in approximately 25 minutes and produce, in most cases, reliable and valid estimates of the morale, climate, or learning environment of the class. The scales have been translated into several languages, and used in a number of countries of Africa, Asia, Europe, and South America, as well as Australia and the United States. Some investigators have omitted certain scales or reduced the number of items per scale to save student time. Occasionally, some scales have required modification to make them more suitable for a particular research setting (e.g., Fraser 1978).

The *My Class Inventory* (MCI) is an adaptation of the LEI for elementary school research. It consists of 60 items and only five scales are included (cohesiveness, satisfaction, friction, competitiveness, and difficulty). The vocabulary level of the items has been simplified, but occasionally items must still be read and explained to poor readers.

Table 6.2 shows the relation of the LEI and the two other most carefully investigated measures of classroom environments, the Classroom Environment Scale (Trickett and Moos 1973) and the Individualized Classroom Environment Questionnaire (Rentoul and Fraser 1979). Numerous analyses (Fraser 1980) confirm that classroom perceptions cluster into dimensions of task orientation or completion of educational and personal tasks, affective and social relations among class members, and organization of the classroom work as shown in the table.

Table 6.2
Classification of Variables in Three Domains Represented in Three Instruments

Instrument	*Task*	*Affect*	*Organization*
Learning Environment Inventory	Speed Difficulty Competitiveness Goal direction	Cohesiveness Friction Favouritism Cliqueness Satisfaction Apathy	Diversity Formality Environment Disorganization Democracy
Classroom Environment Scale	Task orientation Competition	Involvement Affiliation Teacher support	Order Rule clarity Teacher control Innovation
Individualized Classroom Environment Questionnaire	Independence Investigation	Personalization Participation	Differentiation

Studies in Australia, Brazil, Canada, India, the United States, and other countries demonstrate the substantial predictive validity of learning environment scales in general, and the LEI in particular. These scales are capable of predicting cognitive, behavioural, and affective gains that occur during instruction. The predictive validity of these scales was established by Anderson and Walberg (1974) in a review of the unique criterion variance accounted for by learning and by IQ. Using the LEI to operationalize the learning environment, Anderson and Walberg set to answer the question "Is the Learning Environment Inventory a useful predictor of student learning?" To answer this question, they examined the results of other well-known predictors of student learning to determine whether or not such instruments as the LEI predict substantially more variance in learning than does IQ, and whether it predicts different variance from that predicted by IQ. Student perceptions of the social environment of learning accounted for a median of 30 percent (range = 13 percent to 46 percent; all significant) of the variance in cognitive, affective, and behavioural postcourse measures beyond that accounted for by parallel precourse measures. By contrast, IQ accounts for only a median of 7 percent (range = 0 percent to 9 percent) of the residualized variance (Anderson and Walberg 1974). Efforts at generalizing these results suggest consistency across different school subjects and different languages and cultures (Anderson and Walberg 1974). Although in classroom research the usual treatment (aside from content opportunity) and its interaction with aptitude add little to the prediction of learning variation beyond that accounted for by aptitude, student perceptions of the social environment of learning add considerably.

Essentially the same conclusions were reached by Haertel *et al.* (1979) in a recent synthesis of research on the relation of sociopsychological environment to learning outcomes. A total of 734 correlations were analyzed, from a comprehensive collection of 12 studies of 10 data sets on 823 classes in eight subject areas, encompassing 17,805 students in four nations. All of these data were taken from studies carried out in naturalistic classroom settings, kindergarten through to 18-year-olds, and all were simple, part, or partial correlations between student perceptions of the sociopsychological climate and end-of-course learning. A tabulation of the signs of the relationships is shown in Table 6.1.

Psychological perceptions of classroom environments have important influences on student achievement, performance, and self-concept as well as on other valuable educational outcomes. Climate measures are practical, inexpensive, and valid; and they predict learning gains more accurately than do so-called objective variables such as students' social class, teacher behaviours and other characteristics, school and class sizes, and educational expenditures.

Constructive educational climates may be viewed as means to valuable educational ends or as worthy ends in their own right. Information on educational climates may be conveniently gathered and fed back to school staffs for the planning, execution, and evaluation of data based educational improvement programmes. Climate measures can also be included along with standardized tests and other assessments in national, local, and school accountability, evaluation, and research efforts.

Because learning environment assessments are convenient, practical, and inexpensive, because of their demonstrated predictive validity and revealing, reliable sensitivity to educational innovations, and because research information from them proves interesting, meaningful, and suggestive to educational policy makers and practitioners, they are being used in a wide variety of evaluation and research projects in many countries. It seems likely that this thriving, young tradition of environmental assessment, because it balances and complements the older traditions of behavioural assessments and standardized cognitive measures, will continue to grow in size, theory, and utility.

7

Teacher and Instruction

"Teacher expectation", "self-fulfilling prophecy", and "teacher faith" are terms associated with the hypothesis that teachers create realities commensurate with their perceptions of students. The corollary is that the learner, in turn, makes his or her other reality—a reality substantially grounded in the reality of the teacher. This describes the mediating mechanisms that potentially bring about these expectancy phenomena. It is suggested that teacher act on their perceptions about individuals so as to provide differential treatment to them, and that such treatment can interact with pupil self-expectations to produce expected outcomes.

A landmark study by Rosenthal and Jacobson (1968) stimulated both interest and controversy when they announced to the educational world findings that pupils mirror teachers' expectations in their school performance. The researchers submitted to elementary teachers a list of randomly selected "academic bloomers" who were given an intelligence test, ostensibly to norm the test. According to the researchers, this externally imposed information induced expectancies in teachers' minds which, in turn, were reflected in significantly greater intellectual gains in "academic bloomers" than in other children.

Publication of the Rosenthal-Jacobson study met with immediate enthusiasm from the educational community but methodological and generalizability concerns were raised by many about the study.

The concept of the self-fulfilling prophecy has generated volumes of research (Finn 1972, Brophy and Good 1974, Braun 1976, Darley and Fazio 1980). The concept continues to generate research, theory, and controversy. This is testimony to the importance of the construct, which is central to many of the practical implications of the sociopsychological dynamics in classroom settings.

While investigations continue to generate considerable evidence confirming the expectancy phenomenon in experimental settings, and in nonexperimental social interaction settings, the educator should bear in mind some of the problems which have clouded some investigations and many interpretations since the Rosenthal and Jacobson study. First, whether or not expectancies are artificially or naturally induced must be considered in any interpretation. It is reasonable to expect that self-generated expectancies are more potent than artificially induced expectancies (Braun 1976). Further, the result of some of the investigations remain equivocal partly because they have failed to examine teacher self-generated expectancies and children's academic performance in relation to different levels of the social environment of children, at different levels of the intellectual scale, and for different age cohorts of children.

Perhaps, the most critical caution is that the expectancy context should not be viewed as a simple, social dyad involving a student and a teacher as two non-interacting components. Much of the earlier research suggests a simplistic, direct "teacher-alone" effect on children. The expectancy relationships which might develop within the interactive dyad involve: (a) teachers' expectations about student's academic ability; (b) students' expectations about their own abilities; and (c) teachers' and students' combined expectations about the latter's abilities.

The purpose of the discussion here is to examine, in detail, the processes underlying the complexities of classroom interaction. Earlier discussions attempting to elucidate the process are those by Braun (1976), Cooper (1979), Brophy (1979), and Darley and Fazio (1980).

THE GENERAL TEACHER EXPECTANCY CYCLE

The mediating mechanisms by which a perceiver's (teacher's) beliefs and conceptualized as a cyclic sequence of events. Such cyclic flow does not connote a consistent one-way process, but rather an interactive feedback flow. The general flow can be conceptualized as follows: (a) the teacher forms differential expectations about different learners as a result of observations, beliefs, and stereotypes which he or she has encoded about learners (input factors); (b) the teacher reconstructs or modifies expectations of particular learners on the basis of particular interactive constellations "input" and develops a "set" for action; (c) the teacher acts toward different learners in accordance with the "set" developed (teacher output factors); (d) the learner interprets the meaning of the teacher's action based on his or her unique set of beliefs about self, and self in relation to the teacher and forms self-expectations; (e) the learner acts on the teacher's "output" in accordance with his or her perception of the total situation (pupil output); (f) pupil "output" provides new data for teacher "input" either to confirm original expectations, to modify, or to refute them; (g) the learner interprets his or her own action. This interpretation may vary from acceptance of the action as appropriate and caused by the teacher's action to a new inference about the self as a learner (Darley and Fazio 1980).

The cyclical sequence outlined above is a modification of an earlier process model (Braun 1976) and bears many similarities to the cycle suggested by Darley and Fazio. In fact, the latter provide a number of explanatory notes which help elucidate the complexities of the interaction sequence. First, they suggest that the sequence may represent a cyclical process in that the perceiver's (teacher's) expectancy may have developed from previous "passes" through the sequence, or it may represent the beginning of the interaction. Second, the authors point out that while one of the individuals involved in the interaction is designated as the perceiver and the other the target, such a process can be "symmetric" in nature. By the same token, the identification of who the perceiver is in the sequence is often non-arbitrary in which case the interaction is "non-symmetric".

Having presented the general flow of the expectancy cycle, some of the mediating mechanisms and intermediary linkages can how be examined.

TEACHER EXPECTANCY—POTENTIAL SOURCES OF INPUT

The interaction sequence is initiated by the teacher's formation of expectancies about the behaviour of the learner. There is no doubt that expectancies can be inferred from several "inputs", each with various possible sources of bias (Darley and Fazio 1980). It is these biasing sources that must be borne in mind when examining "input factors."

Sources of "input" into teachers' expectancies are well-documented. Elashoff and Snow (1971) summarize the impact of a few of these sources:

> Teachers...form impressions based on physical appearance and conduct...achievement, IQ scores, or general characteristics of older siblings or parents. These impressions based on a day's or a week's experience may produce expectations about pupil behavior and future achievement...When teachers characterize pupils they are likely to label them as "good," or "bad." Clean children "good," dirty ones "bad"; or they may be "fast" or "slow" learners.

It is interesting to note that physical appearance heads the list of "input" factors. Research studies have claimed varying degrees of potency for this factor. Clifford and Walster (1973) concluded that attractive children were perceived by teachers to possess a higher IQ, greater educational potential, and more interested parents than less attractive children. Further documentation is provided by Dion (1972) who found that attractive children were perceived as less likely to be antisocial than unattractive children. He reported that attractive children who commit unacceptable acts were perceived as more honest and pleasant than unattractive children. While several studies have reported contradictory evidence, these studies involved artificial settings.

The dynamics underlying the relationship between sex bias and achievement are less clear than the fact that the bias exists. Such bias appears to be operative for young children as well as older students.

The sex bias may, in part, relate to the common belief that girls' behaviour in classroom settings is more complaint and more consistent with general academic expectations (Braun 1976). It is suggested that acts of disapproval may often be stimulated by an expectancy that boys will need correction. Felker (1974) has hypothesized that girls have more areas in which they can receive approval and positive feedback than boys in a school setting. An interesting and illuminating investigation by Leinhardt et al. (1979) adds an entirely new dimension. They found that teachers made more academic contracts with girls in reading and with boys in mathematics. Teachers also spent relatively more cognitive time with girls in reading and boys in mathematics.

Another "input" factor is that of the learner's general psychosocial environment including race and social class which have been shown to lead to differential assignment of personality traits to stereotypes.

It has been shown that middle-class students are expected to receive higher grades than lower-class students, and that white middle-class students are held more internally responsible for failure then other students.

The interactive nature of environmental "input" variables is further elaborated by Marjoribanks (1978). He concluded that if children come from a deprive social environment or have a low intelligence level, and are perceived by teachers as having unfavourable school-related behaviour, then they suffer a compounded deprivation in school achievement. However, if children are perceived as having favourable school behaviour, then they are able to overcome, at least in part, the restrictions imposed by environment and intelligence test performance.

Another important investigation is that of Rotter (1975). Her study took into account teacher variability in relation to race and socioeconomic status (SES). She found that previous performance of children was the most significant variable in controlling expectations. When such information was not available, race and SES effects were nonsignificant. The author noted a "learning backwards" effect for race, that is, black teachers tended to grade white middle-class pupils higher than other types, and white teachers tended to grade black lower-class pupils highest. However, Cornbleth and Korth (1980) found that teachers rated white students higher can black students with respect to potential achievement and classroom behaviour. They also rated white students as more efficient, organized, reserved, industrious, and spoken. Overall ratings were higher for white than for black students.

Much research is needed to explicate the intricacies and complexities of social environment influences on expectations half for other and, more particularly, how such expectations translate into differential treatment.

There are a few findings from research regarding the impact of teachers' perceptions of the intelligence of students. Barnard *et al.* (1968) found that teachers tend to rate brighter pupils in a more favourable light, attributing more positive characteristics to high-ability than to low-ability children. Further, Willis (1972) found a positive relationship between teacher judgment of student ability and teacher evaluation of student attention, self-confidence, maturity, and ability to work without supervision. Kehle (1974) attested to the importance of test information in interaction with information on sex, attractiveness, and race.

There is a cluster of variables related to "input" which includes students past and present achievement and psychological reports and a fairly consistent body of research documenting differential teacher/pupil interaction based on the teacher's perception of high or low achievement (Braun 1976, Brophy and Good 1974, Good *et al.* 1980, Rosenthal 1974).

A study by Mason (1973) provides information regarding the potential biasing impact of psychological reports. This research directed its focus toward an examination of the effect of psychological reports containing fictitious material on teachers' perceptions of a child's performance and expectations for the child. A further purpose of the study was to investigate the impact of knowledge of the effect of biases on pupils' performance. Subjects, after having heard a lecture on the effects of biases, observed a videotaped due to the psychological report or lecture. However, the psychological report had a significant effect on expectations even in subjects who just been warned against such biasing effects. One of the conclusions drawn by the author was that teachers are more influences by negative information about students than by positive or neutral information.

The relationship between expectations based on record-type information (i.e., standardized test, previous teachers, family, physical characteristics) and the quality of reported performance was investigated by Cooper (1979). He found a positive relationship between the variables. More interesting is the finding that the perceived accuracy of these expectations was relatively uninfluenced by the perceived reliability of the source that generated them. Further, expectations stated after more direct exposure to student performance continued to be influenced by preobservation expectations. While the study was conducted in a simulated setting, it does provide useful insights into potential ways in which reported information can be used.

At least two studies give credence to knowledge of siblings as a potential "input" source of teacher expectation. Seaver (1971) found that younger siblings of good students obtained higher achievement scores if they were assigned to the former teachers of older siblings than if they were assigned to other teachers. Seaver (1973) further substantiated the sibling effect. He obtained first grade achievement scores for 79 younger siblings who had been preceded in school by "bright" or "dull" older siblings. Again, he found that children taught by the same teacher as their older siblings performed better than those taught by a different teacher if their older siblings had been good students, and that they performed worse than the controls if their older siblings had performed poorly.

The foregoing "input" factors involve classes or categories of traits which trigger inferences about the actions an individual from these categories ought to display. These categories or stereotypes often become overgeneralized leading to degrees of inaccuracy in behavioural prediction (Brigham 1971). It is important to note that prediction are not necessarily based on observation of an individual's behaviour but rather on inferences drawn from race, gender, ethnic, and other categories. Such a caution is particularly relevant when new categories and stereotypes are generated in the educational realm, categories and stereotypes are generated in the educational realm, categories which frequently have elusive, ill-defined, arbitrary designations. Such is the case with categories of handicapped children. A study of particular relevance is reported by Palmer (1979). He investigated regular classroom teacher's attributions and instructional prescriptions for normal achieving, educationally handicapped, and educationally mentally retarded pupils. Background descriptive information about pupils given to teachers affected teachers' failure but not success attributions as well as the manner in which they revised their failure attribution ratings. In addition, it was found that teacher's initial instructional prescriptions were anchored by descriptive information reflecting characteristics of normal achieving, educationally handicapped, educationally mentally retarded pupils. Pupils' subsequent achievement, however, did modify instructional decisions.

There is little doubt that the labelling process in education, and especially in special education, can serve to induce negative expectations. While most of the evidence to support this claim is impressionistic, a few recent studies lend empirical evidence (Foster 1975, Lee 1975). They demonstrated that teacher trainees in special education could be biased in their assessment of a child's behaviour by applying different labels to the child prior to (or during) their observations. That such bias potentially affects performance is documented by Sutherland and Algozzine (1979).

It would be naive to assume that expectation "input" factors lead to direct, unqualified channels of "output" on the part of the teacher. It must be understood that most of the "input" studies base their findings on "average" reaction of teachers, and many of the conclusions are derived from correlations analyses. It is perhaps as dangerous to stereotyped teachers on the basis of their perceptions as it is to stereotype their charges (Braun 1976). While "input" or "inputs" cue a set for action, or "output", teachers do not necessarily remain static in the implicit personality theories which they hold. Further, teachers may modify or reconstruct stereotypes which they hold. Then, too, there is wide variability with respect to teacher's inclinations to act on "input".

It would seem that teacher personality is a prime factor in orchestrating action or nonaction based on pupil "input". Suggestibility, or the degree to which teachers give credence to externally imposed information would appear to be one such factor, as would teacher sex and knowledge of behavioural theory.

Indeed, the link between teacher expectation and teacher "output" is not as direct as assumed by early expectation experimental studies. "Input" data are filtered through a complex of personality/dispositional, attributional, self-image, and knowledge variables.

THE INSTRUCTIONAL ENVIRONMENT—TEACHER OUTPUT

While the impact of expectations held for different learners and groups of learners interacts with specific teacher variables, there is no paucity of research to support the fact that both quantitative and qualitative "outputs" are influenced by expectations. Teachers' expectations lead to "output" than often consist of grouping, tracking, or streaming students, usually to facilitate more appropriate treatment in the classroom. These are planned and explicitly reasoned outputs. There are, however, more subtle outputs. For example, the amount of attention and contact varies with students for whom differential expectations are held. It has been suggested that teachers pay less attention to low achievers, call on them less often, and interact differentially with high and low achievers at both elementary-, and secondary-school levels. Willis (1970) found that teachers ignored comments of low-efficiency students more frequently than comments from high-efficiency students. Even nonverbal behaviours emitted toward students labelled bright or dull have been shown to differ. Such behaviours include more smiling, learning closer, more nodding, and more direct eye gaze for so-called bright than for dull students (Chaikin et al.1974).

Further qualitative aspects of teacher contact include praise and blame. Evaluative feedback may well be the most potent classroom socializing and academic variable. Low-expectations students do receive less praise and more criticism than high-expectation students (Brophy and Good 1974). Cooper and Baron (1977) proposed that the teacher's sense of control over interactions might explain the linkage:

> Low expectations imply that future interactions with these students are more likely to be unsuccessful and more energy- and time-consuming. Since interactions initiated by the child are less controllable in both timing and content than teacher-initiated interactions, criticism may be dispensed more freely and praise less freely to low-expectations students to decrease these student's seeking out behaviour.

It should be remembered that the distribution of praise and criticism is likely to vary widely among teachers. Consistent with attributional theory, praise and blame should be most pronounced when the causes of behaviour are perceived to be personal in origin.

Task and performance expectations lead to differential treatment on the basis of high- and low-ability perceptions. Teachers may set tasks either stifle or stretch the achievement of a groups or individual within that group. These differential expectations may be apparent in the range of comprehension questions posed to individual children. The group for whom expectations are low may have little opportunity to grapple with questions that require inferential and critical thinking. Brophy and Good (1969), for example, found that black children received more memory questions that did white children for whom higher expectations were held.

The treatment of children for whom the teacher has low expectations may have a dual effect. First, the teacher's treatment may reduce the motivation of the learner. Further, because the learner is exposed only to lower level tasks the teacher's low expectations is confirmed.

Pidgeon (1970) reports evidence of the relationship between expectancy and levels of tasks teachers set for children. In discussing the inferior arithmetic performance of California children compared with English and Welsh children, he attributes the difference in achievement to differential expectations reflected in the curricula:

> In California much less was expected of pupils in arithmetic; more limited objectives were formulated for children of primary school age and less emphasis was placed on rapid progress in mechanical arithmetic than was customary in England and Wales.

Perhaps more subtle interaction variables related to the amount of prompting and probing that teachers do for individuals children. Brophy and Good (1974) indicate the teachers' expectations clearly determine whether learners will be prompted to respond or whether they will be stifled by the impatience of the teacher. Rosenthal (1973) refers to "expectant voices" of teachers that are often fulfilled by the child's responses. He reports that 11 out of 12 studies support the notion that teachers encourage greater responsiveness of students from whom they expect more. They call on such students more often, ask them harder questions, give them more time to answer, and prompt them toward the correct answer.

Closely related to prompting and probing is teacher interruptive behaviour especially in reading. Allington (1980), for example, examined the incidence and type of verbal interruption behaviours of teachers with high- and low-ability readers. He found that not only do teachers interrupt poor readers more often than good readers but also that the type of interruptive behaviour differed. Teachers tended to provide poor readers with remarks that directed attention to graphophonemic characteristics of the target word, whereas good readers were directed to semantic and syntactic information.

Further confirming evidence regarding differential task expectations of low and high achievers comes from student perception of teacher interactions with low and high achievers. Weinstein and Middlestadt (1979) found that student-perceived teacher treatment of male high achievers reflected high expectations, academic demands, and special privileges. Male low achievers were viewed as receiving fewer chances but greater teacher concern and vigilance.

Whether group assignment, labelling, or reinforcement comes first, if appears that the amount and quality of pupil-teacher interaction offer important clues to the mystery of possible expectancy cues which the learner internalizes, and ultimately translates into action.

Pupil-teacher and pupil-pupil interaction become a function of how both teachers and pupils perceive the individual child's status within the classroom social microcosm. Assignment to learning groups and special classes is often interpreted as a measure of status by both teachers and pupils. In a sociometric study of first-grade children, McGinley and McGinley (1970) found that lower reading group members chose significantly fewer than expected peers from their own group and significantly more than expected from the top reading groups. Middle group children made fewer than expected choices from lower reading groups and more than expected from top groups. The top group and fewer than expected more than expected choices from their own group and fewer than expected from the lower two groups. The authors interpreted their findings as reflecting the principle that persons are generally attracted to successful persons, to persons sharing a successful experience, and to persons in a success-reward situation. Further, they pointed to the probability of reciprocal success-reward relationships between teacher and children from the top reading groups. These children read well, and were rewarded and attracted to the source of reward—the teacher. The teacher, in turn, was rewarded by the children's success. The opposite cycle of events was interpreted as occurring for the lower reading groups children. Further apparent effects of group assignment involved teacher's expressed feelings about children. Five of the six teachers in the study expressed negative feelings toward children in the lower reading groups.

The effects of groups assignment have also been investigated with older children. Stevens (1971) found that students assigned to remedial reading groups display specific behaviours which make them socially unacceptable. He concluded that remedial readers know how others feel about them.

Tuckman and Bierman (1971) studies the effects of grouping. They moved randomly selected junior- and senior-high-school students into higher ability groups. Students who were transferred to higher groups achieved higher on standardized tests than students who were not transferred. Further, more than half of the students transferred were recommended later by teachers to be retained in these groups. The authors suggested a possible "inertia" function related to the grouping process and commented on the frustration and disillusionment of grouping procedures that "lock student in and out".

There is evidence that the physical structuring of the classroom, on the basis of group assignment, may interact with other variables that will facilitate the permanent "locking-in" or "cementing-in" process. In a longitudinal study, Rist (1970) described how kindergarten children were ranked during the first eight days of their school life on the basis of mere guesses at their learning potential. On the basis of these guesses the children were designated to their social and academic destinies at three different tables—assignment which appears to have led to differences in performances. For example, children assignment to the nonacademic table were farthest from the teacher, so far away, in fact, that they had difficulty hearing the teacher. In addition, these children received considerably less attention than groups closer to the teacher. The author indicated that expectations, translated into group assignment "output", consequently, differential treatment, were perpetuated as children advanced from first to second grade. Certainly, it is fallacious to generalize from a sample of one; however, variations of the dynamics of the Rist study are in evidence in at least some educational settings. Good and Brophy (1977) have supported the covariance of performance expectations with teachers' seating low achievers farther from themselves.

There appears little doubt that grouping, if employed on a long-term basis, affects achievement. Such implications pertain not only to in class grouping but also streaming. Burstall (1970) studies the achievement of children who scored low on tests designed to measure their performance in French. Schools where teachers expressed positive attitudes towards teaching French to low-ability children showed significantly higher achievement for such children than school where teachers expressed negative attitudes. Moreover, children of low ability reached the highest level of achievement in French when they had been taught in heterogeneous classes.

Pidgeon (1970), has commented on the effects of streaming. He found standard deviations on test scores for the International Achievement Pilot Studies to be higher for students in England and Wales than for students in other participating countries. He suggested that homogeneous assignment to classes is probably responsible for the results. He surmised that when childrens are assigned to homogeneous classes, teachers assume that the students have been accurately placed and that within any classroom the ability of the students will be highly similar. Children are, then, treated differentially according to their assignment. Such treatment and the "culture of defeat", which is often prevalent in low stream classes, may account for many of the fulfilled prophecies. Vernon (1957) has postulated that expectancy, high or low, might be responsible for the under-achievement of some pupils:

> Children who are related to a lower stream to suit their present level of ability are likely to be taught at a slower pace.... The initial differences become exaggerated and the duller children who happen to improve later fall too far below the higher streams in attainment to be able to catch up.

Just as teachers vary in their susceptibility to expectation "input" cues, so children vary in their susceptibility to the teacher "output." What are some of the variables that determine how potent this external imposition of cues will be?

The credibility of the source of "output" is perhaps one of the most potent variables. It is safe to make the generalization that, at least for primary-school children, the teachers' credibility rating is high. If teachers communicate to learner continuously that their performance is poor, this will undoubtedly influence the goals they strive to achieve.

The potency of specific expectancy cues also appears to be a function of the self-image of the learner. If a child already views itself as a competent learner, it may require a consistent bombardment of cues, and from credible sources, to change this image. Similarly, there is considerable evidence that a confirmed negative self-image is highly resistant to change and that part of this resistance result from the fact the learner needs to be faithful to the picture of self or else be threatened with the loss of selfhood. Bettleheim (1961) commented on situations where children decided to think of themselves as failures in this way, making it virtually impossible for criticism for poor performance to hurt their self-images. Cues even of the most subtle type will help confirm this negative image, which is like a boundary that limits the learner's actions.

The degree to which one views such boundaries as fixed has critical educational implications. One could argue that individuals who attribute success or failure to effort (rather than to ability) are filtering their performance through an unstable as opposed to a controllable factor. This has implications for the interpretation of and reaction to teacher "output." If learners who perform poorly conclude that they are helpless in changing their performance, then their failure will undermine their motivation, satisfaction with self, and future performance. On the other hand, if learners are encouraged to associate failure with factors which are controllable, then the debilitating consequences of failure may be avoided. By emphasizing the importance of internal, controllable factors as causes, teachers may promote pupils' educational experiences that are both more satisfying and more effective.

LEARNERS' SELF-EXPECTATION—PUPIL OUTPUT

If, indeed, children's perceptions of causes or present and past performance mediate their subsequent expectations of self, it seems logical that these self-expectations are the prime motivational energizers for pupil "output." It is this "output" which can be viewed as a significant mediating link between the teacher's original expectation of the child and the perpetuation (or modification) of the original expectation. Figure 7.1 presents a graphic illustration that summarized the cyclic flow of behavioural events.

It is reasonable that the factors which mediate learner's interpretation of teacher "output" will, at least in part, determine pupil "output." Reference has been made to the significance of learners' perceptions of locus of control of their performance—unstable/controllable, internal/external. Such perception has implications, for example, for the degree to which learners take risks in responding and the degree to which they persist at a task even if success is not imminent. There certainly is a close

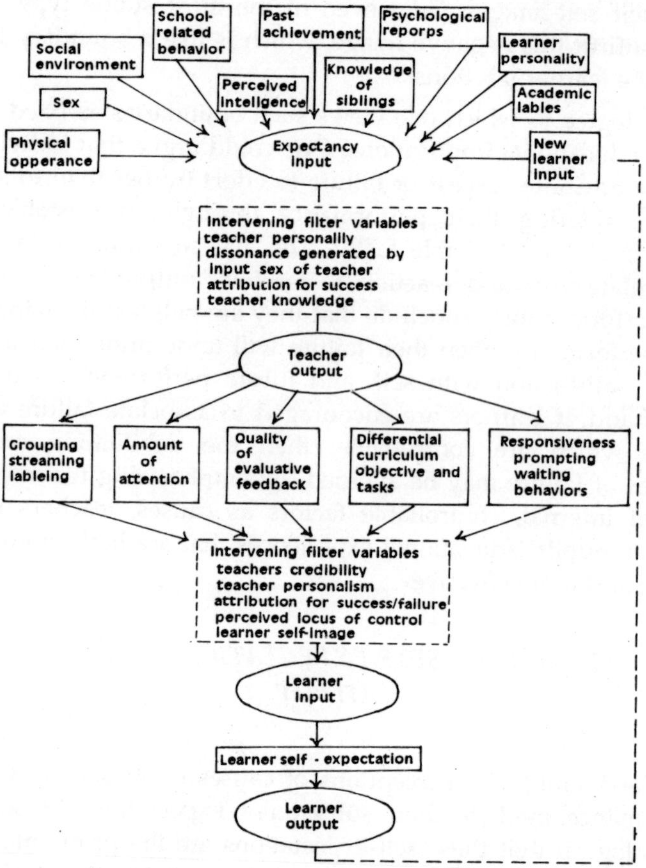

Fig. 7.1 The Mediating Cycle Between Teacher Expectation and Learner Output (after C. Braun, A.R. Neilsen)

relationship between self-expectation of failure in problem situations and withdrawal from such tasks. By the same token there is a close relationship between self-expectation of success in problem situations and persistence with such tasks.

A significant link that may account for the perpetuation of the cycle may be found in an interplay between expectations for success/failure and academic self-concept. If learners think of themselves as inferior, their actions will tend to be those of inferior persons and will confirm to the teacher and their peers the reasonableness of treating them as inferiors.

The cycle is probably maintained more than anything by the intellectual and affective constraints characteristics of the curriculum of the failing child. In the preoccupation to require every child to attain specific competencies, the need for children to explore widely to the point of discovering their own unique aptitudes has been forgotten. Curricular constraints frequently restrict the failing child to sterile, irrelevant, artificially contrived learning experiences.

The consequences for the individual learner of how the cycle (Fig. 7.1) is perpetuated or modified are staggering; the implications for the educator are sobering. Certainly, teacher personnel must become vitally concerned with preventative action. Perhaps the most logical step in this direction is a close examination of personal "input" factors relative to "teacher expectation of pupil." Teacher education courses and inservice programmes must sensitize teachers to the potent dynamics of these "input", and their potential to trigger specific "output" for individual child treatment. Teachers need to be sensitized to the personal biases and stereotypes they hold, and encouraged to examine these in relation to their classroom interactions with students.

8

Colleges and Politics

In thinking about what I might say as your keynote speaker, there was a strong temptations to repeat a speech given about four months ago as part of the 1974 University of Lethbridge Seminar Series on the Politics of Higher Educational entitled "from Autonomy to System: A Provincial Perspective". Doing so would have had two major advantages. It would have acquainted you with my perception of certain aspects of institutional-governmental relations in Alberta, and it would have saved me a substantial amount of time. On the other hand, while I am immodest enough to believe that what was said on that occasion has relevance beyond the borders of my own province, I felt obliged to approach this morning's presentation from a somewhat different angle. The fact that a number of you have already read my Lethrbidge talk, and that many persons were outraged by what I said, obviously constitute less acceptable reasons for not repeating it.

Eventually, I decided to let you have both barrels: to make available my from "autonomy to system" talk and to offer some observations intended to be even more closely linked to the theme of this conference. My initial comments will be about the context in which we in colleges and governments find ourselves. These will be followed by some discussion about the operation of instructions in the non-university sector before a look is taken at their interaction with government. I will then conclude with a few suggestions about future roles and actions.

CURRENT CONTEXT

A very significant and positive feature of the current context is that colleges and governments throughout Western Canada appear to be in agreement about the general functions that non-university higher educational institutions ought to perform. These may be defined as the development, integration and career functions.

The development function applies both to students and to the community. With students it means fulfilling expectations and actually meeting their specific needs through the application of the principle of personalization. This will require more innovation and less imitation in policies governing admission, programming and evaluation. In the case of the community, it means providing leadership-service in the solution of special regional problems, and in the anticipation and direction of future events. Through such interactions with a much wider constituency each college also will establish its own special identity or mission.

Integration is concerned with the harmonious development of the total person in pursuit of the higher order needs of liberation and integrity. Character traits such as self-awareness, flexibility, openness, creativity, courage and the capacity to love may be viewed as prerequisites of personal integration and responsible citizenship. These derive from the general education efforts of the college. As in earlier phases in the educational system, the valuing aspect of learning must be a central part of college experience. Valuing is necessary, not only to establish or reinforce personal behaviour standards, but also as a basis for active participation and influence in shaping the future of the wider community.

Colleges must also be involved in the education of individuals for an occupational role in society. For some they must provide first-entry occupational preparation. For others they must offer opportunities for upgrading previously acquired skills and knowledge. For still others they must provide for retaining in a different occupation. Performance of this career function requires that stress be placed upon the use of knowledge over knowledge for its own sake. In this way it will be possible to prepare persons who will be readily employable and productive within a minimum period of time. Nonetheless, care must be taken to avoid narrow prescription that might result in occupational obsolescence and that might restrict the awareness of the student of the broader social and personal implications of the specialized role that he may be called upon to play.

This agreement about functions come at a time with higher education in its traditional institutional form appears to be in a steady or slow growth state because of the interaction of a variety of well-known circumstances. less well-known—or at least less publicly acknowledged—are some of the actual and probable correlates of having a relatively modest rate of increase in revenues during the next few years.

First, and most obvious of these correlates, is the attempt on the part of those currently obvious of these preserve their jobs. while the phrase "feather-bedding" is probably too harsh a term, most of us have already observed efforts on the part of staff to safeguard their own positions. Tenured staff members develop even stronger arguments for the tenure system and agree that scrutiny for those aspiring to tenure be made more searching in order to limit rationally the total number of individuals permanently linked to institutions. Non-returned staff begin to look more favorably at unionism and a negotiated contract on the assumption that a contract might well be better job security, particularly for the young, the part-time and the peripheral instructor that would an orthodox tenure system. Similarly, it can be expected that administrative officers will probably spend more time in their present posts and will be reluctant to move in the absence of quite explicit provisions for job security. All of this is likely to result in an aging teaching staff and administrative core, finding each year it is easier espouse conventional wisdom than to withstand the physical and emotional costs of change.

Secondly, institutions experiencing competition for the clientele previously served are quite likely to embark on explorations for new mass markets which can generate increased revenue. The first step is for institutions to invade regions in which undercapacity still exists. This often gives rise to territorial disputes. The losers then search for completely new markets. This frantic pursuit of additional enrolments has led in the United States, according to a news item in the *Chronicle of Higher Education* (Magarrell, 1974), to a demand for "truth-in-education" laws to protect student interests. The area of the "education huskster" is closer than we care to admit.

A third correlate is curiously mixed in that it involves both rejection and utilization of educational technology. There are those who will eagerly embrace such things as computer-assisted learning, television, individually paced instruction, and the like, in the hope that these devices can bring about economies by reducing salary costs. Yet concurrently others will adamantly resist the application of technology except in a complementary or supportive role to the teacher. This resistance, is, of course, rationalized in many ways, including the old argument of impersonality and dehumanization. But significant also is the fear that a computer, or a programmed textbook, or a television set might replace a flesh-and-blood instructor.

Traditionally within higher education, tension has existed between those who teach and those who administer. However, in a steady or slow growth state a fourth correlate is likely to be greater animosity and mutual suspicion. Staff will remain convinced that central administration has access to money which it could use to increase their salaries or add appointments if it chose to do so. Administrators or board members, on the other hand, will frequently embrace the [...] belief that staff members are inflation oriented, if not lazy, and unwilling to assume heavier work loads in order to insure the economic viability of the institution.

Another probable correlate will be a tendency for central administration or the oligarchic staff leadership to isolate itself from reality. The scenario might run something as follows: administrators who served during periods of rapid growth and acknowledged success, and who attributed or allowed others to attribute these developments to their own leadership, upon finding that the institution is experiencing difficulty may tend to blame staff, obstreperous students, or some other group. Alternatively, they may be inclined to assume that if others would just follow their instructions, thing could return to happier norm. As these ideas persist they tend to talk more and more to their immediate associates and drift farther and farther away from the concerns of the majority of the people involved in the institution.

A sixth correlate is that institutions will be tempted to cut back on research and development activities designed ultimately to improve or terminate existing programs and to identify desirable new one and to concentrate on business-as-usual, stressing their seemingly successful ones. As institutions try to cope with little or no increase in financial support they first cut back on physical plant maintenance, secretarial help,and library acquisitions. Then they cut back on student-related activities like counselling and health services while upping the cost of housing and food services. Eventually, they may get around to curtailing staff appointments and finally to actually terminating some existing staff. The rarely used but opposite point of view is that only through intensified research and development activities is a no-growth or declining industry likely to reverse the tide of adversity.

These six potential correlates, while understandable, are all potentially pathological, destructive, and disruptive. Job preservation, frenzied search for new markets, fear of technological change, mutual suspicion on the part of staff of expenditure, unwillingness to change with the times, cutbacks of expenditure on research and development, and the insulation of central administration from the actualities of changing conditions could lead some institutions into even more precarious conditions than they presently face.

At the same time, every college is being buffeted by a world-wide impulse that has promoted the development of adult education systems and the management of these systems at the national or provincial level. That impulse can be identified as follows: societies, whether modern or modernizing, are experiencing an increasing demand for access to higher education and, at the same time, an increasing requirement for trained citizens that only higher education can produce. This demand and this requirement have forced a steady expansion of colleges and universities around the world. They have also brought about growing diversity in institutions, programs and services to meet the specialized needs of students and society. No longer can one institution, or even one type of institution, hope to provide the myriad specialities that now comprise post-secondary education. Today, the total requirements of higher education are met through a system of diverse institutions and agencies. Each part of the system servers some special purpose or a particular geographic area, but collectively the system offers a fuller range of educational choice.

In an interconnected and interdependent system of institutions, programs and services, the offerings of individual institutions can no longer be left to chance. Large-scale planning is necessary to coordinate the many parts of the system, and since this is obviously beyond the capacity of any single institutions, agencies for this purpose have emerged or are proposed as the newest feature on the academic landscape invirtually every country of the world.

SYSTEM OPERATION

Two of the key components in the system of adult education in Western Canada are colleges and governments. The college components consists of a number of institutions that vary in size, name, age, services, internal structure and relations to government. They are, however, quite similar in functions, clientele, and financing. Yet it is still difficult to define with precision this component, and its constituent parts, because our data base or statistics are incomplete and unnecessarily complicated.

Thus it is not surprising to find in the report on *New College Systems in Canada*, prepared by Cicely. Watson (1973) of the Ontario Institute for Studies in Education, the assertion that the statistical records of colleges are of such poor quality that it is difficult to see how administrators can make rational educational policy decisions. This is a very serious weakeness in the non-university sector which colleges and governments are already working in concert to overcome.

Another cause for joint concern and action identified in this same report is that the relevant legislation, regulation, staff manuals, calendars, functional descriptions of offices, and public statement of officials of this sub-stems portray a picture which very often differs from that found upon visiting the various institutions. Watson and her colleagues marveled at the ingenuity with which senior officials make institutions mirror their own philosophy, reinforcing or distorting the sub-system as designed. The regulations of the CAATs in Ontario provide for no faculty or student participation in the operation of the college, yet they seem to have at least as important a consultative role as that of their counterparts in the other provinces. The Alberta public colleges provide officially for student and faculty participation, but from descriptions of procedures obtained in the institutions themselves, their consultative activities seems rather minor and their initiating power less than the actual practice in Ontario. Although formally extremely democratic, most of the CEGEPs in Quebec actually seem to be run in quite authoritarian fashion. This state of affairs cannot be assessed other than subjectively, on the basis of the statements of administrators and the documented public stances of the faculty. Authoritarianism is a measure of the difference between one's expectation of being permitted to participate in decision-making and the degree to which one is given the opportunity to participate. Some staff and students may hold unrealistically high expectations; others are content because their expectations are humble. Generally, all of these institutions were found to more conservative and hierarchical than was previously supposed.

At the same time, the Watson study supports the view that college administrators and associated government officers are imbued with a strong sense of mission and social cause. Those involved in the non-university sector are convinced that colleges are a liberating force, enabling students to realize ambitions they could otherwise never hope to achieve and allowing faculty to provide a service and enjoy a useful sense of purpose hitherto generally denied to teachers at this level. And there is little doubt that our colleges are serving a broader segment of society than our universities. They are indeed broadening the horizon for adults whose opportunities have hitherto been too narrowly limited. They are free from many of the constraints of academic tradition, but they are not free from the social constraints which lie beneath some of the academic selection devices. In the past, Western Canada has been able to provide considerable scope for human development to people from other countries. because its rapidly expanding economy created these opportunities. Yet in many ways these were not matched with a careful cultivation, through education, of our own human resources. Our colleges can do much to redress the balance.

But the revolution in quality and quantity of adult recurrent education which they have helped to trigger has barely begun. Nor has it significantly altered college operation. Colleges have, as yet, made virtually no contribution to educational process changes. They have merely mimicked many of the most undesirable features of traditional academic studies. Their programs are fragmented, with large numbers of courses, class hours and specific assignments. There is relatively little freedom of or from study for their students. Their institutional structure is often formal and expensive, using a very large number of highly paid professional staff with considerable overlapping of administrative authority. In the rapid birth and exponential growth phases that many colleges experienced there was ample opportunity for empire building, and the duplication which these empires represent will be difficult to eliminate. Their educational process is equally expensive, characterized by a very large number of teachers and expensive machinery and material. This condition is changing as funds become scarcer. This missionary spirit of college administrators is now being put to the test as they are expected to serve many more students on proportionately fewer dollars. In such a situation, colleges might well become pioneers in reforming traditional teaching/learning processes. The OECD report concludes, however, that they lack two important ingredients to accomplish this: at the institutional level, faculty commitment to experimentation; and at the system level, administrative commitment to empirically based research and evaluation.

The apparent absence of these two ingredients or commitments may be, at least in part, a reflection of a developmental pattern which many formal organizations seem to follow. First comes the "birth" period when relationships between all staff are informal and not appreciably controlled; tasks are relatively unspecialized; reunite procedures are not well established; goals and operational objectives are in the process of being developed; there is freedom to experiment in a tolerant environment. This is followed by the "youth" period when interpersonal relationships become formalized; tasks become more specialized; procedures become more routine as the number and complexity of activities increase; size increases rapidly; the environment becomes less supportive and more critical of the organization. A "productive" period then emerges in which formal interpersonal relationships become stabilized; the number and kind of specialized tasks and standard activities are limited; the rate of size increase decreases; innovativeness is less encouraged; the amount and intensity of activities to influence a less supportive environment increase. Concluding this unfolding is the "mature" period when structures and functions become fixed; broad goals become emphasized; decentralized decision-making is encouraged; size and program changes occur slowly; some control over the environment has been obtained.

The existence and influence of such a four-fold developmental sequence in Alberta colleges was recently examined by Heron and Friesen (1973), who reported three main sets of conclusions.

It terms of levels of decision-making, as colleges grow older they tend to become more decentralized and to become more independent of their boards of governors. Though decision-making, especially for operational problems, does not necessarily become more widespread at any one level, it does seem to become distributed among more and lower levels in the college hierarchy. At the same time, a clearer distinction between operational and policy decisions appears to occur, with operational decisions being made by the chief executive officer and his staff and policy decisions by the board and the provincial government authority.

In terms of the degree to which staff behaviours are both specialized and standardized, there is a strong suggestion that increased structuring is directly related to the introduction of increasing numbers and kinds of specialized programs. Not only does specialization suggest the need for more standard types of control but it also appears to result in an increase in the number of support staff. This increase in specialization appears also to result in more decentralized decision-making.

Mechanisms for controlling and regulating employee behavior also tend to be different at different periods in the structural development of colleges. In the initial stages of growth, colleges tend to exercise control by centralizing decision-making at the level of the chief executive and the board of governors. This centralization and the wide reporting spans enjoyed by the chief executive also suggest a sensitivity to the surrounding environment to which the college is accountable, namely, the various constituencies represented on the board of governors. In the "youth" state, college appear to exercise control by instituting many direct reporting relationships between subordinate and supervisors. There was a strong suggestion that control could be obtained more readily through surveillance and reporting procedures than through the establishment of more impersonal and procedural mechanisms. In the later stages these reporting relationships were either stabilized or even reduced. They became supplanted by the gradual introduction of more and more written documents to define and record the performance of employees and to communicate rules, regulations, and guidelines for standardizing procedures.

In summary, Heron and Friesen argue, as does Watson, that in the dimensions of structuring staff activities, of decentralizing decision-making and of changing hierarchical configurations, colleges exemplify the process commonly referred to as bureaucratization. In other words colleges, as has been postulated for other formal organizations, seem to move from a participative, open-climate stance in their early years to a more authoritarian, closed-climate stance in their late years. They also appear to become less influenced by community wishes as these are expressed through a board of governors or advisory committees. In addition, these progressions seem to occur independently of such factors as changes in chief executive, in legislation, in the compositions of the board of governors, in location in physical plant, and in numbers and kinds of programs. Given this kind of strong internal momentum in institutions of higher education, it is little wonder that government sometimes resort to the use of equally strong measures to restrain or redirect it.

I am unaware of any comparable appraisals of provincial coordinating agencies—government departments or otherwise.

Yet I suspect that many of you, on the basis of personal experience, would be inclined to agree with me that in Western Canada these government organizations exhibit similar characteristics. Certainly the trend seems to be more clearly toward centralization to effect greater accountability, more accurate and complete information, and more effective complementation of efforts. Closely related to this trend is growing central agency concern about issues that have often been primarily within the jurisdiction of institutions, such as faculty functions and work load. To a considerable extent this concern reflects disenchantment with traditional institutional approaches to budget justification and quality evaluation in terms of inputs rather than results. Related to accountability, effective management, centralization and internal operation is a more fundamental concern of legislators over adequate means for evaluating higher education, including its outputs in relation to societal needs. Recent controversies about surpluses of highly educated manpower in some areas and shortages in other mirror the increasing demand for more effective planning to conserve and develop human resources. There are also counter trends in every province related not to real need analysis, but to special-interest pleading and what can only be described as vested interest and local pride.

Although circumstances and means vary in British Columbia, Alberta, Saskatchewan and Manitoba, there is an obvious determination to gain the commitment to experimentation and to empirically based research and evaluation which the OECD report claimed was needed Currently, it seems that governments are more determined that this should occur than are the colleges. Witness the various new carrot-and-stick funding arrangements and the more rigorous program review policies and procedures appearing on the Western scene.

The apparent difference in determination for reform may arise from differences in development periods between a specific college or group of college and a given government, including its designated coordinating agency. For example, a "mature" college is likely to be critically suspicious of a government during its "birth" period or of a coordinating agency in its aggressive "youth" stage. Similarly, a college in its "birth" and/or "youth" phases is probably going to be a source of frustration and anxiety to a "productive" and/or "mature" central authority. In either case, the resulting cross-impacts are apt to yield visible differences in externally versus internally induced initiatives for change.

FORWARD TOGETHER

Having noted the existence of some points of congruence and disparity in the intentions and behaviors of colleges and governments in a changing contextual framework, it seems appropriate to conclude with a few suggestions about what colleges and governments might do so that together they can better serve the electorate.

The first of these is that the ideal comprehensive by institutions should be abandoned. Instead each ought to focus on sharply delineated markets desiring specialized services. The ideal of comprehensiveness which, of course, is essential at the system level, holds that all community colleges should offer university transfer program, technical-vocational education, general education, further education, counseling and guidance while serving as a focal point for community cultural, recreational, and intellectual interests and aspirations. Even technical institutes, vocational centres, agricultural colleges and proprietary schools are seen as offering comprehensive programs in liberal or general education. Rejecting such an ideal at the institutional level means trying to select a competitive domain in which a given institution can or does have an advantage and building upon that strength and opportunity. It means identifying a distinctive and continuing clientele through sensitive market research, and developing programs of specific interest to that group. It means assuming a "broker" role in relation to other relatively unique institutions to help facilitate the delivery of comprehensive services by the system to various regions in a province. And it also means curbing narrow faculty, administrative or community desires or aspirations so often rationalized through arguing a social or economic need. There is emerging indicative evidence that serving a specialized clientele produces stable or expanding enrolments and financial viability. When coupled with extra-institutional services arranged or purchased for specified periods for particular clients, this approach also promises to extend educational opportunity. Only the system can reasonably strive to be all things to all people.

A second, and closely related suggestion, is for colleges and governments to exhibit parsimony with respect to claims. Public malaise regarding higher education earlier in this decade was considerably precipitated by the grandiose claims of educators to be able to do too much too frequently during the times of expansion. The institutional question was phrased, "Is there a demonstrable social need for something?" with the answer, "If there is, the institution should attempt to do it." Such rhetoric produced rampant program proliferation. It is quite significant that researches discovered that one of the correlates of institutions in serious financial difficulties was rapid program expansion. It is also significant that an investigator who examined the case histories of recently dead institutions discovered that all had manifested a pattern of frenzied creation of new programs during the last years before death. A better question might be, "What is the least an institution can do in order to meet its mandate and to warrant the financial support necessary to ensure institutional continuation?" Again, in order to determine a parsimonious catalog of purposes of institutionally mounted programs which will appeal to distinctive clienteles, careful market analysis to detect trends and discern likely saturation points is essential a both the local and provincial levels.

Third, increase the use of an external performance audit. Performance audits by outsiders—people who would not be representing the provincial agency or the institution—would provide a less biased appraisal of existing programs or services in terms of their states objectives. Moreover, only an external evaluation is ever likely to question the validity of the objectives themselves. Further, the audit would assess the organization and operating efficiency of the unit in relation to the delivery mechanism, and also evaluate the extent to which effective quality was being maintained relative to the investment of resources in the unit. By providing for performance audits on the request of an institution or on its own initiative, the provincial agency would not abrogate its authority and responsibility, nor undermine institutional independence. Rather, the general overriding purpose of such an audit would be to develop a report to serve as the basis for discussion between the agency and institution. This audit, this common ground for discussion, would provide the basis for a joint review of high-cost and/or declining enrolment programs with a view to either making them more attractive and efficient or discontinuing them.

Fourth, in setting priorities government must take responsibility for ensuring that the institutions affected both by the priorities and by the actual funding process of fully involved. Higher education budgets, because of their magnitude and potential impact, are a sensitive matter. The sensitivity extends to institutional administrators, board members and civil servants. It also extends to elected representative, who have the responsibility for establishing priorities and eventually approving public dollars for the delivery of higher education. Apprehension and suspicion are common. Institutional administrators fear that the justifiable—even essential—items of program and service support will be deleted from their budget requests through ignorance or bias. Officials of the government agency with responsibility for the budget review of higher educational institutions are concerned that provincial priorities will not be acknowledged and given adequate consideration. In addition, members of the legislature and board members may be concerned about actions that may be detrimental to their constituents. In this kind of atmosphere it is imperative that the establishment of priorities and their translation into funding at the provincial level occurs not in isolation but rather with the full knowledge and, to the extent possible, effective involvement of all responsible parties.

A CONCLUDING OBSERVATION

These four suggestions may not be particularly startling. But they could help all of us achieve a little more satisfaction from the state of affairs projected for the immediate future. A relocalized faculty might contribute once again to the development of a feeling of community. A more parsimonious set of goals might allow time and energy to be devoted to the more effective achievement of those goals. And if understanding and acceptance of reality is the correlate of satisfying mental and organizational health, then widespread understanding and acceptance of a more realistic view of programs and services could contribute to greater tranquillity on the campus and increased levels of support by government.

In such circumstances it is likely that the joint commitment of colleges and governments to an open society in which the fewest possible number of educative decisions are irrevocable will be attainable. And the concept of recurrent education is then not just a matter of rigging a safety net for those who fall, but a perpetuation of the idea of a learning community in which it is always possible to acquire knowledge and organized experience, whether for vocational reasons, for cultural reasons, of pleasure or for a combination of all these. This is a luxury which Western Canadians should be able to afford in the last quarter of the twentieth century.

9

Swedish Higher Education for Human Resource Development

ABSTRACT

The Swedish 1968 Educational Commission (U 68) completed its main report in 1973. The Commission recommends a very wide definition of the concept of higher education so as to include any qualified education or training for adults, whether academic or vocational in nature. Higher education should be seen in the context of an overall educational planning, with the aim of distributing educational resources to meet the needs of every citizen. As a consequence, U 68 proposes a *numerous clausus* for higher education as a whole. The geographic distribution of higher education is also being stressed, and the creation of one comprehensive institutional organisation for the main part of all higher education is proposed.

The proposals of the commission should be seen in the perspective of recurrent education. The author points to the possible development of a new educational structure, the main feature of which is the division into compulsory and post-compulsory education.

THE 1968 EDUCATIONAL COMMISSION

In the course of 1973, the Swedish Educational Commission (U 68), appointed in 1968 by the Swedish Minister of Education, has completed several reports. The following discussion is intended to present the main issues of the commission's report and the debates surrounding it.

The use of Government-appointed *ad hoc* commissions for planning purposes has long traditions in Sweden. One of its essential features is the open circulation of the commission's final reports to all authorities, institutions and groups involved in the problem and the collection of their views before coming to a final decision. In the case of U 68 the deadline for this "formal" discussion was the Ist February 1974. At the time of writing, it was too early to form a comprehensive idea of the reactions to the proposals of the 1968 Educational Commission.

This openness in the decision-making procedure already existed within the commission. Thus U 68, whose members have been the Under-Secretary of State for Education (chairman), the Chancellor of the Swedish Universities, and the Directors-General of the National Board of Education and of the National Labour Market Board, has had three adjoint Reference Groups. Through these groups, representatives of the political parties, of teachers and students, and of the various labour market organizations, have taken part in the work of the commission.

According to the schedule suggested by the commission, Parliament should take a decision in principle on the proposals in late 1974. It is envisaged this implementation would begin in the year 1976/77.

THE BACKGROUND

Most countries have seen a rapid development of education and research in recent decades. Compared to the educational situation in most Western countries, the Swedish system thirty years ago was rather old-fashioned and relatively small. Today the level of enrolment in all forms of Swedish education (with the important exception of pre-schooling) is amongst the highest in Europe and the structure of the school has been completely remodeled. Thus, for good or ill, the changes in education in Sweden have been more profound than in many comparable countries.

In a sense, 1962 was the pivotal year of this development. Parliament introduced a *nine-year comprehensive school (grundskola)*, compulsory for all youngsters aged 7–16. The curriculum of the comprehensive school is common to all pupils in grades 1–6. In grades 7–9 a certain specialization takes place according to the interests of the pupils, but there is no streaming with definite consequences for future choice of education or job.

A decision by Parliament in 1968 gave a more coherent organization to the *upper secondary school (gymnasieskola)*, which has been in force since the school year 1971/72. The present capacity of the upper secondary school corresponds to about ninety per cent of the 16-years-olds. However, only three quarters of the pupils who complete the ninth grade of the comprehensive school go immediately to further studies. Many of the pupils in the upper secondary school have returned to studies after a period of work.

The upper secondary school consists of a little more than twenty branches. Five of these, representing together about one-third of the intake capacity, are three- or four-year programmes that qualify, in the present organization, for university studies. The majority of the other branches, all of which are two-year programmes, have a mainly vocational goal, although all of them also give a certain amount of preparation for further studies.

Higher education is intended for adults. No description of the environment of higher education is fairly complete without inclusion of what is often called, with a rather narrow use of the term, *adult education*. Sweden has old traditions in this field through its folk high schools and voluntary educational associations. The number of participants in study circles is close to two million, a quarter of the total population. In recent years a very essential part of the country's educational effort has been labour-market training which in 1972/73 involved some 140,000 persons. The magnitude of the very extensive educational efforts within private and state enterprises is difficult to estimate.

The quantitative development of higher education in the 1950s and 1960s is illustrated in Table 9.1. The last few years have shown some decline in the number of entrants in post-secondary education, as is indicated in Figure 9.1. With some simplification which can, however, be supported by statements in government papers, it can be said that the expansion of technical, economic, medical, and other clearly professionally oriented studies with a *numerus clausus* has been motivated by labour-market needs, whereas the open faculties have catered for the private demand of higher education. In practice, the line of division between *numerus clausus* and open admission has also, to a considerable extent, been a question of unit costs.

Table 9.1

Quantitative Development of Higher Education in Sweden

Year	*Net no. of newly enrolled students*	*No. of Students present*
1950/51	3 500	17 000
1960/61	8 000	37 000
1970/71	26 000	125 000

It is natural that practical considerations have played a predominant part in educational planning during a period of such explosive development as the 1960s. The creation of new universities and colleges and the organization of higher education so as to meet the most immediate needs of modern society are impressive results of the planning commissions of 1945, 1955 and 1963. An important part of the fundamental policy goes back to the Wicksell-Jerneman commission of the early 1930s, which considered the relationship between higher education and the labour market. Their recommendations emphasized the need for information on labour-market prospects, for educational and vocational guidance and for the development of alternatives to the traditional university education. As for the much-debated question of unrestricted admission to higher studies, the commission pointed out the disadvantages of a "mixed" system of faculties, some open to all, others with a limited intake, but turned down the idea of a general *numerus clausus* tied to manpower forecasts.

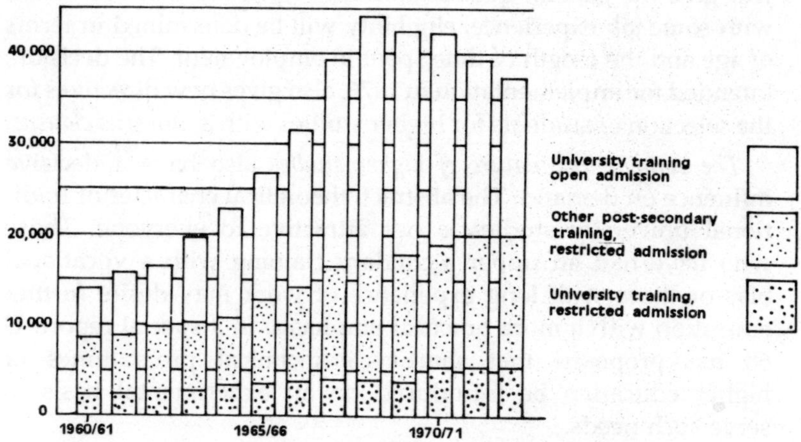

Fig. 9.1 Net Number of New Entrants to University and Other Post-secondary Training.

In the late 1960s, both the enormous quantitative development of higher education and the thorough change in the structure of the school system called for a review of all aspects of higher education. The 1968 Educational Commission was given the task of working out proposals for plans for the number of students, the location and the organization of basic higher education. Research and research training have not been within the domain of U 68, but the connections between basic training and research have called for obvious consideration.

HIGHER EDUCATION FOR WHOM

For whom is higher education intended and who participates in it? It is well known that a number of factors have an important influence on the selection of students. One is the underlying *school system* and its academic or vocational character. Another critical factor is the admissions procedure. The traditional entrance qualification in Sweden has been completion of one of the academic streams of the upper secondary school, but a decision in principle by Parliament in 1972 introduced new rules: any section of the upper secondary school, be it academic or vocational in character, will give the general qualification for higher studies. For adults with some job experience, eligibility will be determined in terms of age and the length of time spent in employment. The decision, intended for implementation in 1976, also gives new directives for the selection of students for higher studies with a *numerus clausus*.

The content and nature of higher studies also have a decisive influence on demand. The abstract, theoretical character of traditional university studies is not attractive to everyone. Those who have had an upper secondary training with a vocational bias or those with long experience of work may desire further education with a more practical emphasis. In a special report, U 68 has proposed that short-cycle technical programmes of higher education be introduced on an experimental basis to serve such needs.

The *location of higher education* and the forms for its dissemination are of great importance for the geographical and social patterns of recruitment. U 68 proposes that new provision of basic higher education should be almost entirely in locations other than the traditional university cities, with an emphasis on decentralized teaching so as to reach as many as possible of the potential students of the area. On the other hand, the commission assumes that research and research training should in the future, as now, be concentrated in seven cities (Stockholm, Goteborg, Malmo-Lund, Uppsala, Linkoping, Umea and Lulea). Thus, of the nineteen proposed higher-educational areas, twelve will have facilities only for basic types of higher education. This will require close co-operation between institutions in order to provide links between basic training and research. Other decisive factors are financial support, educational guidance and information. They are taken care of by other commissions and by regular planning activities.

The present capacity of what is generally called post-secondary education corresponds to almost one-third of an age-group. The proposals of U 68 assume that higher education will expand and develop in order to fulfil the need for highly qualified training of potentially everyone. This does not mean that the commission is unaware of the constraints imposed on the development of an organization by the character of its present resources, its traditions, its "inner logic", and so on. It does mean, however, that long-term planning, and its gradual realization, should aim at a much broader and more varied concept of higher education than at present. The vision of U 68 is not mass production of higher education but an organization that serves complex educational needs, the excellence of which is to be measured along many dimensions.

Such a programme gives to overall educational planning the responsibility of distributing educational resources in accordance with the needs of every citizen, irrespective of economic and social status, sex, religion, place of residence, and, last but not least, age. The century-old tradition of open access to some of the university faculties has therefore to be questioned on grounds of equality. In fact, U 68 proposes a *numerus clausus* for higher education as a whole.

With this general outlook it is natural to use the term *higher education* for a vast field of educational opportunities. In the U 68 proposals, for example, the training of ship masters, nurses, physical therapists and pre-school teachers is considered to be part of higher education. This implies an important attitude towards the future: institutions of higher education should take responsibility for a much wider spectrum of educational efforts than at present.

HIGHER EDUCATION AND THE LABOUR MARKET

The terms of reference of the U 68 commission state the principle that higher education should prepare students for their future occupational activity: this does not exclude broad educational programmes, with application in wide vocational fields. In its main report, the commission develops this theme further. Every kind of education usually has both elements that are adapted to the present state of an occupation and elements that aim at change and development. Education should train the will and ability to arrive at an overall analysis of the occupational activity and its conditions. It is also stressed that only part of the occupational preparation in basic higher education should be concerned with immediate needs. A very important task is to prepare for on-the-job training and for broader responsibility and greater independence in later years.

Against this background it was found suitable to consider the structure of higher education in *two dimensions* as illustrated in Table 9.2.

Table 9.2

Examples of the Two-Dimensional Classification of Higher Education

Base Fields / *Occupational Training Sectors*	physics and chemistry	chemistry and biology	behavioural sciences	social sciences	mathematics and systems sciences	linguistics	history, aesthetics, science of religion
technology	Engineer						
administration and economics				Law			
medicine and social work		Physician	Social worker				
teaching						Language teacher	
cultural work and information							Priest

Educational programmes have been divided on the one hand into five occupational training sectors and, on the other, into seven "base fields." For example, the training of physicians falls into the occupational training sector "medicine and social work" and into the base field "chemistry-biology." The two dimensions express a tension which is inherent in all education and which is reflected in the U 68 proposals. The occupational dimensions represent an exterior element in education, whereas the base fields stand for an inner structure of knowledge. There is no unique ideal for the balance between the two elements, valid for all kinds of higher education or for all times. It is, however, a firm assumption in the U 68 proposals that existing educational programmes in which one or the other dimension is lacking do not represent an ideal balance.

It has been fashionable among educational planners to frown upon *manpower forecasts*. Since they are unreliable, it is claimed that one had better neglect them totally: flexibility and generality is to be the cure of all troubles. U 68 endorses the traditional criticism of an educational planning wholly adapted to forecasts and states that planning, as far as the total capacity of higher education is concerned, should be guided rather by private demand and by considerations of the optimal distribution of total educational resources in order to serve the needs of all citizens.

The Forecasting Institute of the National Central Bureau of Statistics has made two extensive studies that have served as a basis, in the spirit outlined above, of the commission's proposals. These forecasts aim at covering the whole surface of contact between the labour market and the educational system. They illustrate the problems of balance at large rather than the future prospects of single occupations. Some of the results are shown in Figure 9.2. The shadowed areas are meant to indicate the caution necessary in interpreting the forecasts for purposes of educational planning. The reader is invited to speculate on the conclusion to be drawn for the 1980s. The proposals for quantitative planning are summarized in Table 9.3 below. The idea of a

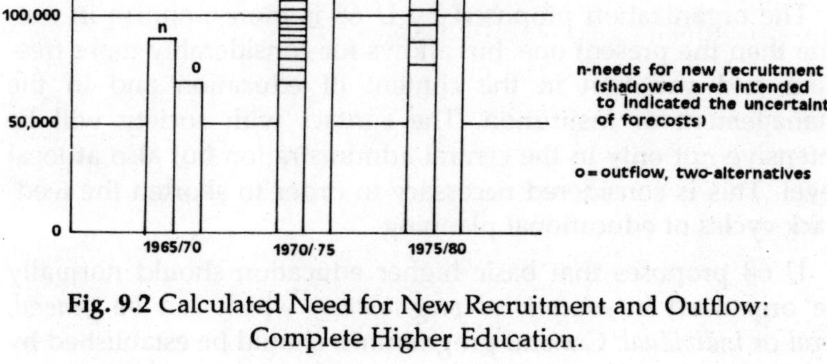

Fig. 9.2 Calculated Need for New Recruitment and Outflow: Complete Higher Education.

numerus clausus has been received rather favourably by most of those concerned, with the exception of the student organizations, which defend the traditional academic freedom also in this respect. When the universities accept it, they do so reluctantly. However, very few of those that accept a more conscious quantitative planning do so with the motivation given by the commission.

THE ORGANIZATION OF HIGHER EDUCATION

If higher education is potentially to serve the needs of every citizen and if one of the goals of every educational programme is preparation for a future occupation, then contacts with society become a central issue in its organization. But the organization has also to meet the demands of the inner structure of knowledge, carried by both tradition and the frontiers of fundamental research. With such points of departure, it is inevitable that any proposals, however well balanced they may seem to the commission, will be looked upon as dangerous by the defenders of the present balance of status, power and influence. A more immediate contact with society and occupational life is opposed by those whose contacts are today indirect, bureaucratic and lagging behind. The arguments very often invoke the undeniable values of freedom of learning and the training to criticize, and the democratic claims of participation in decision-making. An integration in a bigger organization, which would facilitate fruitful contacts with other kinds of education and common use of resources, is opposed on the grounds that it reduces traditional contacts with society.

The organization proposed by U 68 is more uniform in outline than the present one, but allows for considerably more freedom and variation in the content of education and in the management of institution. The contact with society will be intensive not only in the central administration but also at local level. This is considered necessary in order to shorten the feedback cycles of educational planning.

U 68 proposes that basic higher education should normally be organized in *educational programmes*, which can be *general*, *local* or *individual*. General programmes should be established by the Government and local and individual programmes by the local higher-education authorities (in the case of an individual programme after application from the student). Table 9.3 shows the proposed capacity of the general educational programmes in the various occupational training sectors and of local and individual programmes. As a rule, an educational programme should be made up a *courses* giving credit points corresponding to estimated study time. A student may want to study only one or more separate courses of an established educational programme. Sometimes a course will be given in its own right, without connection with an educational programme. The commission proposes a very considerable increase in the numbers of such *single courses*, corresponding in 1976 to about 20,000 full-time students or an equivalent greater number if some of them are part-time.

In order to facilitate combinations of courses over the whole field of higher education, a common marking system is proposed (with marks of Fail, Pass and Credit) as well as a uniform system of documentation. Certificates of basic higher education should draw the attention more to content and quality; they should not contain titles associated with the education received. The obvious aim is to concentrate the attention of students and employers on education itself and detract it from the false goal of certification.

As far as *institutional organization* is concerned, U 68 proposes a division of the country into nineteen higher-educational areas, in each of which there should be (with few exceptions) one joint organization of all state higher education, covering where applicable also research and research training, under a Board of Higher Education. This board should have some ten members, appointed by the Government after proposals from relevant authorities and organizations. It is proposed that the majority of the Board should represent public interests, but also representatives of students, teachers and other personnel should be included.

Instruction and research take place in the institutes. The forms of administration of these are mainly left to the local authorities. It is assumed that an institute will be able to carry through instruction within several educational programmes, and within different occupational training sectors. It is proposed that, contrary to the present situation, the classification into institutes should be a local responsibility. It can be foreseen, however, that the institutes will in many cases represent the "intrinsic" dimension of the "base fields" (Cf. Figure 9.2). The occupational dimension of basic higher education is represented in the proposed organization by educational committees, each responsible for the planning of one occupational training sector. Where suitable, these are supplemented by programme committees for educational programmes or groups of programmes.

Table 9.3

Admission Capacity of Educational Programmes, by Occupational Training Sector (Round Numbers)

Sector		*1971/72*	*1976/77*	*1983/84*
Technological training	U	5 300*	7 300	10 000
	L		6 700	9 000
Administrative and economic training	U	6 500*	8 800	10 000
	L		7 700	9 000
Training in medicine, social work, etc.	U	7 500	8 800	10 500
	L		8 400	9 500
Teacher training	U	9 500	9 900	10 000
	L		9 400	9 000
Training for cultural and informative occupations	U	1 000*	2 000	3 000
	L		1900	2 500
Local and individual educational programmes	U	—	5 000	4 500
	L		3 500	3 500
Without stated occupational aims	U	7 000*	—	—
	L			
Total	U	37 000	42 000	48 000
	L		37 000	42 000

U = Upper planning limit
L = Lower planning limit
* The present capacity within the training sectors for administrative and economic occupations, and for cultural and informative occupations, lies partly within the free faculties, and only an approximate estimate is possible. Except as regards the training of subject teachers, training at the faculties of mathematics and natural sciences that prepares students for e.g. technical functions has been assigned to "training without stated occupational aims."

RECURRENT EDUCATION

The term "recurrent education" is of recent origin but as an individual pattern of behavior there is nothing new of it. A more or less systematic interplay between productive work and formalized training has always been looked upon with benevolence, although the trend of the last few decades has been against recurrent education. The motives for recurrent education are threefold:

(1) better contacts between education, working life and society at large;

(2) promotion of equal educational opportunity by offering new possibilities of education for those who chose a job in their youth or who had then no other alternative;

(3) pedagogical efficiency.

None of these arguments points uniquely to one particular realization of the idea of recurrent education as the optimal solution in any single case. Moreover, it is easy to find recurrent arrangements that are pedagogically inefficient and that promote differences in educational opportunity. The point to be made is that we have to consider the problem of how to distribute educational resources over the life span of every individual rather than, as at present, concentrating them in one continuous period in youth. This holds true as much in industrialized western societies as in developing countries.

Even a short list of problems will illustrate the difficulties involved:

(1) Should school for the 16–19 year olds prepare every pupil for further studies and for an immediate period of work?

(2) In the pattern of recurrent education, what should be the balance between basic higher education and further training? What should be the division of responsibility between society, employers and the individual?

(3) How can the admission of students with work experience be encouraged? Should experience primarily be connected with and of specific value for the higher studies?

(4) How can we prevent recurrent education from developing into an even better ladder of self-development for the suc-

cessful, instead of making it a means to a more even distribution of educational resources?

(5) How should financial support be designed in order to make it possible for adults to return to studies in spite of their economic responsibilities?

It is obvious that the proposals of one single planning commission cannot solve these very intricate problems. U 68 lays no claim to final solutions: the very definition of recurrent education involves so many factors that any practical decision has to be a compromise between conflicting demands. It is, however, easily seen that some features of the present Swedish reforms of reform proposals are designed to promote recurrent education. The new rules of admission to higher education, the increased capacity of single courses, the emphasis on new places and new forms of dissemination of higher education, and the short-cycle technical programmes may be mentioned. In a more general sense, the more conscious distribution of educational resources leading to the general 3numerus clausus, and the stress on contacts at all levels between higher education and society, should be seen in the same context.

When launched for discussion, the idea of recurrent education was received favourably not only by the various organizations of the labour-market but also by educationists and by the public at large. The final report has caused some concern in that it contained no proposals for *the system* of recurrent education, but the commission believes that recurrent education is not something to be introduced on a specific date or organized in parallel with existing schools and universities. It is a pattern, already existing, that has to be developed carefully, sometimes cautiously, by gradual steps and which should permeate *all* institutions of education. In the longer term, then, ideas related to recurrent education may lead to a fundamentally new structure of education. The difficult and crucial problem of the education of the 16–19-year-olds was mentioned above. It may well be that the questions of the length and content of compulsory education have to be restated in the framework of recurrent education. The traditional division of education into primary, secondary and tertiary levels seems, for example in the analysis of the Organisation for Economic Co-operation and Development (1973), to be replaced by the notions of compulsory and post-compulsory education. The function and structure, in this perspective, of what is at present called higher education is well worth a serious analysis.

10

Accountability and Development

In this book, *Sense and Sensibilia*, the philosopher John Austin once equipped that much of recent philosophy was dominated by 'a worship of tidy-looking dichotomies'. Austin's observation might well apply to recent writings on educational accountability, for here we find a tendency among many educationists to view systems of accountability in a dichotomous way. Thus we find writers either opting for managerial models, which stress the need to make schools accountable to some higher bureaucratic authority, or preferring democratic models, which suggest that schools should be self-governing. The former emphasize economic considerations and the need to ensure efficient use of resources, measured against a well defined set of objectives, while the latter stress more cultural criteria, and the need to promote experimentation and more diverse educational outcomes. But must these two approaches to educational accountability always be viewed in contra-distinction to each other? Is it possible to develop a position that cuts across the dichotomy in terms of which most recent writers have presented the issue of educational accountability?

To consider this issue more fully, we need first to acknowledge that 'what is accountability?', 'what is its purpose?' and 'how might it be achieved in a devolved system of educational governance?' have always been questions that have posed special difficulties for those who are committed to school-based decision-making and management. State schools are part of a wider system of educational provision funded through the public purse to carry out functions that the state considers desirable. How the state should ensure that these functions are carried out within a framework which recognizes teachers' professionalism and schools' local autonomy is an issue that needs to be resolved if we are to claim to have cut across the dichotomy between the managerial and democratic models of accountability.

This is not a straightforward issue, for it requires deliberation over questions about the role of the state in educational decision-making, the nature of the contractual relationship between the state and schools, the purpose and uses of accountability in educational administration and the adequacy of the mechanisms of public accountability. Nor is it the type of issue which admits an abstract universal solution. Ultimately, it is a practical question, one which must be explored in the particular circumstances in which it has relevance. It is the nature of practical questions that they do not admit final answers, applicable to all contexts, proving entirely satisfactory to all interests alike. As Burnheim (1985) argues, the process of deliberation over such practical questions 'calls for continual, detailed reflection, speculation, evaluation and struggle.'

The best way to examine the issue of educational accountability might, therefore, be to examine the available data on experiments which have sought to carve out a practical position between the need for public audit for the efficient use of resources and the goal of school-based decision-making. In an attempt to see whether it is possible to resolve the tensions posed by these competing requirements, this chapter seeks to describe the practical politics of a program of reform committed to school-based decision-making. It discusses how the Participation and Equity Program (PEP) in the state of Victoria, Australia, viewed the notion of accountability and constructed a decision-making structure that enabled schools to develop ways of working that suited them best and at the same time ensured that they worked within the framework of certain centrally established guidelines. Drawing upon an extensive overview evaluation of the program (Rizvi and Kemmis, 1987), this chapter evaluates the PEP strategy, analyzing its strengths and weaknesses, and suggests that the requirements of public accountability and school-based decision-making and management are not as irreconcilable as many educational writers have suggested.

APPROACHES TO ACCOUNTABILITY IN EDUCATION

The purpose of a system of accountability in education is to ensure that public funds are used in accordance with the guidelines set down, to improve the quality of educational provision and, where possible, to provide information to show that this is being done. Few would deny that public schools are accountable. However, this is an empty assertion unless we also state clearly the form, extent and character of their accountability. That is, we ask questions such as to whom are schools accountable, for what, and how are proposals for accountability to be implemented and whether these procedures are consistent with specifically *educational* criteria. Answers to all these questions require that we also examine the issues concerning the nature of public schools and their responsibilities to the state and society.

A review of the literature in this area shows that educationists have adopted two broad approaches in response to these questions. The traditional models of accountability view schools in a hierarchical and instrumental relationship with the bureaucratic centre. Within the framework of 'line authority', teachers are accountable to principals, principals to regional bureaucracies, the regional bureaucracies to the centre and, in the Westminster system of government, the centre to the representatives elected to govern the state. Accountability is in terms of measurable, preferably behavioral, outcomes. Teachers are accountable for the achievement of prespecified performances by students. Although there are variations of this approach to accountability in the management literature, such as management by objectives, program budgeting and performance contracting, its basic thrust involves a unidirectional contractual obligation: that is, the obligation of individuals to report to their superiors, but not the other way round. The teacher is directly accountable to the organization, and only indirectly to the school community. Hugh Sockett (1976) has dubbed this model 'utilitarian' not only because of its orientation toward a teleological ethic, but also because it is suggestive of Bentham's mechanistic felicific calculus.

The idea behind management by objectives (MBO) is that educational managers and teachers should agree on the results by which performance is to be judged. Each objective is prespecified and judged individually. The teacher is no longer accountable to pupils, parents or colleagues, but is judged against the criteria of a neutral technology. The supposedly impartial bureaucracy is given the authority to judge performance. The assumption that a neutral accountability technology is possible is also embodied in the idea of program budgeting which requires a structure in which all results related to common objectives are compared for cost and effectiveness. While in MBO each objective is assessed individually, program budgeting involves comparative judgments across the widest network of related objectives. In this way program budgeting is a more flexible tool: it requires that priorities among objectives be established, and that resources be allocated according to the amount that programs contribute to them. But it is also a more difficult mechanism to implement.

Both MBO and program budgeting were developed by US armed forces researchers in the 1950s, but in one form or another they have provided the basis for many of the accountability systems generated by educational bureaucracies over the past thirty years (see Lacey and Lawton, 1981). But are systems applicable to the military, which has rigid authority and penalty structures, applicable to education? Clearly not; because education is a more diffuse and socially complex enterprise, the dynamics of education involve considerable uncertainty: it is not possible to prespecify all the objectives of education, let alone prioritize them. Since good teaching requires making choices continually, having to work from objectives might very well be self-defeating because the objectives might become mechanisms for avoiding rather than making choices. Both MBO and program budgeting rest on the assumption that practical reason can be reduced to technical-instrumental concerns—the application of means to achieve given ends. But as Codd (1988) has pointed out, such an assumption is based on the mistaken positivist dichotomy between facts and values, implying that measurement and observation can avoid the problems of value justification.

The managerial models of accountability have other problems. First, they mistakenly assume that pupil performance is a fair and valid way of accounting for a teacher's skills. The teaching-learning process is affected by variables which exist both within and outside the school, beyond the control of teachers. Socio-economic status, ethnicity, language, resources available in the school are just some of the factors which cannot be ignored in accounting for results. Second, the managerial models involve the assumption that all educationally desirable experiences can be stated in terms of measurable objectives; this is to distort and trivialize both the nature of human activities and the process of education. A Pincoff (1973) has argued, educational goals consist in the development of 'excellences', which are not the kind of dispositions that are determinate and can be prespecified. Finally, managerial models have politically unacceptable consequences. They encourage educational consumerism, since their concern is primarily economic rather than cultural and educational. The criteria of efficiency and economy are treated as unproblematic, given priority over all other values. The emphasis is on optimizing the use of resources, rather than creating sites where students get opportunities to develop their needs and interests. The criteria for judging what is worth-while are thus external to the schooling context, imposed by the state to meet its own requirements.

The managerial models of accountability in education are concerned with one-way accountability: the subordinate in the hierarchy gives an account to a superior for the resources used to achieve certain results. In contrast, the democratic models view accountability as a two-way process: the teacher is accountable to a of constituencies, including the pupils. Sockett (1976) has characterized these models in terms of four major characteristics. First, accountability is for the principles of practice rather than for specific results. Second, accountability is rendered to diverse constituencies. Third, the teacher is to be regarded as an autonomous professions, rather than a social technician. Fourth, the purpose of accountability is allied to providing information for constituents. Accountability is thus tied to the emerging needs of the school. The school communicates information to the whole community, so that the contingent outcomes of the teaching-learning process can be widely known and debated. The emphasis here is on process, rather than outcome.

Viewed in this way, schools are seen as self-accounting. That is, they can no longer be labeled simply as good or bad, but are judged in terms of the criteria of excellence that they themselves develop. Accountability means being responsible for actions that are internal to agreed values and beliefs about the evaluation of educational performance. In very general terms this approach is justified against what is thought to be involved in a democratic way of life. MacDonald (1978) has suggested that democratic accountability models seek an incorporation of democratic social values, implying a rejection of the language of control and management. In them, distinctions between facts and values, between means and ends, give way to a concern with empathic understanding, practical deliberation and a commitment to value pluralism.

More specifically, Simcon (1981) has suggested that the case for democratic school self-evaluation is based on a number of other claims. First, self-evaluation enables schools to develop a more accurate understanding of teaching-learning processes. Second, cyclical processes of review allow schools to determine the extent to which they are providing the quality of education they espouse, and what areas require attention and remediation. Third, in an effort to develop collective understanding, self-evaluation allows teachers to cut across arbitrary bureaucratic boundaries, such as departments. Fourth, it provides more learning opportunities for everyone involved in schools. Finally, teachers get further opportunities 'to develop their professional decision-making skills, enlarge their perspectives and become better informed about the roles, responsibilities and problems of their colleagues' (Simon, 1981).

While these arguments have considerable merit, the democratic approaches to accountability in education are not without their own limitations. The most serious of their problems is the assumption of an idealist epistemology. They emphasize the 'subjective meaning' of social action, but ignore the reality of social structure. As Carr and Kemmis (1983) point out, such a view 'tends to assume that social conflicts are always the result of different social groups having conflicting *inter-pretations of reality* rather than contradictions *in that reality* itself.' Such a limitation prevents these approaches from providing an adequate basis for social change. This fact implies that democratic approaches to accountability have conservative political consequences in their relation to existing social order.

In a sustained criticism of MacDonald's views on evaluation, Lakomski (1983) has elaborated upon this point. She has argued that the value pluralism implicit in the democratic approach implies a 'sophisticated relativism': that is, there is an assumption that when groups disagree, there is no way of establishing one of them as correct. Apart from the paradox involved in any attempt to refute this claim, Lakomski (1983) contends that this view is located in the framework of a liberal pluralism that is profoundly conservative because it allows the self-justification of its own assumptions; and since it.

> ... *takes for granted* the political framework of liberal pluralism so it accepts uncritically the very program it evaluates. More specifically, it does not raise the question of how and why *this* programme came to be conceived and implemented. Worse, it cannot even *raise* the question given its grounding in social phenomenology.... The consequence of the inability to account for the social and educational programmes and to judge their worth leads democratic evaluation implicitly to affirm the *status quo*.

If schools are to be self-evaluating in their own terms, then any outside authority is denied. But this makes the idea of judgments *across* schools a relatively meaningless notion. Without cross-school comparisons, however, we have no way of coherently talking about educational inequalities. Since schools are left to develop their own way of organizing relationships, they are also left free to maintain the status quo within and across schools, even if that status quo means leaving such 'inherently unequal provisions between the among private and public sector schools as exist in Australia effectively intact. Ultimately, the democratic approaches to accountability provide us with no clear way of dealing with the issue of educational inequalities.

For a program like the Participation and Equity Program (PEP), this was fatal limitation because educational inequality constituted the central idea around which the program was designed. The program designers in the state of Victoria had recognized the limitations of both the managerial and democratic approaches to evaluation and accountability and emphasized that program activities had to be assessed against a set of measurable program-wide criteria, but they also stressed the importance of school-based decision-making and participatory democratic processes. In this way they had to carve out a position between some of the requirements of managerial and democratic approaches to educational accountability. In what follows, I describe how PEP conceptualized accountability and discuss the main achievements and problems with its strategy.

THE PARTICIPATION AND EQUITY PROGRAM IN VICTORIA, AUSTRALIA

The Participation and Equity Program (PEP) was a program of educational reform initiated by the Australian Labor Government in 1983, in a context of, among other things, high unemployment among young people, their social alienation, and, by OECD standards, their comparatively low retention rates in upper secondary schooling. Some concomitant educational concerns for the national government were to facilitate curriculum change, to seek changes to the organization of secondary schooling and, through these measures, to promote equity. At the organizational level the Australian Commonwealth Schools Commission, given responsibility to devise its philosophical base, saw PEP essentially as a school-based program. In its documents the Commission eschewed centre-periphery conceptions of educational change, rejecting the notion that changes as far-reaching as those proposed by PEP could somehow be imposed 'from the top'.

Within the context of the Australian federal system, while it was the central government that initiated PEP, it was the state governments tnat had to implement it. In the state of Victoria the central government's understanding, communicated through the Schools Commission's *PEP Guide, of what needed to be done to achieve school improvement was reinforced by the philosophical orientation of the Victorian Government's ministerial papers, released in 1983. Just as the Commonwealth Schools Commission's PEP Guide* (1975) stressed an active partnership between home, school and the wider community, and wanted schools to develop 'real processes of genuine accountability, instead of merely reporting to a passive school community the outcome of policies it has had no hand in shaping', so the Victorian ministerial papers also emphasized the principles of genuine devolution of authority and collaborative, participative decision-making processes.

Arguing that the processes of education must be informed by the values of participation and equity, PEP construed the process of reform itself as an educational process. The program's rhetoric emphasized the importance of devising administrative structures that would encapsulate PEP's democratic aspirations, and so would provide models for the operation of the program at school and classroom levels. Particularly during its first year, the administrators of the program in Victoria repeatedly quoted these sentiments as they struggled to develop a structure that reflected the commitment to collaborative decision-making processes. How were these democratic sentiments translated into an administrative structure? In attempting this task, those charged with the responsibility fur establishing and implementing the program in Victoria had some help from the guidelines provided in the Commission's *PEP Guide. One senior PEP officer described these guidelines in the following terms:*

(a) Talk heavily about people and not resources as being the main items of expenditure.

(b) Ask States to take a non-submission approach.

(c) Suggest large scale funding per school to be intensively directed rather than using the margarine approach i.e. spread a little everywhere.

(d) Have a system of targeting which pre-determines what schools are in the Program...

The Schools Commission had specified that 75 per cent of total program funds be allocated to targeted schools, through at a later stage this requirements was reduced to 55 per cent. The rest of the funds allocated to each state could be spent on other system level initiatives and administrative costs. Target schools were not to exceed or fall below the level of 40 per cent of all government secondary schools in the state. From the Commission's perspective the targeting of schools was to form the backbone of the program: the targeted schools were to be drawn into the program whether they liked it or not. The Schools Commission, however, had little to offer in the way of explicit criteria for the identification of target schools. It expected that states would have available the 'relevant data such as school retention and participation rates and the concentration in particular communities of students from groups on whom the Program is focus...' (*PEP Guide*). In Victoria the 1981 version of the Disadvantaged Schools Index (DSI) was used as a measure to identify schools to be targeted. In all, 178 schools were initially targeted, though in later years the list was changed when a more up-to-date DSI became available.

The program also rejected a submissions-based funding system on the grounds of equity: it was believed that that strategy would once again benefit schools with expertise in submission preparation. Targeting particular schools could, on the other hand, help schools which were relatively unskilled, unorganized and unpractised at securing funds through submissions. It was also felt that schools were generally reacting against submission strategy. The program was keen to try another way of generating school reform, to invite schools which had not previously participated in special programs to be part of a program that encouraged them to re-examine their curricula and organizational practices. According to a senior officer of the program, the submissions strategy had become self-defeating: earlier submission-driven programs had inhibited learning or policy development since much attention was given to the politics and administration of funding rather than to the educational activities for which the programs were created in the first place. Program consultants and support staff had come to be perceived as acting in administrative and inspectorial roles rather than as facilitators of learning.

It was argued that while the main reason in the past for the submissions approach was accountability, this had proved inadequate. Schools had simply devised ways of presenting the desired information for yet another year's funding. Program officials had no way of telling whether the accounts presented were accurate (Stephens, 1984). In Stephens' view, PEP represented a new way of funding schools and approaching the accountability issue. Schools were targeted on the basis of trust, and a complex support structure was established to help schools develop activities to achieve the program's central objectives.

The targeted schools were each allocated funds to evaluate current curriculum practices and organization in order to determine the extent to which they met, effectively and equitably, the needs of *all* students. Schools were to identify their particular educational needs in collaboration with parents, teachers and students. The information collected was to be used to initiate activities in nine specific areas: curriculum; teacher renewal and support; teacher parent student interaction; assessment, accreditation and credentialling; groups with particular needs; education and the arts; school structure and organization; post-school experience-school links; and public support for education. With such a comprehensive list, target schools were given considerable latitude to devise activities that they considered most important. As far as the program was concerned, schools were in the best position to judge what their priorities are. Both its central requirements—that schools initiate activities which catered to the needs of all students and worked for more equitable outcomes and that decision-making processes of the program include parents, teachers and students—were thus formal ones.

The program's key implementation strategy related to the idea of time-release. The PEP funds allocated to schools could be used to release teachers from timetabled duties to work together in the investigations and actions proposed by their schools. The program officials believed that for perhaps the first time in the history of special programs in Australia the government had recognized the importance of teachers' reflection upon and evaluation of their own practices. Schools were asked 'to set aside time to consider clear goals and educational strategies for achieving them in a collaborative decision-making process involving teachers, parent and students' (*PEP Guide*). The program also allowed schools to use funds for the employment of extended or casual emergency teachers, for the employment of school council appointed personnel to work with the school and its community and for other school-based program development activities.

It is important to note that the designers of this strategy had in mind a particular view of how schools change. It was argued that substantial change in schools could not occur unless whole-school communities reflected on their total practice, including curriculum, teaching-learning styles and organization. The emphasis was on processes of negotiation and consensus at local school levels. Radical transformation of education was sought through an emphasis which required a systematic and consciously active approach to learning about how current practices reproduced inequalities, and how access and success in curriculum were only possible when school communities were able to think together and make informed decisions together. This approach to school improvement was thought to imply a view of evaluation as a continuous and participatory process that linked reflection and plans for action. Many in the Victorian program referred to PEP as 'a learning program'. The role of regional and central consultancy was to support school-based initiatives and encourage their development rather than be prescriptive about the nature and pace of changes. The role of administration was to create conditions that enabled schools to proceed with curriculum development without the unnecessary bureaucratic restrictions that had bedeviled earlier reform efforts.

This approach to school change was consistent with the observations of a number of activists in Victorian education. As Hannan (1984) argued: 'I have to say that PEP needs a vision of how change happens in school. My own views on this are rather firm. I don't believe in top down change. Change comes through the involvement of practitioners. Practitioners have to be at the centre and in control of schemes for reform. Support from outside—in this case from or through or in the name of PEP—then consists of people to help with fact-finding, theorising, comparison and criticism.' Hannan's view also reflected the principles of the School Improvement Plan (SIP) outlines in *Ministerial Paper 2*. SIP saw evaluation as a cooperative task for the whole school community involving a process of continuing critical review and renewal. Learning was considered an essential concern of SIP which had, as a primary focus, the aim of improved educational outcomes for all students. In target schools PEP complemented the SIP orientation in giving the idea of school-based decision-making additional rhetorical force.

PEP's strategy of targeting schools and giving them considerable latitude, however, did not receive universal approval among the program's designers. Some believed that the strategy would be too difficult to manage, would be confrontational and might involve very high risks. Schools, they feared, might not use the grant money for the purposes of genuine reform. To allay these fears, the Victorian *PEP Guide* carried a section entitled 'Activities Specifically Discouraged.' This list of proscribed practices also served to define the nature and scope of the program's objectives. The following activities were precluded:

- both top-down centralized control and laissez-faire local approaches, either in the Program as a whole, or at school level, PEP requires cooperative problem solving;
- token participation in decision-making processes;
- development of separate or alternative courses into which students are streamed on the basis of perceived academic potential or performance;
- practices which exclude students on the basis of gender, ethnicity or disability from access to mainstream learning;
- emphasis on competition in learning;
- labelling and testing procedures which discourage continuing participation in education;
- development of programs which lead to the exclusion of some students from the study of traditional intellectual disciplines;
- school organizational arrangements which make it possible to pay attention to individual needs and learning paces. (*PEP Guide*)

Even with this statement, the discussion of program goals in the *Guide* and the nomination of the broad areas for action, some members of state PEP committees and program administrators remained uneasy. They argued that there was still no administrative mechanism for ensuring that these guidelines were adhered to. The program had to confront the issue of accountability, but this had to be done within the requirements of a commitment to school-based decision-making.

PEP'S APPROACH TO ACCOUNTABILITY AND EVALUATION

Victorian PEP acknowledged that a level of managerial accountability could not be avoided but it sought to view the structure of this accountability in a very general way through which each targeted school was required to provide a statement of its purposes, structure and activities to the program's central managers, and through them the state government and the Commonwealth Schools Commission. Other more specific elements of managerial accountability were rejected because the program designers believed that they were incompatible with the principles of participation and equity. In Victoria PEP was regarded as an open and experimental program, objectives of which could not be stated in behavioral terms. In particular, objectives such as reflecting, evaluating, negotiating and understanding could not be easily translated into measurable terms. Moreover, PEP encouraged a diversity of activities, rendering it impossible to develop a undimensional scale against which the heterogeneous efforts of all schools could be measured. The designers of the program thought, moreover, that a managerial accountability mechanism, even if such a thing could be devised, would not only not promote learning, but in some circumstances might prove to be a disincentive for some schools to be experimental by engendering defensiveness.

The managerial model of accountability was also thought to be politically unacceptable since many in the program agreed with House (1973) that it embodied control assumptions. Committed to school-based decision-making as the program was, its designers were reluctant to establish a scheme in which education was organised like a corporation which required subordinates to the strictly accountable to the organization and in which the organization was not accountable to the individual. In a program committed to democracy, accountability must be reciprocal, based on the assumption that all members of the school community have direct access to decision-making processes. The program sought a mechanism in which educational values and the idea of public interest were continuously negotiated, rather than agglomerated in some central bureaucratic dictate. It wished to provide school communities with ample opportunities for learning and for disseminating information, including what it called 'practitioner crafted accounts' of curriculum innovations and organizational experiments.

It is within the framework of these principles that PEP developed its notion of peer accountability for schools. The program wished to see accountability as horizontal rather than vertical. The idea of 'horizontal accountability' involved emphasis on accountability to school communities, to parents and students, as well as to other schools, rather than to a central committee or the educational bureaucracy. It was seen as a major step towards devolution. The program's centre gave itself the minimal role of overseeing developments, and ensuring in a very general way that schools did not abuse the guidelines established by the Victorian PEP Committee in order to meet the broader accountability requirements that the Schools Commission, with most of the real powers of decision-making, transferred to schools themselves. The major accountability function was handed over to the Schools Reference Groups (SRGs).

Schools Reference Groups were created to serve the purposes of 'horizontal' accountability. The size of SRGs varied from three to seven grant schools, which normally included both technical and high schools, and from 1986 special schools. The membership of each SRG normally consisted of at least three representatives from each grant school, including at least one teacher, one parent and one student. These representatives were to negotiate their understanding of the broad objectives of the program and moderate each other's plans for curriculum reform. This accountability scheme acknowledged that schools themselves had considerable 'expertise' to develop their own curriculum.

But beyond the peer accountability function, SRGs were also established to provide schools with a wider forum to reflect on the planning and implementation of their program activities. In the jargon of action research this process was referred to as 'the sharing of learning through collaborative reflection'. Each SRG was serviced by a regional consultant whose task it was to keep records of meetings and provide information and advice on regional and central issues. SRGs normally met at least three times each term to consider an agenda which they had determined for themselves, and to assist one another in whatever ways they saw fit.

In turn, the work of the SRGs was, at least partially, coordinated by Regional Reference Groups (RRGs), though the relationship between SRGs and RRGs was not considered to be that of a line authority, and not all regions saw the need to create these groups. Program officials insisted that the relationship between the program's central office and SRGs was not of a hierarchical kind. The centre was to provide all kinds of information that it thought the SRGs might find useful. It also made available particular consultancy services, but only when these were requested by the SRGs themselves. In turn, SRGs were requested to submit profiles of school PEP activities and school plans so that these might be collated to obtain state-wide information.

In line with the non-submission-based approach to funding, and in line with ideas from the ministerial papers, a model for accountability within the program was constructed, as shown in Figure 10.1.

While the membership of Schools Reference Groups included representatives endorsed by the school council from each target school including a teacher, a parent and a student, all of whom were directly involved in the school's PEP program. SRGs also had the power to co-opt other members. The formal structure of SRG was seen as creating conditions necessary for 'horizontal accountability' by allowing peers from participating schools to discuss proposals and to offer criticism and advice. Target schools were expected to submit a formal plan for the use of their PEP funds to the SRG for consideration. On the basis of feedback received they were then expected to amend proposals

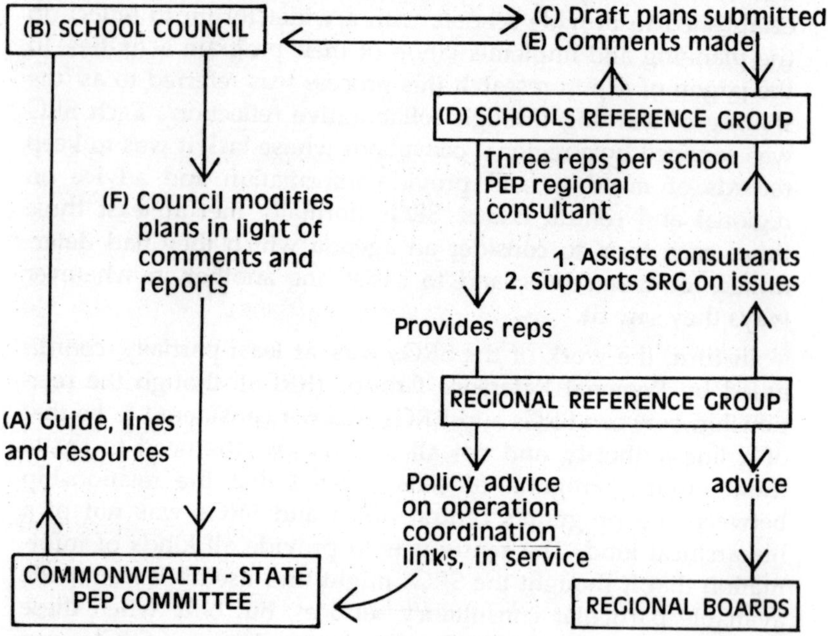

Fig. 10.1 PEP Accountability in Victoria.

until they fell within an agreed understanding of the program's guidelines through debate at the SRG level. In this way it was intended that the judgment about the adequacy of plans would not be made by 'outsiders' who did not have a responsive stake in the outcomes of action at the school level, but by people who were directly involved in translating the program's broad guidelines into practice. Some regional consultants in the program referred to this approach as 'responsive accountability' (as opposed to control accountability), since schools were required to be sensitive to the attitudes and values which structured their audience's interaction with them under the particular cultural and political conditions which prevailed in the local contexts.

Of major concern to the program's designers in Victoria was the need to ensure that its approaches to accountability and evaluation complemented each other. Evaluation along broad action research lines was to be a key principle. The first Victorian *PEP Guide* (1984) set the tone for this: 'Evaluation is not simply a requirement imposed for the purposes of (hierarchical) accountability. As the Program aims at improvement of the organization and practice of education at the level of systems organizations. Program administration and support services, whole-school curriculum and individual approaches to teaching, evaluation becomes a major tool in the achievement of the Program's aims.' Evaluation was seen not so much as a means of finding out the program's effect but as key strategy in achieving the program's objectives. All schools were expected 'to engage in the cyclical process of evaluation, planning, implementation and ongoing evaluation to improve school organization and curriculum.' The program stressed that 'improvement depends on a capacity to learn, both individually and collectively, to make progressively better decisions by monitoring the outcomes of current action, and plan future action on the basis of the best information possible' (*PEP Guide*, 1986). Clearly, school-based evaluation approaches were primarily to serve the needs of the school rather than some outside agency.

In SRgs the requirements of evaluation and accountability merged. While at the school level evaluation represented a starting place for investigation and action, at SRGs participating schools reported accounts of developments to each other with the expectation that their accounts and further plans might be subjected to criticism and advice. SRGs were designed to moderate school-based decisions but also to promote a 'shared approach to school based curriculum development' and encourage 'sharing of resources between schools and the development of broader curriculum options between schools' (*PEP Guide*, 1986). Instead of viewing accountability as a one-way process which required schools to report to its SRG, PEP conceived it as a two-way process: participating schools were accountable to each other; the information they collected was essentially for their own use, written in a form that was accessible to schools communities, including teachers, students and parents, represented on the SRGs. How did this accountability strategy fare? In the next section, I want to describe some of its successes, and discuss the problems schools encountered in trying to develop effective SRGs.

SCHOOLS REFERENCE GROUPS

The Schools Reference Group strategy represented a major innovation which the program itself did not adequately appreciate. Much of the recent debate over school accountability has been between those who advocate centralized control systems and those who support the notion of democratic accountability. On the one hand, educational bureaucracies have put forward various management approaches such as performance contracting, Michigan State accountability system and national assessment of education progress, while, on the other hand, educational researchers such as MacDonald (1978) and Elliott (1980) have proposed the ideas of teachers as autonomous accountable professionals and self-accounting schools. The SRG strategy represented a fresh way of looking at the issue, one that cut across the hoary dichotomy between school autonomy and centralized control. It placed school learning at the centre of reform efforts, and developed a mechanism that viewed accountability as a two-way process in which educational criteria played a dominant part.

For some schools, the SRG strategy enabled them to have direct formal contact with their neighbouring schools for the first time. While inter-school sports competitions were common enough between many other schools, they seldom had the opportunities to discuss educational matters together. Such contact led to targeted schools becoming familiar with the plans that other schools had devised for the use of their PEP funds, how the schools saw their educational priorities and what problems they encountered in promoting the goals of participation and equity. Schools learned of a broader range of curriculum options and procedures by drawing on the experiences of other schools. As one teacher pointed out in late 1986: 'As far as I am concerned, even if PEP doesn't achieve anything else, SRGs would have been a major achievement. It has allowed schools to share their experiences, their difficulties and their successes together. I knew nothing about.... High School, now I am better informed. I know now that some of the problems we have had at this school are not unique. I reckon that even when PEP goes, as it no doubt will, SRGs will be an idea well worth keeping in some form....'

However, as might have been expected, the SRG strategy had a slow and confused beginning. Despite schools being saturated with the rhetoric of school-based decision-making contained in the ministerial papers, they had remained highly routinized places, suspicious of programs of reform that promise democracy yet do not deliver resources and support needed to practise it. It was in this context that PEP represented an experiment in developing a non-bureaucratic and non-hierarchical approach to school reform. As an organizational innovation, it sought to bring the needs of accountability and self-evaluation and learning together. These ideas represented a radically new way of working for most targeted schools. Imbued with an understandable level of cynicism, in 1985 most schools seemed unclear about the *real* purposes of the Schools Reference Groups. Lacking a clear understanding of the program's emphasis on schools devising their own ways of working together, many SRGs wanted clear directives from the central office and the PEP committee. Past programs had given schools manuals to guide their work; in contrast, PEP was encouraging schools to develop their own manuals, to become responsible for their own actions. The regional consultants found it difficult to respond to many of the schools' queries about how to conduct SRG meetings, for many of them had not themselves developed a clear model. The SRG strategy was as much of an experiment for them as it was for schools. As a conference of the regional PEP consultants in May 1985 it was clear that there were competing views about the nature and scope of SRGs. Some saw them a decentralized groups which collected information for accountability, as mechanisms for ensuring that central guidelines were adhered to; others saw them as open-ended structures, to be developed into forms that the participating schools desired.

These consultants did not wish to impose any particular view of how schools ought to work together on SRGs. They wished to see schools themselves negotiate the best way of working with each other. Lacking any established pattern for their work, SRG meetings were variously seen as learning exchanges, in-service activities, show-and-tell sessions and administrative committees whose task it was to approve school plans. As one regional consultant argued in late 1985, SRGs had not developed as 'forums for critical debate about curriculum, democratic processes in schools and the specific curriculum of member schools. Only on rare occasions do Schools Reference Groups question the practice of individual schools or identify to what extent member schools are ignoring or addressing the needs of disadvantaged groups within those schools.' Teachers from one school were understandably hesitant to evaluate critically the school plans of another. Some teachers found it difficult to reconcile the notions of school-based development and cross-school critical commentary. In one region in particular, where a 'rationalization' process was under way with the accompanying threat of closures or unfavourable amalgamations, there was a reluctance to be open about the problems schools were facing for fear of political misuse of such information. In such circumstances schools in some SRGs adopted a 'you scratch my back, I will scratch your's attitude. It was clear that the SRG strategy had to work within a broader bureaucratic structure, the values of which could not be easily reconciled with PEP's approach to evaluation and accountability.

As might be expected, there was considerable variation in the role and function of various SRGs. While all groups, after initial hesitation, facilitated and supported evaluation and the development of school plans, the degree to which they were committed to these tasks varied. At some SRG meetings nothing more than show-and-tell occurred, while at others broader educational issues were taken on immediately and examined systematically before the approval of a plan was granted. Schools were made to justify their plans of action in terms of the goals of participation and equity as had been negotiated earlier.

Throughout 1985 a number of schools perceived SRGs to be inconsequential and ineffective. The morale of participating schools received severe knock when the Federal Government announced that the PEP budget would effectively be cut in half. PEP was not a very significant part of the overall concerns of the schools anyway; now there appeared even less at stake. Cynicism that had already existed in schools about the commitment of governments to reform programs was intensified. In such a climate even the evaluation tasks that SRGs had to undertake became difficult to arrange and were mostly completed superficially. For some teachers attending SRG meetings became a chore: 'another meeting to attend on top of everything else'. In such cases the regional consultants saw their task in terms of a challenge to raise the level of critical thinking and debate in SRG meetings. For a number of reasons, however, this objective was difficult to achieve.

First, the membership of SRG groups changed often, with new representatives of schools attending meetings when others lost interest. This meant that there was little continuity in the conduct of tasks: the same ground had to be covered repeatedly. Often the same committed few teachers and parents attended the meetings.

Second, considerable distrust existed between schools which had historically regarded themselves in competition with each other, making communication between them difficult to achieve in SRG meetings. A technical school in the western suburbs of Melbourne, for example, refused point blank to work with its neighbouring high school, forcing the regional consultant to medicate in the dispute, which was not easily resolved.

Third, at meetings where principles attended (usually those which dealt with funding matters), they tended to dominate the proceedings, often making students and parents feel redundant and unwelcome. At some SRGs only junior members of staff attended; these teachers were perceived as having little authority to speak on behalf of the whole school, let alone commit their schools to particular plans of action.

Fourth, as already indicated, some schools were reluctant to reveal their problems to other schools in their SRG for fear that information might be misused. This was particularly so in the south-central region where a plan for reorganization and rationalization of schools coincided with the establishment of the SRGs. In a political climate where closures and amalgamations of schools were a real possibility, some schools felt it prudent not to divulge information that could be seized upon and used against their interests. For the SRG strategy to succeed, it was essential that schools trust each other; yet in the context of the rationalization process many teachers and school administrators understandably found it difficult to be frank and open about the problems and issues their schools confronted.

Fifth, some schools found the role of the students on SRGs unclear. Since there had been little precedent for students working on issues of school reform; many teachers found it difficult to discuss openly the organizational and personality issues confronting their schools.

Sixth, since meetings were often held after school, the idea of student involvement gave rise to practical problems. In particular, questions such as how the students were to travel to the school where the SRG meeting was to be held, and under whose guidance, had to be clarified.

Seventh, some SRGS found it difficult to understand the role of the regional consultants. They were often seen as having the requisite information and skills to judge particular plans of action, but other SRGs found regional consultants intrusive and viewed their presence on SRGs suspiciously. The role of regional consultants on SRGs continued to be poorly understood. While in most cases consultants provided a supporting role, in some others they were viewed as the experts. Consequently, directions were sought from them not only on administrative matters but also on matters of educational policy. Developing non-hierarchical ways of working in an educational system still governed by notions of accountability to the centre and line authority was never going to be easy.

Eighth, some SRG members found they did not meet often enough to develop good working relationships, to establish trust between schools. They believed that more time was needed to develop an adequate understanding of the notion of horizontal accountability. As it was, few schools continued to abuse the consultative processes. School plans were approved which did not receive adequate attention or scrutiny. Many of these plans required intervention from the "Schools Unit, and had to be rejected because they full outside the broad guidelines developed by the program. In a few remote cases school-approved accountability processes were ignored cynically; more generally, some schools continued to find it difficult to come to terms with the evaluation and accountability part of their role, not only because they believed that they did not have the appropriate skills but also because the idea of evaluation through action research was poorly understood. Accountability was also seen by some SRG members in narrow, financial terms, and not in the broader educational context PEP had envisaged.

Finally, there was the problem of deciding exactly whom the teachers, parents and students attending SRG meetings represented (the schools, themselves, or their constituencies) and what authority they carried to commit schools to certain plans of action. The relation between school councils and SRGs remained unclear. Those who attended SRG meetings were not always members of their school council, and they were not sure whether their reports were being adequately discussed by the school council. Many of these participants felt that despite the PEP's rhetoric of mainstreaming, at their school the program activities were considered marginal.

Despite these difficulties, towards the end of 1986 there was some evidence to sustain the view that most SRGs were beginning to come to terms with their roles. While many of the problems remained unresolved, they were being tackled in the belief that the SRG strategy was well worth experimenting with. As a result of considerable trial and error, schools were beginning to define the role and mode of working of SRGs in a way that suited their interests, making SRGs into bodies that were not simply imposed from above but forums that could even survive after the demise of PEP in late 1987. Indeed, many regular participants on SRGs, and the regional consultants in particular, believed that as a new way of conceiving the issue of accountability, the strategy had great potential. Most schools agreed that SRGs had provided important forums for educational discussion and for learning from the experiences of others.

In addition to the specific administration and evaluation tasks they were required to undertake, Schools Reference Groups tackled a range of educational issues and problems, including tertiary access and credentialling; accreditation for student participation on decision-making committees; the nature and scope of PEP task forces; the ministerial papers; the Blackburn Report and the issues of retention, the new VCE and assessment procedures; and the previous proposals for school rationalization, where these were applicable. In various SRG meetings schools helped each other by thinking through strategies for improving communication with parents, discussing ideas about the use of PEP funds, exploring strategies for the use of funds provided through PEP funds, exploring strategies for the use of funds provided through PEP's capital grants program and more generally examining, and attempting to resolve, the problems associated with teachers' time release and the availability of emergency teachers. SRGs also provided schools with an opportunity for pooling resources and coordinating activities among member schools, enabling inter-school visits and, in a few notable cases, developing collaborative curriculum projects.

By the end of 1986 most schools conceded that the SRG strategy was at least a useful discussion forum for those who attended. Others were considerably more enthusiastic about its success and saw enormous possibilities in its further development, though they were unclear as to how this might happen. The following remarks by a teacher were typical:

> The SRG has been very useful to this school. Normally five or six of us attend and we have all got a great deal out of being involved. We have all got a great deal out of being involved. We have discussed the issue of retention rates, the problem of descriptive assessment and student participation on curriculum committees. We also talked about *Ministerial Papers 2* and *6* as well as major curriculum initiatives that have been debated through teacher journals like the Hannan article on 'Towards a Democratic Curriculum' and the key issues raised within the Blackburn Report. Students in particular have gained a great deal from going to SRG meetings. We have also organized visits to other schools to see how they have organized their PEP... and that has been very useful.... Our program this year is much better because of SRFs than it would have been without it.

DISCUSSION

In the development of the SRF strategy the role of the regional consultants turned out to the crucial. The strategy was based upon an assumption that it was possible to develop collaborative and trusting relationships between schools. The regional consultants were given a major task in enabling SRGs to develop into critical self-reflective communities. However, as a regional consultant noted, 'Consultants had to develop their own role as well as school participants. No one had experience of SRGs and how to operate in them as it was a new way of networking schools. The concept of horizontal accountability and action research evaluation is new to schools and it needs a lot of time to develop an understanding of these concepts and to realize the valuable potential of SRG meetings.' However, the limited time was not the only difficulty the regional consultants faced. Other difficulties were linked to the more general theoretical problems with the program's conception of horizontal accountability and its location within a broader bureaucratic structure that remained largely untouched by the program's ideological thrust.

Regional consultants provided the primary focus of support for program development and a link between schools and the PEP Committee and the regional officers. Their work was crucial in developing the confidence schools needed to implement activities and projects designed to achieve greater participation and equity. Yet their work was not always appreciated by schools which were only too willing to vent their anger over such matters as the announcement of the cuts over which they had no control. The consultants also faced the brunt of school's wrath over such administrative difficulties as schools had in getting emergency teachers through the Ministry's Human Resource Branch to cover for the time release promised by the program. Since the program was committed to mainstreaming, it was required to rely upon Ministry's existing services. But those employed to provide these services were not always in sympathy with the administrative innovation which the program's distinctive orientation entailed. It was clear to the consultants that until the values embodied in the notion of horizontal accountability were accepted by the Ministry as a whole, they faced an uphill battle in convincing schools that the idea could work.

Schools had differing expectations of the PEP consultants. Some regarded them as having administrative responsibilities only, while others were prepared to view them in ways that the consultants themselves preferred, as change agents, facilitators, general curriculum consultants and educational listening posts. Some regional consultants saw themselves as buffers between the centre and schools. The educative change agent role of the consultants was particularly difficult in schools which showed a lack of interest in the program, at least during its first year, and which refused to make problematic those features of school life which schools themselves refused to open to question, especially in relation to issues of equity.

The consultancy role was bedeviled by a conflict of loyalties. Many consultants were appointed for their skill in supporting school-based activities; at the same time, however, they believed that they were increasingly obliged to perform administrative tasks expected of them by the program's committees and its central and regional administration. Ironically, they found themselves in the classical bind of school inspectors in former years: they wanted to see themselves as educational change agents and servants of schools, yet some schools continued to view them in terms of their administrative responsibilities, as servants of central and/or regional administration.

The regional consultants occupied an ambiguous position in the program's organizational structure. Part of the problem lay in the efforts of the program to regionalize consultancy support on the one hand, and to centralize the decision-making processes about key operational issues on the other. As things turned out, the consultants believed that not everyone involved in PEP's central office was committed to the idea of regionalization. Regional bureaucracies, on the other hand, had little understanding of 'PEP's goals, and many had no evident commitment to them. Far from receiving support from regional bureaucracies, consultants were confronted with the major task of having to convince regional officers to take the program seriously. In the end the PEP consultancy role became as much servicing the regional office as schools. In an effort to mainstream PEP reforms, consultant faced a fundamental dilemma. They wanted to mainstream PEP into general, regional concerns and yet they were conscious of the need to avoid being subsumed within the culture of the regional bureaucracy. On the one hand, they wanted to be critical of the developments occurring in regional offices that were contrary to the principles of PEP, but on the other hand, they were required to be loyal to the bureaucracies they served.

The time that regional consultants did spend with schools was devoted to ensuring that representative structures were put in place in schools and in SRGs. A great deal of every was expended in trying to get more parents and students attending task force or SRG meetings regularly. So much so that at some regional offices PEP consultants were often regarded as special program consultants, concerned with establishing participatory processes. The perception highlighted a major theoretical problem with PEP's notion of 'horizontal accountability'.

The 1986 Victorian *PEP Guide* maintained that 'accountability is essentially about the relationship between actors and decision makers working within the framework of policy', and 'to be accountable, all those who initiate decisions must be responsible to those affected as an outcome'. However, fearing that this definition was stated at an unacceptable level of generality, the *Guide* went on to state conditions for the needs of accountability that must be met at each level of the program:

- decisions were reasonable and based on available information;
- the decision-making processes were based on a democratic and participatory framework;
- adequate steps had been taken to gather information to enable informed decisions;
- decisions taken have fallen within the framework established by Program guidelines and state education policy and related regulations. These conditions were widely understood to highlight participatory processes. Schools were not accountable for the achievement of specified results; rather; they were asked to explore options and experiment with curriculum and organizational innovations. They were accountable to the various constituencies through their SRGs for adhering to certain principles governing decision-making practices. Schools were to demonstrate to SRGs that they had abided by certain procedural principles.

While this emphasis by Victorian PEP on accountability for the adherence to principles of decision-making and accountability to diverse constituencies rather than to the centralized bureaucracy represents a major advance on the mechanistic hierarchical views of accountability, it does pose a major theoretical problem. It suggests far too fundamental a division between accountability for certain outcomes and accountability in adherence to certain principles of practice and decision-making processes. Arguably, processes and outcomes cannot be so easily dichotomized. This problem is similar to that discussed by White (1986) in relation to PEP's definition of curriculum.

White objects to the Victorian *PEP Guide's* definition of curriculum as the 'sum of all experiences, planned and unplanned, developed by the school community. It includes not only what is taught, and approaches to teaching and learning, but also the way the school is organized'. The definition, as White points out, was developed by teacher activists in the 1970s as a useful way of demanding that schools look at what they were really doing. But in the mid-1980s, under PEP. While maintains, the definition became removed from the context of its formation and has become less useful, being taken to mean almost anything that takes place in schools. The definition lacked a value orientation; it made no distinctions in respect of what constitutes quality in schools, except on extraneous grounds.

Given the formalistic nature of this definition of curriculum, Victorian schools struggled with the dilemmas concerning the desirable outcomes of education. Since on this definition everything done in schools is equally curriculum, schools themselves had to determine what was good curriculum and what was not. Schools had to give content to the objectives of participation and equity. Similarly, lacking a detailed analysis of 'participation' and 'equity', the program left SRGs with no clear way of judging the content of the many activities schools proposed. It is true that SRGs were important forums where the program objectives could be and were further explored, but ultimately they could not reject idiosyncratic understandings of the program's objectives, as long as the principles of decision-making processes were adhered to.

In the final analysis it has to be admitted that the Victorian PEP's understanding of accountability and its construction of the SRG strategy represented an important experiment through which the goals of school-based decision-making and public accountability could be expressed. Rejecting the notion of self-monitoring schools. PEP established a mechanism which provided groups of schools with forums in which to discuss issues of mutual concern and at the same time meet the requirements of peer accountability. However, this accountability remained confined to principles of practice and not to outcomes, and even in this limited way it was mostly marginal to the broader concerns of schools. PEP's location within the larger structure of the Education Ministry meant that its success was always going to be dependent on the bureaucracy conceding some of its power and influence. Such was not the case; needed, if anything, in Victoria the bureaucracy has reasserted itself.

11

Managing Stress in Schools

Effective management of human and physical resources or of the curriculum is only possible if those concerned with managing them can operate without the dysfunctional effects resulting from excessive stress. Managers as individuals need to be able to manage their own stress but they also have a responsibility to manage the school as a whole in such a way that stress levels are reduced for all staff. The chapter starts with a review of the dimensions of stress by defining it, identifying its symptoms and causes and reflecting on who is prone to stress. It then puts forward a framework for managing stress in school and this is applied in practice by use of a case study. One of the specific causes of stress, poor time management at both individual and whole school levels, is analysed separately in the next chapter.

DIMENSIONS OF STRESS

Over the last few years there has been a general recognition that many in the teaching profession are working under considerable stress. This is perceived tobe a result of the pressures caused by the rapid rate of change and the increases responsibilities at the school level. Unfortunately, there has been a dangerous tendency to accept this problem without attempting to alleviate it.

(i) What is Stress?

Stress is the body's biochemical response to a threatening situation (stressor) and, although it is intended to ensure self- survival, the frequent changes in blood pressure caused by regular exposure to stressors can lead to cardiac (and other illness in the future.

Kyriacou and Sutcliffe (1978) have defined teacher stress as:

> a response of negative affect (such as anger or depression) by the teacher...resulting from aspects of the teacher's job...

Although stress is usually seen as something which is negative and threatening, it is important to remember that it can also be stimulating, acting as a valuable human response to challenge and change. While healthy tension helps to improve performance by providing a challenge, excessive pressure can be distressing, leading to loss of effectiveness and, ultimately, to ill health and breakdown. Success in managing stress therefore depends on the ability to recognise and respond to an individual's position on this continuum. Figure 11.1 shows the

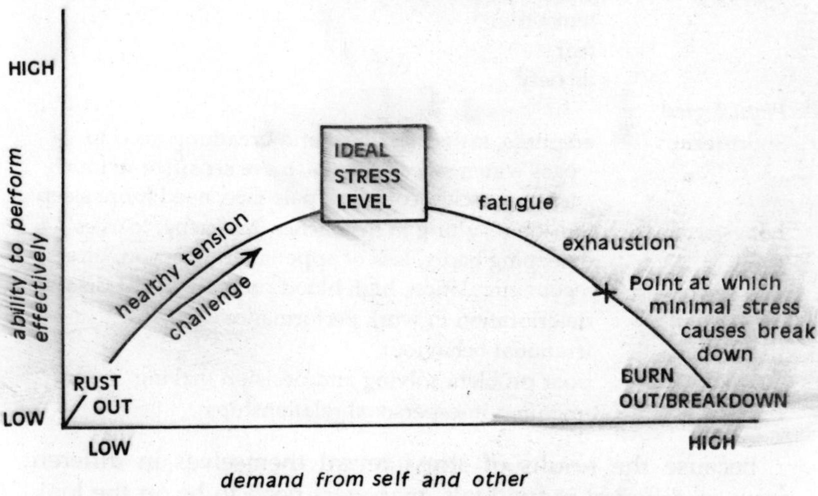

Fig. 11.1 The Stress/Performance Curve.

relationship between pressure and performance with the conditions at the extremes being described as rustout and burnout.

Although much of the stress facing teachers arises from aspects of the job, the level experienced will vary from one to another because of varying demands and differences in ability to cope with problems.

(ii) The Symptoms of Stress

If we accept the model described in Figure 11.1, it is important for managers in schools to be aware of the various positions which individual staff occupy on the stress and performance curve. This recognition will enable management to provide increased challenge or to reduce stress factors for individuals or the staff as a whole so that they are working at the ideal level and have the best chance of being effective.

The symptoms of 'rustout' (or tedium) could manifest themselves as boredom, fatigue, frustration and dissatisfaction. Excessive stress is currently more prevalent and has a variety of symptoms which can be divided into categories (although this is not intended as a medical guide):

Psychological	frustration tension fear anxiety
Physiological	
Short-term	edginess, faster heartbeat and breathing need to pass water, sweaty hands, more sensitive to touch, tense muscles, cold feet, pale face, need more sleep
Long-term	tension resulting in headaches, backache, 'nerves', sleeping badly, loss of appetite, indigestion, ulcers, poor circulation, high blood pressure, heart disease
Behavioural	deterioration in work performance irrational behaviour poor problem solving and decision making impaired interpersonal relationships

Because the results of stress reveal themselves in different ways in different individuals, managers need to be on the lookout for any combination of these symptoms within the school.

If individuals are experiencing high levels of stress and moving towards 'burnout', there will be evidence of both personal and organisational symptoms. The personal symptoms will be taken from all three categories above, while the organisational ones, which will have a very detrimental effect on school effectiveness, will include:

- increased absenteeism
- lack of direction
- high levels of complaining
- lack of communication, trust and positive feedback
- increases in conflict and greater difficulty in resolving it
- difficulties in motivating staff
- lack of co-operation and unwillingness to accept change/innovation.

(iii) The Causes of Stress

Although stress was defined earlier as a reaction to pressures, there are other factors which come into the equation such as an individual's characteristics and the existence (or otherwise) of control mechanisms. A healthy balance of pressures and these compensatory factors would keep an individual at the ideal stress level for effectiveness. On the other hand, an imbalance on one side would result in the individual moving towards rustout or burnout.

It is generally recognised that high levels of stress are caused by a life event such as the death of a spouse. Even going on holiday entails a degree of stress. People become particularly prone to ill health when a variety of these life events occurs at the same time, for example:

- changing jobs
- moving house
- increasing mortgage
- changing social life
- experiencing financial difficulties.

Such a combination is often found when teachers move to a post in another LEA.

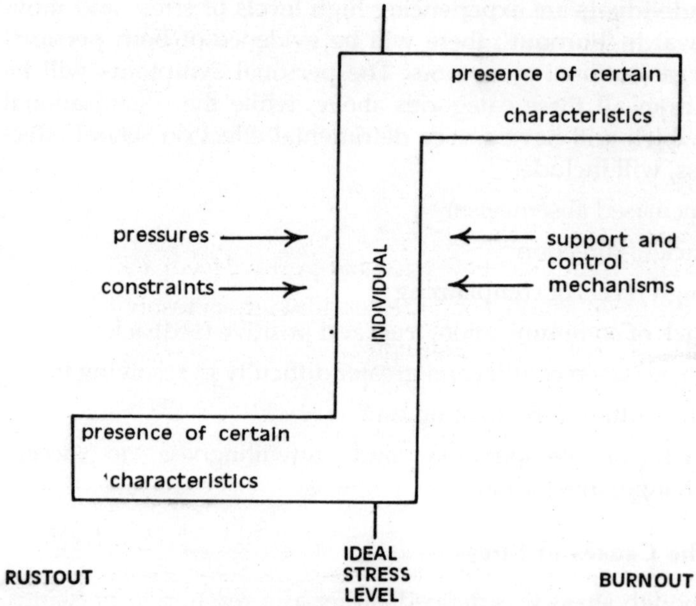

Fig. 11.2 Factors which affect stress levels.

As well as general research into the causes of stress, much has been written over the last 30 years about the specific stressors in teaching. Most of the research highlights the same stressors although they have become more widespread (and the literature more prolific) in recent years, particularly in relation to senior management. There are both core and marginal issues in creating stress. The former will comprise the basic assumptions and ways of doing things within the school while the latter includes factors related to the core issues and also more individual problems. The major stressors which have been identified (excluding personal ones) can be grouped under the following headings (which are based on the work of Rees (1989)):

(a) *Pupils*

large classes and high levels of continuous assessment work
lack of support from senior staff for those experiencing discipline problems
excessive administration for those with pastoral care responsibilities

(b) *Working environment*

poor maintenance, inadequate heading and lighting
lack of resources
overcrowded classrooms
inadequate staff facilities and ancillary support

(c) Organisational factors—management and structures
time wasted, fruitless meetings
mounting paperwork as a result of bureaucratic procedures
job ambiguity and role conflict

(d) Interpersonal relations
lack of time to maintain good social relationships
the divisive nature of the incentive allowance system

(e) External demands on the school from parents and society
changing demands causing confusion about precise responsibilities
perceived poor standing in society
lack of opportunities for career development
a largely hostile media exacerbating the situation

(f) Time i.e. work overload
(underload is not usually applicable)
excessive workloads, hence the need for earning and week-end
work at home (which can lead to family problems)
covering for colleagues on in-service training in-service working
outside the school day

It is important to remember that these potential stressors do not have the same dysfunctional effect on every teacher. Nevertheless they are now accumulating and applying to many more people therefore creating an increasing problem for the individuals concerned and for those who manage schools.

(iv) Who is Prone to Stress

The amount of stress which a person can withstand depends largely on the individual, because a problem will only be perceived if there seems to be a discrepancy between demands placed on the individual and his/her ability to cope. Some people thrive on stress and may then be viewed as ideal candidates for managerial responsibility, while the attitudes of others result in them appearing to be more slow and steady. Friedman and Rosenman (1974) have identified the former as Type A (restless, over- conscientious, work aholics) and the latter as Type B (calm, relaxed) personalities. Excessive demands (which may be self- initiated) can cause Type A people to be adversely affected by fairly low levels of stressors so that their responses become out of tune with the degree of danger and they 'blow up' at a minor inconvenience which their Type B, or less stressed, colleagues would take in their stride.

It is difficult to assess the extent of stress in teaching because of a lack of understanding of description used in questionnaires and an unwillingness to admit to stress problems. Rees (1989) surveys the research on teacher stress and concludes that the various findings cannot be amalgamated in order to identify the individual characteristic, e.g. age, sex, seniority or type of school, which may cause increased predisposition to stress. Although males and females tend to identify different concerns, this could be a result of sex bias in certain roles. Some research (for example Coates and Thoresen 1976) shows that new entrants to teaching tend to experience higher levels as they have not yet developed coping skills. There is also evidence (Kyriacou 1987) that stress is seen to be connected to job satisfaction, reflecting the idea discussed earlier of positive stress as presenting a challenge.

MANAGING STRESS

Although many in the teaching profession are experiencing undesirably high levels of stress, this manifests itself in different ways. The tendency to believe that admitting stress indicates a weak, ineffective character results in many people failing to discuss their stressors and their reactions. Wilce (TES 26 May 1989) reports that:

> One of the big problems is that there is a conspiracy of silence. You don't like to tell your colleagues you're having difficulties, so you go round holding it all in and creating more stress for yourself.

The personal nature of the problem and the varied ways in which it reveals itself demand that there is a sensitive approach to managing stress, although the possibility of difficulties should not be a reason for avoiding the issue. Because of the need for organisational and personal effectiveness, it is important that management, as well as individual, attention is given to stress reduction in the school. Although the symptoms are individual, the causes are largely organisational or school-wide and, therefore, need tackling at the level of the whole school. For example, there may be a need to improve the climate within the school.

Figure 7.3 outlines the components of a stress management plan and there follows a consideration of some of the practical approaches which can be used to identify and tackle stress in schools. These focus on overcoming high levels of stress, rather than on the less common cases of rustout (which could be tackled by providing more challenging work and delegating responsibilities). Although many of the ideas could be adopted at either the individual or the school level, it is the author's belief that open and supportive discussion with colleagues proves particularly valuable and that some form of whole school review can provide the opportunity for highlighting and discussing problem areas.

The stages and key elements in this plan (at either the individual or whole school level) will now be worked through in some detail.

Stage A—Recognition and Analysis of the Problem

At the individual level, it is possible to recognise the signs and causes of stress and then to manage these stressors. Gray and Freeman (1988) suggest that an individual should try to classify what he/she sees as intolerable behaviour (for example on the part of pupils, colleagues and parents). They believe that sharing this list with a colleague will improve each person's understanding of the similarities and differences in areas of tolerance. In knowing ourselves we can improve our own situation and that of our colleagues.

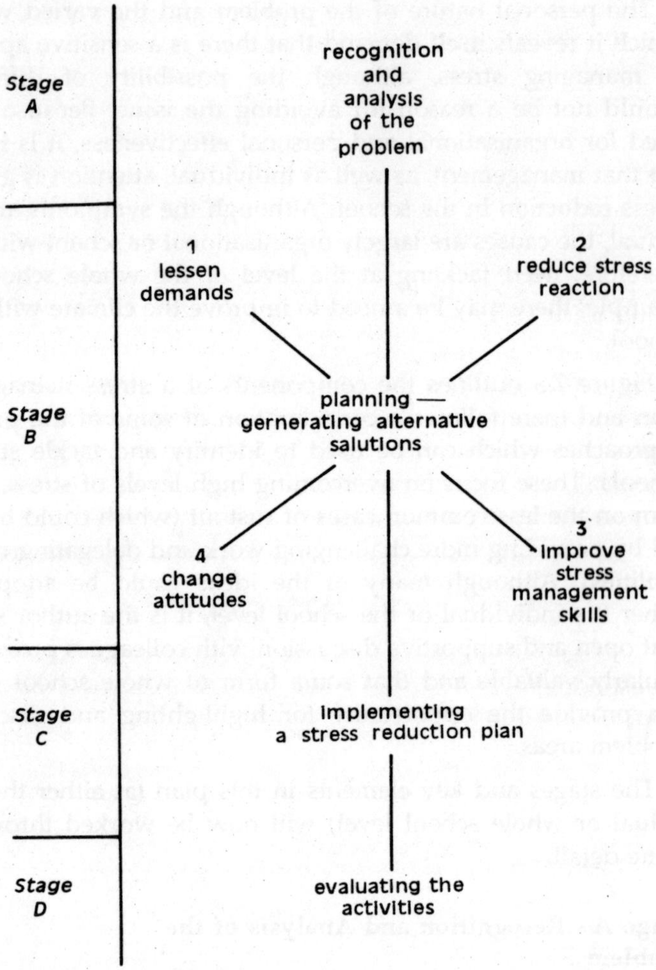

Fig. 11.1 The Stress/Performance Curve.

Although there is considerable value in this 'self-help' approach to understanding stress, the role of management is to develop a proactive strategy for stress reduction for the whole school. Recent evidence shows that if a school is well-managed, for example where staff are involved in decision making, then stress levels will be lower anyway.

In order to identify stressors, it would be possible to ask all the individuals to list the causes of stress within the school. However, this would probably mean that people would classify factors in different ways and it would produce a vast amount of data which would be difficult to analyse and to attack. There is a need to raise certain issues and to pinpoint the stressors fairly accurately without offending anyone and with some consistency over terms, descriptions etc. A specially designed questionnaire is probably the most appropriate mechanism. A well established instrument, such as DION (Elliott-Kemp and Williams 1980), could be used to identify areas which are causing concern and 'hot spots' which require immediate attention. Alternatively, a more informal questionnaire (see below) could, for example, contain statements with which each person could agree or disagree. A calculation of agreement/disagreement with the listed stressors could then take place in order to shed light on common stressors.

ANYTOWN SCHOOL

Questionnaire to be completed by individuals by ticking the appropriate column:

Organisational structure

	Agree	*Disagree*
1. New regulations frequently require me to change the way I do things.		
2. My school is very hierarchical.		

Individuals' responses could be summarised and an average produced for the school as a whole, although averaging in a large organisation may result in distortion of certain problems which are concentrated in only one part of the organisation.

Analysis of the data would identify the core and marginal issues in creating stress and this would help to give focus to the stress-reduction programme. The major areas of concern across the organization could be tackled on a collaborative (organisation) or group) basis, although individual variations from this norm would still need recognition and attention, for example, by individual counselling.

Stage B—Planning: Generating Alternative Solutions

The first stage in dealing with common problems would ideally take the form of some sort of open forum/discussion/brainstorming session, perhaps led by an outsider such as a counsellor or educational psychologist. This has the advantages it.

using that person's skills
depersonalising some of the more contentious issues
providing a less preconceived view of things.

Alternatively, or as an extension to this, a planning team could generate solutions and propose strategies which could be implemented by individuals or the organisation. The sharing of strategies and expertise in coping can solve the problems of individuals and bring about greater cohesiveness in the organisation.

As indicated in Figure 11.3, the strategies can be divided into four categories and each of these will be examined in turn.

1. Lessen the Demands

This direct approach to handling stress is the most practical and the easiest to understand. The actual cause of stress is reduced or removed and the results are clearly seen by the individual and throughout the organisation. Many of the strategies which could be employed are detailed in the next chapter.

Briefly, individuals should be helped to plan their work and to prioritize so that the most essential tasks are not overlooked. There should be more readiness to delegate, especially to others with time and expertise, and to say 'no' rather than take on too much work. Although the literature on stress suggests that only one task should be tackled at once, the author feels that, because of the complexity of roles, this would not always be practicable for teachers. At the whole school level, the establishment of realistic goals will ensure that they are attainable and staff will feel less frustrated than if there is a sense of working hard and never actually reaching the goals. Administrative procedures should be designed to suit the particular school and to support the staff in their work, rather than be based on an LEA-wide model.

There is considerable scope for a school-wide review of structures and responsibilities in order to meet changing demands in the most effective way. This may involve the redefinition of job descriptions, changes to teaching groups, the use of non- teaching assistants etc. If lack of resources (money, time, expertise etc.) seems to be the root cause of the problem, this should be discussed and taken into account when planning the budget.

If the demands can be lessened there will be more time for implementing the stress-reduction strategies described in the next section.

2. Reduce the Reaction to Stress

This involves the use of techniques which moderate the perception of threat, not by tackling the cause but by overcoming the response. Chivers (1989) has evidence that:

> many gifted and experienced teachers are adopting personally and professionally detrimental strategies. Increased smoking, alcohol dependence or over-use...are all serious problems for teachers.

The aim must be to avoid such props and to seek palliative action which is not detrimental to health in the long term. Behaviour must be modified so that the individual becomes less aggressive and more able to accept crises philosophically. Approaches to raising the stress threshold can be grouped together and most of the ideas will be put into practice at the individual level, although the school may be involved in a facilitating role. Those under stress should consider adopting some of the following:

(i) Improve the diet—eat regular, healthy meals which are not too heavy; cut down on artificial stimulants such as tea, coffee and use herbal remedies instead; drink less alcohol. Relax before a meal as this prevents overeating.

(ii) Practise relaxation techniques—the art of 'letting go'—physically and mentally. This can cover simple activities like stretching, shaking, and breathing techniques, e.g. deep breathing and slow exhalation or counting to 20 when stressed. Schools can help by providing a quiet room for staff.

(iii) Practise *yoga* which teaches mental and physical control, increasing one's awareness or the inner self, or *meditation* which relaxes the mind, increasing awareness of self and potential, lowers blood pressure and decreases breathing rate. *Visualisation* (calling briefly to mind a pleasant scene) can allow control to be regained during a stressful incident, for example, a heated conversation.

(iv) Take regular exercise which release pent up energy and improves the efficiency of the body; teachers may feel that they do quite enough of this during the school day but if it is to relieve tension, the exercise needs to be removed from the job, e.g. swimming or jogging.

(v) Develop creative rather than competitive hobbies and take an annual break from routine and the usual environment. Most teachers follow the latter piece of advice during the summer but, because of the nature of the job, they should also allow themselves a break at half-terms whereas many are involved school trips or simply in 'catching-up' at this time.

An individual should learn to recognise his/her own stress situations and then be able to relax in order to cope. A mixture of physical and cultural activities is known to be stress-relieving but it is best if such activities take place on a regular basis and are adopted from an early age.

3. Improve Stress Management Skills

Staff can become better able to deal with stress if they enhance their skills in relating to others. Instead of just talking *at* colleagues, it is important to *listen* to what *they* have to say. If people can relate well to each other, they can function as groups and, through effective teamwork, develop mutual support systems. These skills, and the opportunity to benefit from them, will arise from the implementation of appraisal-led staff development.

In the case study school *synectics* was used as a means of sharing problems and attempting to generate solutions. This is a form of brainstorming combined with creative thinking which, briefly, involves the following.

(i) The 'owner' airs a problem, explaining its background.

(ii) The other members of the group note the situation and then generate a large number of possible solutions (all prefaced by 'I wish' or 'How to') which the 'owner' might consider. The important point is that all suggestions should be accepted and written on a board. No one should be made to believe that an idea is 'silly' as there may be the germ of a solution there.

(iii) From about 30 possible solutions, the 'owner' selects two or three for further exploration and then scores the most appropriate actionable idea', giving marks out of 10 for newness, appeal and feasibility (the NAF rating). An idea which scores eight or more in each of the three areas has potential.

There are various other ways to improve stress management skills:

- relax over meals and talk to friends and colleagues (not just about work) as this helps relationships as well as helping the body to reduce its reaction to stress
- get up earlier so that there is less rush; it is possible to be relaxed and to eat a meal
- adopt practical coping skills, for example when tired decide to organise things later when refreshed
- practise compartmentalisation, i.e. shutting off one aspect of life (which may be causing a problem) when dealing with another
- learn to prioritise and pace activities.

4. Change Attitudes

A school which takes a collaborative look at stress has already begun to adopt a changed attitude to it. People are given encouragement to express their feelings with the minimum of embarrassment and without the bitterness or aggression which can accompany frustration. Just talking over a problem can help people to cope with stress, particularly when it originates outside the school and there is little which can be done to remove the cause.

Ad hoc or structured counselling (e.g. as part of appraisal-led staff development) may demonstrate that a person is particularly unhappy in the his/her job and this may highlight the need for an internal change of role/responsibility or for a move to a different school or even outside teaching.

Gray and Freeman (1988), when discussing how colleagues can be supported, mention the value of humour. Because laughter relieves tension people should be helped to seer the funny side of a stressful situation so that they rationalise the problem. There is a tendency, especially when under pressure, to worry over trivia. Not all problems are as serious as people think, and keeping a sense of proportion helps ourselves and each other. It is better if people accept in a relaxed way that certain things cannot be changed or controlled.

There is a need to consider the relative importance of being busy and successful or of being happy and to concentrate on the present rather than dwelling on the past or living for the future.

Stage C—Implementing the Plans

The preceding sections should have demonstrated to the reader that there is a wide variety of strategies or combinations of strategies which can be adopted by individuals, groups or the organisation as a whole. The most appropriate strategies and means of operationalising them need to be chosen to suit the situation, with the aim of helping staff to take responsibility for their own lives and to solve their own problems (collaboratively if that is best). Staff may wish to consider the following as organisation-wide possibilities for tackling the stress problem:

- training day for whole staff
- on-going INSET work
- use of the Educational Psychologist, e.g. for counselling and group skills
- intervisiting (within or between schools)

- development of practical skill, e.g. through course on management or stress
- counselling, appraisal, staff development
- change in organisational structure/responsibilities/administration
- change of resource use through LMS

If the 'training day' approach is chosen, it is important to appreciate that stress reduction is an on-going process and therefore some follow-up will be necessary.

Sometimes a minor change can have a very beneficial effect. Wilce (TES 26 May 1989) reports that one primary head realised the importance to classroom teachers of a break from the children and the chance to relax with colleagues so she took over some of the break duties. This type of approach is particularly relevant in small schools where the burden of duties falls heavily on all staff.

In general, though, management of stress at the whole school level requires that the strategies are applied at a *macro* rather than a *micro* level. Effective prioritizing and planning will filter out the less immediate tasks so that these can be picked up at a later date. This particular strategy was employed extensively by classroom teachers in the early stages of National Curriculum implementation when most other developments were subordinated by the need to alter the content of the curriculum.

Stage D—Evaluating the Activities

Any activity should be evaluated in order to consider its effectiveness. While the results of a stress reduction programme should be apparent in increased organisational effectiveness, a more formal evaluation is possible. This will particularly be the case if a questionnaire approach was used at the outset; it can be repeated at a later stage and used for comparison. However, one note of caution—staff's increased awareness of stress as a result of the programme could distort their replies.

The outcome of a successful programme should be that problems are seen in a better perspective. Individuals should feel that they have retaken control of their lives and that they are able to make constructive decisions about their work. It is to be hoped that the coping strategies which are employed do actually bring about their work. It is to be hoped that the coping strategies which are employed do actually bring about stress reduction, otherwise people will feel a sense of failure and be even more aware of their inability to cope with pressure. The case study which follows is intended to show the practical application of the key elements discussed above.

A CASE STUDY—MANAGING STRESS

The following case study describes the process of attempting to alleviate stress in a large urban primary school and it provides a framework which could be adapted by any school. Although its main focus is on the individual, whole school issues are allowed to surface and can be tackled in the subsequent weeks. The stages in the process are based on the principles described in chapter 3:

1. Recognition and analysis of the problem
2. Planning the aims, objectives, activities and evaluation
3. Implementation
4. Evaluation.

1. Recognition and Analysis of the Problem

The LEA recognised the existence of teacher stress and Educational Psychologists organized a series of awareness-raising courses for representatives from the schools. (An alternative scenario could be that those within a school notice the symptoms.)

As a result of this course, two teachers from the case study school decided to try to alleviate the problems of stress in their school, proposing to devote a training day to the topic. Because of the possibly controversial and personal nature of the subject, they first consulted all their colleagues in a staff meeting in order to develop confidence in the idea. Although apprehensive, the staff indicated a willingness to participate in a series of activities which aimed to provide positive advice for individuals and for the school.

Before setting objectives for the day, the planners needed to identify priorities by investigating the existing individual and

organisational stressors. They achieved this by distributing a questionnaire to colleagues, asking a variety of questions which, when analysed, put the stressors into the rank order illustrated.

Work overload Environmental Role conflict Job ambiguity	verage scores above 50 per cent
Managing people Personal Organisational structure Interpersonal Work underload	average scores below 50 per cent

2. Planning

Having identified aims and priorities, the following objectives were developed for the day:

(i) to provide a pleasant and relaxed atmosphere so that staff could derive maximum benefit from their experiences;

(ii) to help individual staff and groups to minimise the problems of work overload;

(iii) to provide a forum for the airing of concerns such as the poor physical environment, the problems of role conflict and job ambiguity;

(iv) to provide a mechanism for evaluating the day and its subsequent impact.

The programme for the day was planned on the following lines:

relaxation techniques
time management
problem solving using synectics
personal plans
evaluation

3. Implementation

Lack of funds prevented the organisers from achieving the first objective as they had wished (by using a teachers' centre) so they rearranged the school library, introducing flowers and relaxing music at the start of the day. Many staff had been worried about taking part in the relaxation techniques but found that they were not embarrassing, rather that they were soothing and calming.

The session on time management covered analysis and present use of time, and suggested ways in which this could be improved. Some of these ideas are discussed in the next chapter.

Micropolitical problems and changes in senior management meant that it was difficult to tackle some of the priorities in a direct way, so it was decided that staff should be introduced to synectics beforehand so that they could identify problems for airing on the training day.

It was felt that this new approach to problem solving would be beneficial because time-wasting in meetings, accommodation problems, lack of role clarity etc. could all be tackled in this way. On the training day the staff divided into two groups for the synectics session and, in each case, many valuable ideas were put forward.

However, the author felt that the most important outcome of this session was not the ideas generated, but the increased openness and sharing of problems amongst the staff. This would have many future benefits within the school.

The final sessions on personal plans and evaluation were fairly brief. Staff were left with forms which would help them to assimilate the day's experiences and to plan a stress reduction strategy for the future.

4. *Evaluation*

The evaluation of the day's activities produced a very encouraging response from the staff who, despite initial worries, found that they had a worthwhile day. The organisers planned to reassess the levels and causes of stress in the school six months after the training day to see it it had any longer-term benefit. Their final evaluation may not, however, pick up the more general benefit of an increasingly open, supportive atmosphere in the school.

CONCLUSION

This chapter has looked at the important area of managing stress. Its significance can be seen if one considers that effective resource management and curriculum management are only possible in an environment where individuals can cope and adapt to changed policies and respond to them effectively. Two aspects of stress management have been put forward. The first is at the individual level where self-awareness and self-discipline are improved. The second is at the level of the whole school where key strategies are applied to wider staff and pupil activities. This latter approach may involve considerable change within the school so that there is a new management culture and an improved climate.

12

Time Management

The case study towards the end of chapter 7 reflects national research which identifies lack of time in relation to workload as a major stressor in schools today. The concern is not only directed at teachers, but at the need to make more creative use of pupil time so, as to deliver a broad curriculum within tight time constraints. This chapter develops and model of the time management process which begins by considering the existing use of time and then looks at a variety of ways in which time may be deployed more effectively. This should allow schools and individuals to reduce levels of stress and to increase organisational effectiveness.

Drucker (1970) emphasises the importance of time:

> Time is also a unique resource...one cannot rent, hire, buy or otherwise obtain more time. The supply of time is totally inelastic. No matter how high the demand, the supply will not go up...time is totally perishable and cannot be stored. Yesterday's time is gone forever and will never come back. Time is, therefore in exceedingly short supply.

Although much attention is given to this topic in business management training, it is an issue which is often ignored in education. The main reason for this is the fact that the dual role of the teacher/manager (in whatever proportion, at whatever level) means that there is 'no time for management' (Handy

1984). This implies that there is no spare time in which to fulfil one's management role and, indeed, many teachers see this role as a minor inconvenience. Because there is so little time to be managed, it is of paramount importance that any which is available should be used to best advantage. An additional constraint is that schools and indeed, people in the community, have deeply entrenched, traditional views of the timing of the school day and of the divisions within it, especially at secondary level. It may be that one of the keys to improved time management in the schools of the 1990s lies in questioning the validity of such views, and that by attacking the problem at the whole school level, we can resolve the individuals problems.

Drucker (1970) has observed that effective managers start by finding out how they use time and then they manage it, aggregating spare time into usable blocks. The time management process can be seen to comprise four stages:

recording
analysing
managing
consolidating

each of which will be examined below.

RECORDING THE USE OF TIME

Before deciding how to improve the use of time, it is essential to consider present use. This can help to identify tasks or times of the day on which to focus. Teachers may well find it valuable to examine the whole day rather than the working day as this will give a truer picture of the way in which their burdens cross the home/school boundary.

The method chosen to record use of time will vary according to the roles and responsibilities of the individual. It is probably most effective if a rough outline is drafted, tried and then rewritten to find the most useful format. The following may be included:

time of day
task
who originated the task?
was it prescribed (fixed/compulsory) ,e.g. teaching at 11.00 or discretionary (voluntary/movable), e.g. tidying the filing cabinet at 12.30?
how long did it take?

Some people consider that to record everything is a waste of time, particularly in education where there is so little discretionary time. It can be more effective to concentrate on a particular problem which seems to be consuming a lot of time, such as pupil record-keeping. Other general points to bear in mind are:

- recording should be done daily for at least a week to gain a true picture
- a 'typical week should be chosen, not the end of term or examination time (unless specifically looking at this)
- recording should be done regularly throughout the day, otherwise accuracy is lost
- there may be a need for a 'shadow' to do the recording—this is not always feasible but could be applied to a limited part of the day and there may also be a possibility of having one's use of time observed as part of the appraisal process
- it helps if specific note is made of time-wasting/unproductive activities.

Broader school issues could be examined such as the amount of time spent in meetings and the involvement of those present. Legislation requires some schools to record the use of pupils' time in respect of the national curriculum, but an occasional look at their day may reveal disproportionate amounts of time being spent, for example, on moving around the buildings.

ANALYSING THE USE OF TIME

Once the use of time has been recorded, it will be evident that, for the majority of teachers, much of the school day is spent carrying out prescribed activities such as teaching, registration and duties. Closer investigation of some of these activities may indicate that elements contained within them do not make the best use of time. Any discretionary time which might usefully be managed is found to be scattered throughout the day in small pockets, for example before school, breaks, lunch-time and possibly some 'non-contact' time.

The individual should begin by considering his/her job description and identifying the important responsibilities. The following questions can then be asked:

1. was the activity really necessary or could the time be better spent?
2. how successful was the outcome and are there any habitual failures?
3. how much time was spent on each of the various types of work—'must do', 'should do', 'could do' (least important duties)?
4. where did the work come from?

    is a superior delegating too much?

    are subordinates too dependent?

    are you setting yourself too many tasks?
5. could the task be delegated?

    if yes, to whom?

    if no, why not? is it your job?

    have you made yourself indispensable?
6. was the activity planned or was it an interruption? Could it have been planned?

The author's work with teachers suggests that the following are seen to consume a disproportionate amount of time:

photocopying
trying to contact people by telephone
dealing with other teachers' discipline problems
attending poorly thought-out meetings
trying to gather management information
poor communication
reading documents especially from the LEA/DES, especially at head/deputy level and in times of great change
having to carry out routine tasks because of lack of support staff.

The highlights another contrast with the business world where research shows that frequently cited timewasters include drop-in visitors and talking on the telephone, although there are similarities such as the inability to say 'no'.

Having analysed the use of time, it will be possible to see the unproductive demands on time and these should point to what might be done by the individual or the organisation. A positive approach to managing this valuable resource can then be developed.

MANAGING THE USE OF TIME

Having completed the diagnosis stage, one should have some idea of which activities take a disproportionate amount of time and it would be expedient to focus on one or two of these as a first step. It is generally recognised that 80 percent of our time is spent achieving 20 percent of our results so, when considering how to manage time better, we should be aiming to achieve more by doing less, reflecting the view of Mackenzie (1972) that 'working smarter, not harder, is the real goal of effective management.' Possible objectives may include:

- to increase efficiency when reading documents
- to increase the opportunities for delegation
- to reorganise information systems to improve communication and decision making
- to create more time for planning and, thus, avoid crisis management
- to make meetings more worthwhile
- to allow more creativity in the use of pupil time.

Because so much of the school day involves prescribed activities, attention may fall on the use of breaks or the lunch hour. This would contrast with industry/commerce where such time would probably be considered to be outside the brief.

Figure 12.1 suggests a variety of approaches which may be adopted in order to improve the use of both 'directed' and 'discretionary' time for the individual and the organisation. A combination of approaches will usually be the most appropriate.

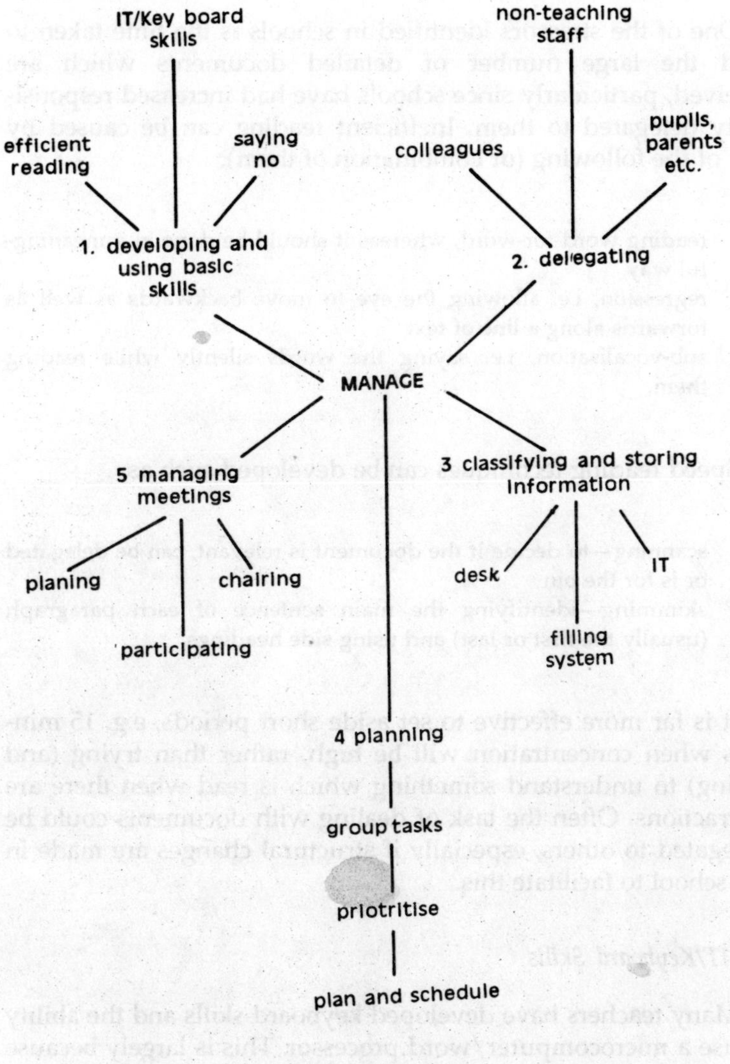

Fig. 12.1 Approaches to Managing the Use of Time.

1. Developing and Using Basic Skills

These approaches to time management will be put into practice at the individual level.

(i) Efficient Reading

One of the stressors identified in schools is the time taken to read the large number of detailed documents which are received, particularly since schools have had increased responsibility delegated to them. Inefficient reading can be caused by any of the following (or combination of them):

- reading word-for-word, whereas it should be done in a meaningful way
- regression, i.e. allowing the eye to move backwards as well as forwards along a line of text
- sub-vocalisation, i.e. saying the words silently while reading them.

Speed reading techniques can be developed such as:

- scanning—to decide if the document is relevant, can be delegated or is for the bin
- skimming—identifying the main sentence of each paragraph (usually the first or last) and using side headings.

It is far more effective to set aside short periods, e.g. 15 minutes when concentration will be high, rather than trying (and falling) to understand something which is read when there are distractions. Often the task of dealing with documents could be delegated to others, especially if structural changes are made in the school to facilitate this.

(ii) IT/Keyboard Skills

Many teachers have developed keyboard skills and the ability to use a microcomputer/word processor. This is largely because of a lack of ancillary support and a desire to produce materials specifically tailored to their pupils. In particular, the ability to amend a document, i.e. to understand how to use a word-processing package, can be a great time-saver. However, it would often be a far better use of the school's resources if a clerical assistant were to do the original keyboard work.

While we acknowledge the use of computers throughout the school as a teaching aid, many people have not yet developed the ability to use them as aids to management and administration. As with curricular use, this does not require programming skills, but, simply, an understanding of the way in which software packages can store, manipulate and retrieve information for the individual teacher or for the whole school. Carefully used, IT can alleviate many of the time-linked stressors in the school. Alternatively, if it is badly applied there can be vast quantities of paperwork generated, increasing the workload with no corresponding increase in school effectiveness.

(iii) Saying 'NO'

Many teachers admit to finding it difficult to say 'NO', especially to requests from pupils or to carry out voluntary activities. The following reasons are often given for saying 'yes' when the answer should, realistically, be 'no'.

having unclear priorities
a fear of offending others
the need to be a 'good guy'
hoping to make others feel indebted to you
a desire to please superiors
the need to obtain a good reference in the future.

It should be possible to learn to say 'no', especially if one remembers that it is the way in which something is said, not just what is said, that matters. Four steps to saying 'no' are suggested here:

(a) Listen to ensure that you understand what is being requested
(b) Give a definite 'no' rather than 'maybe/perhaps'
(c) If it is appropriate, explain the reasons for your refusal
(d) If possible, suggest alternative strategies.

Failure to say 'no' to an unreasonable request may actually demonstrate weakness and cause loss of respect, rather than pleasing someone.

2. Delegating

In the business world it is accepted good practice that managers should be managing rather than carrying out menial tasks. In education there is greater role ambiguity, largely because of the dual role of teacher and manager. It is quite common to see a deputy head of a large secondary school collating and stapling hundreds of newsletters or arranging furniture. Under LMS schools have greater flexibility over staffing and it should be possible to make more effective use of time and money by employing non- teaching assistants to carry out routine clerical or technical work.

Various excuses are given for failing to delegate:

no-one else will do the job as well
it takes too long to explain it to someone else
everyone else is too busy
there isn't anyone else to whom it could be delegated
there is a need to remain responsible and accountable.

There are many reasons why delegation to colleagues can be beneficial in an organisation. There is often someone who is better able to do the job than oneself or, if not, it can form part of a staff development process and enable someone else to cope in a crisis. Delegation also helps to motivate people by giving them challenging tasks as well as mundane ones. Waters (1987) refers to the difficulties (especially in terms of staff development) experienced by primary school deputy heads when the heads do not delegate but, because of the vast increase in responsibilities which they now face, the benefits of delegation should become more apparent.

When delegating a task, the lines of accountability and responsibility must be clear and it is important to delegate the right to make mistakes. Both parties should be aware of:

(a) which items need to be referred back up to the delegator before a decision is taken;

(b) which items need to be referred back up to the delegator after a decision is taken;

(c) which items need not be referred at all;

(d) which items may be delegated further.

Delegation of responsibility is not limited to colleagues, but can be applied by encouraging pupils to be responsible for classroom equipment and for managing their own learning. Parents are often willing to help and, here again, care is needed so that they feel valued and are not just asked to carry out mundane jobs.

3. Classifying and Storing Information

Chapter 2 referred to the importance of information but if this is to be of value it must be easy to find. Unfortunately the plethora of notes, documents, books etc. which a teacher receives often end up in one large pile. Mackenzie (1972) explains that 'we stack our desks with all the things we do not want to forget, but when we look at them we risk becoming sidetracked....' A desk should be a place to process work, not to store it. It is the author's contention that every teacher is a manager and deserves a desk on which to work and at least part of a suitable filing system for personal use. Too many teachers are expected to operate effectively from a locker and the top of a cupboard or coffee table.

Teachers tend to hoard all sorts of things in case they are ever useful (and often they would be, if they could be found). However, paperwork clogs up the system so it is important to be ruthless and to discard or delegate as much as possible.

Each person needs to decide how to classify the important items which are received. One model offered would include boxes or files for each of the following:

IN
OUT
DO TODAY
DO THIS WEEK
TO BE FILED
FOLLOW UP (file according to when)
PROJECTS (labelled folders—leave in until needed)

Because the reading of documents is recognised as a very time- consuming activity in schools, it is important to try and generate as little paperwork as possible. This can be achieved in a variety of ways:

replying to memos by writing on them
using IT to make information accessible to those who wish to receive it but not overloading those who do not want it
using 'Plain English', lists, summaries and the underlining of key-words to improve readability
marking amendments clearly when re-issuing documents.

4. Planning

Managers must ensure that planning and target-setting at the whole school level (as discussed in chapter 3) takes account of priorities and available resources, including time and staff good-will. There is also considerable scope for improving the way in which individuals formulate their shorter-term plans.

In order to manage time effectively, it is necessary to draw up a list of tasks and projects, attempting to group them in a meaningful way. At the individual level such lists will probably be compiled on a weekly and daily basis with the latter, by virtue of immediacy, being more detailed and less flexible. Priorities need to be considered and the standard approach is to classify tasks as follows:

Priority A—those things which must be done
Priority B—those things which should be done
Priority C—those things which could be done, i.e. which we would like to do

The next stage is to decide what needs to be done, when and by whom. It may well be feasible to delegate some of the tasks, especially the more routine aspects of category A, in order to create time for development. Having produced a list of tasks, it is now possible to plan and schedule. The aims should be to produce plans which can be adapted if circumstances change and to spend as much time as possible on activities which lead to goal achievement.

There are many personal planning aids available for purchase or suggested in the literature on time management (see for example Noon 1983, Garratt 1985). these may be inappropriate in schools because of their emphasis on appointments throughout the day but teachers could adapt them and include appropriate categories such as 'write do', 'short task' and 'don't forget'.

While deciding how best to plan the use of time, it is important to bear in mind the points which emerged from the diagnosis of the current use of time and attempt to devise a system which can help to remedy the weaknesses. It is good for morale to start the day or term with a task or project where maximum results can be achieved fairly easily and then to move on to those tasks on which one seems to spend a lot of time, yet sees few results. Particular consideration should be given as to when and where it is possible to achieve the most effective span of concentration. One of the problems in schools is that important matters, such as meetings, are left until the end of the day when a block of time is available but when staff are tired.

5. Managing Meetings

The effective use of meetings is a prerequisite of effective time management in schools. Purposeful, 'limited time' meetings which achieve objectives can increase motivation and commitment where as long, unstructured, time-wasting meetings can demotivate staff and increase stress.

Holding meetings is just one of the many ways in which members of a school communicate so that they are all working effectively towards its goals. Meetings are often informal, held over coffee in a staff room or departmental office but, nevertheless, they can still fulfil their purpose and act as a mechanism for consultation and the generation of ideas.

With the concept of 1directed time' it is now possible for senior management to require teachers to attend meetings outside the teaching day and this has often resulted in a more formalised meetings pattern. Benefits are seen because full attendance is assured so that everyone is well aware of developments but, sometimes, meetings are being held as a matter of routine, with little thought given to their purpose or composition.

The following sections are in the form of checklists to facilitate good practice, both for those who organise meetings and for the participants. They cover the types of meetings which might occur during the school year, the criteria for success and the causes of failure.

(i) Classification of Meetings

The type of meeting determines its size and composition as well as the way in which it is conducted. The categorisation shown may be helpful when planning a meeting.

Type	*Features*	
1. Informing, briefing, exchanging information	'tells'	these meetings can be very large, yet still effective; they usually take the form of 'presentations'
2. Persuading	'sells'	
3. Problem-solving, collect views, generate ideas, brainstorm	'consults'	these tend to be more effective if there is a smaller group involved, preferably not more than twelve: they usually
4. Deciding	'involves' in decision making	involve sitting round in 'boardroom' style

Quite often there will be a mixed agenda, involving elements of all four types, although problem solving and decision making with large groups may well result in very poor use of many people's time. It is also difficult to switch from the type of meeting to another unless there is a break, for example of coffee.

Participants in a meeting should be aware of the type of meeting in advance. This may not always be clear from the agenda. For example, an item such as 'allocation of teachers to classrooms' does not make it clear whether this allocation is to be discussed or whether the allocations have been decided and are to be announced. Such lack of understanding may result in participants wasting time preparing points for discussion when there is to be no debate. Conversely, if staff do not realise that an issue is for debate, they may not have the necessary information ready so as to present and substantiate their arguments.

(ii) Effective Meetings

Successful meetings usually have certain characteristics in common. They have a distinct purpose, they involve communication and there is a controlled situation. The right people are present and the timing is right in terms off frequency, start and finish. On the other hand, failure of a meeting to make best use of time or to achieve its purpose is usually the result of one of the following:

- too many meetings held
- unclear purpose of lack of purpose
- agenda badly prepared—order wrong
- unclear agenda or late agenda—participants therefore not prepared
- late start, meeting too long or too short
- time not divided carefully, therefore urgent/important matters not given priority/adequate consideration
- agenda not kept to, uncontrolled—side discussion etc., repetition
- interruptions
- lack of balance of skills, wrong people there—key person missing/too many people
- uniformed chair
- indecision, lack of conclusions
- unminuted, therefore decisions are unclear, not communicated, not carried out
- poor minutes or too late after event
- lack of follow-up.

Figure 12.2 provides a checklist to assist the chair and participants of meetings. Greater detail can be found in a wide variety of books which have been written on the subject (see for example Warwick 1982, Allan 1989), most of which are intended as general management texts but are directly applicable to management in education.

AS CHAIR	*AS A PARTICIPANT*
Before the meeting	
1. Set the objectives i.e. decide what is to be achieved.	1. Read the agenda and consider whether you have anything to add.
2. check that a meeting is the best way to achieve this.	2. Brief yourself, collecting opinions and documentation which may be required. Consider the arguments and alternatives which you might put forward.
3. Be clear about what sort of meeting it is to be.	3. Be prompt.
4. Draw up the agenda, listing each item unambiguously. It should tell people why they are to be thee and be a plan of the meeting time.	
5. Decide who should attend. Beware of having too many present or having the key person missing. Numbers can be kept down by receiving reports from working parties and by attendance for only part of the meeting.	
6. Decide when and where to hold the meeting. Start and finish times should be clear. Consider the most effective time of the week.	
7. Send out the agenda in good time.	
8. Brief someone to take the minutes.	
9. Brief yourself thoroughly on the issues to be discussed. Collect the necessary documentation and background information which may be required. Work out approximate time limits for each item on the agenda so as to reflect priorities.	

Fig. 12.2 Meeting Checklist.

AS CHAIR	AS A PARTICIPANT
During the meeting	
1. Start promptly, follow the agenda, keep to time and finish on time.	1. Listen to what others have to say.
2. Avoid a hidden agenda.	2. Be concise when speaking.
3. Control the meeting—do not allow sidetracking, side discussions or over-domination by certain individuals.	3. Do not become side-tracked or involved in side discussions. Avoid a hidden agenda.
	4. Stick to the agenda.
	5. Be supportive and positive, rather than destructive and critical.
4. Listen carefully and summarise at intervals so that everyone is clear about what is intended.	6. Keep a note of any follow-up which is required of you.
5. Do not allow AOB to become more than a few very quick points.	
After the meeting	
1. Ensure that accurate minutes are sent out as soon as possible and displayed for other interested parties, e.g., the whole staff.	1. If appropriate, inform your team of the issues and outcome of the meeting and make the minutes available to them.
2. Take any action which you agreed to take.	2 Check that you carry out any actions which you agreed to carry out and that you take action according to the minutes.
3. Evaluate the organisation and operation of the meeting.	

Fig. 12.2 (cont'd.)

The main activities can be summarised as:

Before the meeting	Planning Pre-notification Preparation
During the meeting	Processing
After the meeting	Putting 'actions' into practice

CONSOLIDATING THE USE OF TIME

The aim should be to consolidate discretionary time into the largest possible continuing units so that worthwhile tasks can be carried out. For senior management this may mean an increased emphasis on diary management as there is a tendency to fit appointments round those requiring them giving fragmentation of one's time. Because of the large number of prescribed 'slots', it is difficult for most teachers to group their discretionary time in this way. Secondary schools may wish to give greater consideration to grouping non-teaching periods so as to provide worthwhile blocks. The desirability of non-contact time for primary teachers has, at last, been realised and, in many school, LMS can provide the opportunity to adjust the staffing in order to facilitate this. It is possible to go even further than the ideas put forward here. Osborne (1986) believes that there is even greater scope if pupil groups are kept large and time is blocked, delegating to groups of staff the power to manage those pupils and that time and thus be creative.

CONCLUSION

This chapter has made various proposals regarding the analysis and improved use of time in schools in order to increase effectiveness. Managers must apply them to the organisation as a whole and must facilitate their implementation by individuals. The following rules summarise the main ideas.

1. Have a 'flying start'—get going first thing with something which can be accomplished.
2. It the maximum amount of brain work is needed, carry out the task when at one's best.
3. Priorities, putting off the less important tasks but do not put off important matters.
4. Lean to say 'No'.
5. Do it, delegate it or ditch it.
6. Collect all information in one accessible place.
7. Do things well enough—avoid exaggerated perfectionism.

8. Finish a job if possible.
9. Make a habit of completing a task which is over and above the daily routine.
10. Regularly check the use of time.

13

Marketing of School Education

Every school has a reputation and that reputation has to be managed. All schools in the 1990s have to consider how they relate the service they provide to the needs of their clients. A great deal has been written about processes or techniques of marketing. This chapter seeks not to replicate these but to establish a management perspective on five key issues in marketing a school. It is hoped that the reader will then be able to apply them to analysing his/her own school marketing strategy. This chapter is divided into the following sections to achieve this:

1. What is marketing?—an overview
2. The who, what and why of marketing
3. The place of marketing in the organisation
4. The marketing cycle
5. Establishing a marketing culture in a school.

WHAT IS MARKETING?—AN OVERVIEW

Marketing as a management process is the most recent addition to the field of education management. Its rise in significance is largely attributable to the impact of the 1988 Education Act, introducing as it does the central notion of choice. If parents have a choice then schools will need to be more sensitive and responsive to them. These notions of sensitivity and responsiveness are the essence of marketing. The majority of effective schools have been operating a marketing strategy for years although the label has not always been used. Many of the components of marketing have been discussed in previous texts but usually in the academic and political context of accountability. This chapter argues for the professionalism of the ways in which schools manage their relationships with their clients.

There are two common misapprehensions about marketing, firstly, that it is synonymous with advertising and, secondly, that it is concerned with external relationships. Advertising is one possible outcome of a marketing strategy, however it is not that strategy. Equally, marketing is as much about internal as it is about external relationships. Marketing is about managing relationships through effective communication and, by definition, such communication is a two-way process. Any successful transaction is concerned with the achievement of mutually desired outcomes. It is equally important that the message is delivered consistently and that it is fundamental to internal working relationships. Marketing in education therefore involves diagnosing needs and values, developing appropriate responses and then ensuring that those responses are meeting the needs identified. Marketing is not just about 'selling a product'; it is about identifying the nature of the product required and ensuring that it is delivered and that every facet of the organisation contributes to the quality of the product.

Therefore, marketing is implicit in every component of effective management. It provides the basis for integrating schools' aims, the data for planning and decision making, the criteria for resource allocation and thereby the budget. It will also inform staff selection criteria and help to generate training and development programmes. Equally, marketing will serve to focus monitoring and evaluation procedures. Marketing is implicit in effective management because if effectiveness is about the attainment of goals then marketing helps to ensure that the 'right' goals are being pursued, identifies the extent to which goals are attained and is as much concerned with the processes involved as the outcomes.

It can be stated that marketing is about conformity to client needs. In the context of schools it means the systematic analysis of those needs, the development of strategies to meet them and the deployment of resources to allow such strategies to be implemented effectively. Like all management techniques, marketing is about action but it is specifically about deciding direction and being capable of responding to changing needs. Glossy advertising and good public relations techniques are peripheral outcomes of marketing, skills which have to be based on professional integrity.

Marketing relationships are extremely complex and multi-dimensional. It is not just a matter of the 'school and its environment'. The possible permutations are substantial but may include the following: senior management team and teaching staff, teaching and non-teaching staff, school staff and governing body, staff and pupils, school and parents, school and employers, higher education, etc., school and external agencies, school and LEA. Each of these relationships is distinct, each has its own marketing needs and procedures; all are interdependent in order to achieve their desired outcomes. Each relationship, to be successful, depends upon effective communication and the analysis and meeting of needs.

Most commercial organisations have few problems in identifying the customer/client and the product. For service industries, and education in particular, the issue is more acute notably in the context of defining both the client and the product let alone securing agreement as to the nature of outcomes. These issues will now be explored and developed in more detail in the succeeding sections.

THE WHO, WHAT AND WHY OF MARKETING

This section looks at three questions about marketing schools:

(i) WHO are the clients the school is marketing to?

(ii) WHAT is the school marketing?

(iii) WHY is the school marketing?

It is hoped that the reader will reflect on these basic questions before becoming involved in the 'technique' side of marketing in terms of brochures and publicity handouts.

(i) Who are the Clients the School is Marketing to?

This presents a difficult problem of definition and prioritising for the school. In the primary school most teachers would consider that the pupils are the clients and, therefore, the first priority of the teacher. Secondary teachers often consider that the parents are the clients and that they are responsible/accountable to them. There is also a responsibility to the wider community which funds the school through local business rates and the community charge.

However, the child/parent dimension of who is the client is the key one for schools to explore. The thrust of government action during the 1980s and the underpinning of the 1988 Education Reform Act is to reduce the power of monopoly suppliers and to put power in the hands of the consumers. This certainly has been true of a number of reforms, for example, the reform of trade union legislation. In the education service the legislative and other government action has definitely been to reduce the power of the suppliers of education—the teachers. This can be seen in terms of the very significant reduction in teacher control of the curriculum in favour of centrally determined and controlled developments in GCSE examining and, more latterly, the National Curriculum.

As was seen in chapter 4, one of the key elements in LMS is open enrollments. This gives the power to parents to send their child to the school of their choice, providing the school has the physical space to accommodate that child and the child meets any pre-existing entrance requirements, for example, religious affiliations. This choice depends on two crucial factors, firstly, that there are sufficient schools locally for the choice to be exercised and, secondly, that the parents have the resources (time and finance) to transport the child from the immediate catchment area school.

What impact does this have on a school? Certain schools will still retain a near monopoly because if there are no other local schools conveniently available parents have no effective choice. The nature of the catchment area may also mean that, even where choice exists, the convenience of a local school may overcome broader educational factors. However, whether schools, because of their near monopoly position, are only affected at the margin or are in a much more competitive position, relating to the client is a prime factor in a school's success.

The younger the child the more dominant is the parent in making the choice of school. Children at the age of five exercise very little choice as to the school they attend. This is ironic as primary teachers often see the pupils as 'their children' and put their professional views as being of greater importance than those of the parents. Teachers' perceptions of this relationship often change when their own children go to school and they sit on the opposite of the teacher's desk on parents' evenings. As children get older and attend secondary school and, more significantly, when they transfer to Sixth Form College, Tertiary or Further Education College, the pupils play a more dominant role in the choice process.

It would be wrong, however, to take the simplistic view that the parent is the client with an increasing role being undertaken by the child as he/she gets older. At stages the child and parent influence each other as to the value and esteem in which the school is held. When the child comes home and relates good or bad experiences about the school this influences parental opinion, and the parental response influences the child's perception of the school.

Viewing the parent/child as the client is not fudging the issue but is the fine balance which schools need to achieve in effective relationships with their customers. Schools do not exist to provide teachers with jobs; they exist to provide effective education to their clients. Reflecting on the changing importance, power and definition of who is the client/customer in education is the essential prerequisite for effective marketing of schools.

Outside the immediate consumer is a broader set of clients, the local community who fund the school and who are also significant in marketing terms.

(ii) What is the School Marketing?

That which follows will not be a discussion of the different values and attainments which a school puts across, such as examination results or sports achievements, important as these undoubtedly are. Instead it will consider whether the school is concerned with marketing perceptions or marketing reality. Another dimension of this can be expressed by asking if it is paying attention to overt or covert performance indicators.

Do the clients choose a school because of its examination results and other quantifiable factors like this? Certainly they are major factors but the reputation of a school is made up of a series of complex and inter-related factors. When a child is five the quality of education may not be assessed by the parents in any meaningful way. Overt factors such as test scores may not be as important as covert factors or perceptions. Wearing school uniform, which parents associate with good discipline, and the taking home of their reading books by five-year-olds, which parents associate with homework and academic standards, may be very significant. These determinants of the perceptions which parents have of the school may be more important than the reality of what is actually going on to deliver effective education. The reputation of many secondary schools may be enhanced by the overt reality of good staff/pupil relationships, high academic standards, etc. This reputation may be undone by the behavior of pupils in the local town at lunchtime, smoking outside the school gates and the behavior of pupils travelling to and returning from school on school buses.

A useful management exercise for school staff to undertake is to list the four strengths and weaknesses of the school as they perceive them. Secondly, drawing on the knowledge from the interaction they have with parents at parents' evenings, etc., to list the strengths and weaknesses as perceived by parents. The key management information comes in comparing the two lists. It is not the internal educationists who set the criteria; there may be significant factors in the perceptions of parents that determine the reputation of a school which have little to do with its core educational activities.

Schools, therefore, have to decide whether they are marketing a set of values which is taken for granted but ignoring a number of factors that parents perceive as being key indicators of a 'good' school. While the authors would not suggest that fundamental educational values are ignored at the expense of marketing pragmatism, it is vital that schools do not assume they know what parents want. It is important that if schools are to fulfil their educational mission, they address the concerns of their clients and respond to them. The only way to do this is to sample parental opinion to find out what they consider is significant and not to rely on the existing teacher perceptions based within the internal culture of the school.

(iii) Why is the School Marketing Itself?

This can be summed up by stating that, in the modern world, 'virtue does not of necessity bring its own reward' while virtue with a good marketing strategy may! Whatever the good attributes of a school are they will not, of themselves, ensure continued success and survival unless the wider community understands, values and, above all, knows about them.

Marketing a school is basically a process of relating the school's aims, objectives and achievements to the needs and wishes of the community. This is the prime accountability dimension of marketing in an educational institution.

This has been given tremendous power by the overt introduction of market forces through the 1988 Education Reform Act. And earlier in this chapter, reference was made to LMS and, in particular, to two specific aspects of it; formula funding and open enrolments. As was seen in the diagram earlier, increasing or decreasing pupil numbers as a result of parents operating their power of choice under the open enrollment entitlement has, through the formula-funding mechanism, a direct effect on the financial viability of schools and, hence, on teachers jobs.

While the main reason that a school *should* be marketing is a desire to improve its service and relationship with its clients, the main reason why it *has* to market itself is that, in the 1990s, economic realities make this a precondition of its future survival.

THE PLACE OF MARKETING IN THE ORGANISATION

It would be very easy for schools to appear to be responding to the need for marketing. As with all management activities it would be possible to establish roles and procedures which appear to indicate the acceptance of the principle. Thus the appointment of a member of staff with responsibility for 'marketing', the setting up of a working party, the introduction of the marketing approach outlined below and the production of professionally designed brochures might be interpreted as a school having come to terms with marketing. The reality will probably be completely different.

The messages and images projected by a marketing strategy need to be integral to all parts of the school and every individual must become a 'marketing manager'. The headteacher, teaching and non- teaching staff and every pupil are all essential components of the marketing 'team' and what they say and do will determine the impact of the school's message. In essence marketing is about managing an image and behavior will always be a more important determinant of that image than statements and promises. The problem for schools to come to terms with is that, in managing their image in the community, they have to deal with subjective impressions and these are formulated on a selective basis which may have nothing to do with systems and designated roles. The work of the marketing manager can be totally undermined by one disaffected member of the school. The glossiest brochure can be negated by an incomprehensible letter, the finest art displays invalidated by an attack of graffiti.

For a marketing strategy to work it is therefore necessary to address fundamental issues about the school. In their study of successful British companies, MCBurnie and Clutterbuck (1987) identify what they describe as the 'marketing edge'—the qualities which allow those companies to dominate in their respective sectors. They distil the special qualities of these companies into the '3 Cs'—culture, creativity and commitment; but permeating all three is responsiveness to the customer or client and it is therefore proposed to add a fourth 'C'—the client. Every organisation—company or school—is unique and there is no magic formula or panacea which can be taken 'off the shelf' and imposed. The crucial thing is that organisations evaluate themselves against these criteria and then formulate their own response which is appropriate to their history and context.

(i) Culture

This is the least tangible and most problematic aspect of managing any organisation. However, if practical outcomes and activities are used as the basis for analysis then a number of factors emerge. The single most important determinant of the culture of any organisation is the quality of leadership. In essence, culture is a function of leadership and the qualities of the leader will be reflected throughout the organisation. This has been well documented in industry and commerce and, equally so, in education. The values, attitudes and behavior of headteachers will be the crucial determinant in deciding the extent to which a school is able to project itself to its community.

Positive leadership will help to ensure that the single most important component of effective marketing—awareness of the primary function of the school—is continually at the forefront of all planning and decision making and is fundamental to all aspects of school life. This is in turn reflected in the clarity of a school's aims and objectives and the extent to which they are the basis for action and evaluation.

These values, aims and objectives are derived from a further important aspect of organisational culture—a sensitivity to the environment and a willingness to change in response to it. This in turn involves an openness and honesty in assessing strengths and weaknesses; the school is aware of and celebrates its strengths but is equally conscious of its weaknesses.

It is no coincidence that the principles identified above are very closely related to the notion of the changing school. The first component of a successful marketing strategy is for the school to be clear and explicit about what it exists to do, for leadership to constantly reiterate that mission and to be constantly aware of changing needs and the school's ability to respond to them. Without such a culture a marketing strategy will be superficial, vulnerable and lacking integrity.

(iii) Creativity

Creativity refers to the ability of any organisation to develop a unique, positive and effective response to changing circumstances which solves problems by improving services. One of the fundamental components of successful marketing in education is that schools are perceived as solving problems. In order to do this two qualities are required. The first is the ability to diagnose the components of any problem accurately and in response to the perceptions of those involved. The second is the ability to formulate imaginative responses which resolve the issue to the mutual satisfaction of those involved and yet do not become a new orthodoxy.

Marketing is therefore about anticipating changing needs, being sensitive to economic and social changes and preparing strategies which move the school forward. However, creative solutions need to be creatively communicated. One of the major weaknesses of many schools is that they have been able to generate highly effective responses to new challenges but these have failed because the creativity in managing the curriculum was not matched by creativity in communication. Schools often concentrate on the product to the detriment of the clients. Creativity is needed to develop the most appropriate means of informing clients about the validity of the product—working from their needs rather than assuming that all educational changes are coherent, understandable and self-legitimating.

(iii) Commitment

Organisations which are successful in marketing their products and services set out to cream commitment rather than simply assuming it by virtue of the employment contract. There is therefore an emphasis on communicating a constant reiteration of the values of the organisation and, crucially, the rationale behind them. All those involved in marketing therefore know what the organisation exists to do and, equally, why particular policies and strategies are adopted.

Commitment is thus obtained through communication and explanation. However, this has to be reinforced by selecting people who display the qualities necessary to advance the organisation and by ensuring that the motivation of those involved is understood and appropriately managed. In schools this has obvious implications for the selection, appraisal and development of teachers. However it is equally significant for non-teaching staff and, in the context of rationalisation, for pupils. Commitment is often a function of understanding and this implies that everyone lives the school's values, mission and specific objectives. This means that they have to be understandable, that the means of attaining them are available and that everyone understands their role in achieving them.

(iv) Clients

Marketing is about responding to clients' needs and these are best defined not in terms of specifics but rather, as 'conformity to requirements' or 'fitness for purpose'. In other words, marketing is about demonstrating the extent to which clients' needs have been identified and then met. Thus the components of meeting a specific set of client needs will vary according to the client as will the appropriate vehicle for communication. Equally, it is impossible to draw a neat line between the school and its environment and argue that marketing starts after the line (see Figure 13.1)—numerous individuals will be involved in the generation of a policy or service and they are therefore all part of the marketing relationship.

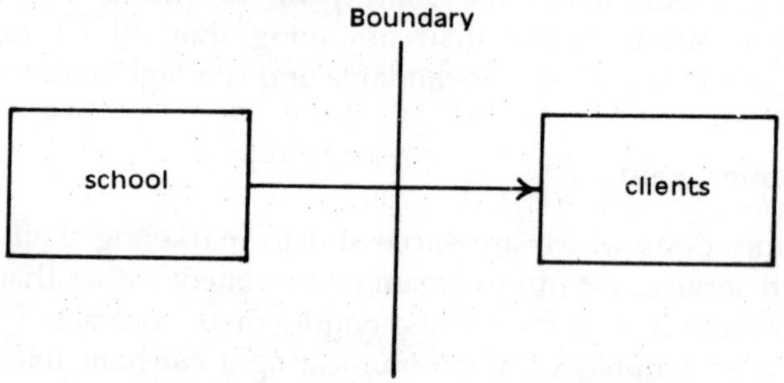

Fig. 13.1 Traditional Marketing Relatioinships.

It is unfortunate therefore that the marketing relationship is too often seen as a one-way process whereby a school tries to sell itself and its services to a perceived external market. This very simplistic view needs to be replaced by a multi-dimensional approach which sees marketing in terms of a continuous process of interaction between the different client groups within the total school framework as seen in Figure 13.2. Here clients' groups are identified as sources of ideas and information rather than simply as 'customers.

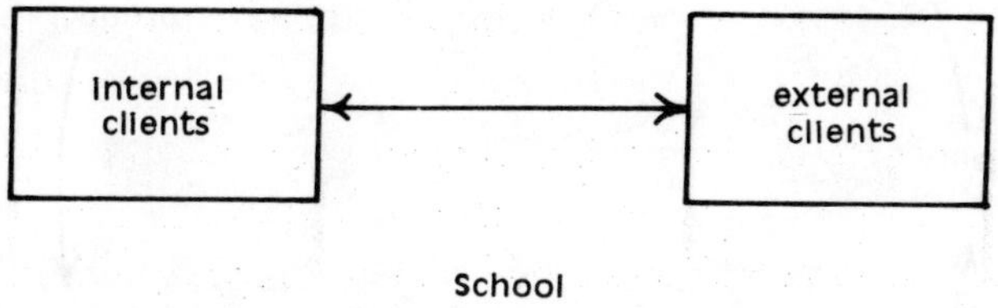

Fig. 13.2 Quality Marketing Relationships.

THE MARKETING CYCLE

Managers in schools should not be seduced into looking at one aspect of marketing in isolation from an overall management approach. Figure 13.3 shows an outline of the seven key stages in the marketing process or cycle.

(i) Market Research

This activity involves defining who is the client to be served and what the product is that the client wants. This, from the earlier discussion in the chapter, involves assessing the parents' and child's relative needs from education and defining what influences them in educational decisions. The earlier discussion of perceived and actual values and outputs in a valuable concept here.

(ii) Analyse Your Product

Product analysis can be carried out using a SWOT analysis, that is, an examination of Strengths, Weaknesses, Opportunities and Threats to an organisation. It needs to be applied to all aspects of the school. A useful checklist approach to this is pro-

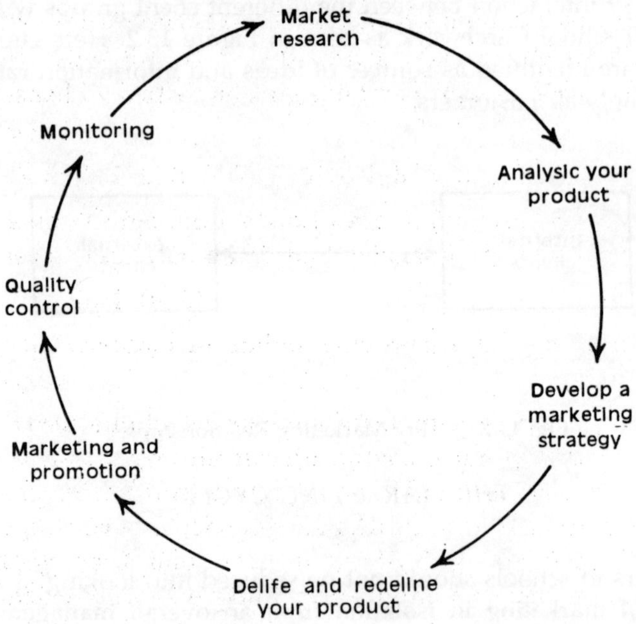

Fig. 13.3 The Marketing Cycle.

vided by Dennison (1989). The analysis can reveal areas which the school can market but, also, areas which will present serious weaknesses unless the school devotes managerial resources to overcoming them.

(iii) Develop a Marketing Strategy

This stage involves laying down the aims of the marketing strategy and the objectives which are to be achieved. It should look forward at least two to three years and not just be concerned with short-term initiatives. Most importantly, the strategy should not be bolted on to other management plans. It should be an integrated part of the whole School Management Development Plan for school improvement. While this strategic view is necessary, it is also vital that objectives can be achieved and that there is a clearly defined implementation schedule detailing the tactics to be employed.

(iii) Define and Re-define the Product That the School is Offering

All staff should have a clearly articulated view of what the school stands for and what strengths and opportunities it is offering to its clients. Some sort of 'corporate identity' or 'image' is necessary if clients are to get a clear picture of what the school is offering.

(v) Marketing and Promotion

The first distinction to be made here is between internal and external markets. Internal markets consist of governors, teaching and non-teaching staff, pupils and parents of existing pupils. All these individuals need to have a clear view of the school's aims and objectives and its current plans for the education of the children in its care. They can only be effective in communicating this to the wider community if they *realise* that they are all ambassadors of the school and are kept informed of and participate in school activities, achievements and plans. Making this key market satisfied and enthusiastic about the school is a pre-requisite for concentrating on external markets. Otherwise any success with the wider community will be offset as soon as they talk to individuals within the school community.

External markets consist of people or organisations with little or no knowledge of the school. These are the people that you have to influence, perhaps for the first time. These could include feeder schools, estate agents, removal firms, Citizens' Advice Bureaux, public libraries, local employers, local organisations that use the school buildings, local media, etc. All need to have relevant upto-date information and promotional literature about the school as they all influence potential parents and children who live locally or are moving to the area.

(vi) Quality Control and Performance Indicators

Schools are working on a series of performance indicators to assess whether they have achieved their objectives. Schools may be able to 'sell themselves' in the short run, but will only retain pupils in the long run if they deliver what they promised they would. These performance indicators can be short-term and tactical, as perceived by parents, or longer-term and more strategic. An example of the former would be setting up a homework timetable. If teachers are not setting the homework then this is a clear indicator to parents of a failed performance indicator. while there are broader indicators such as long-term improvement in language skills, schools should work on both levels to ensure client satisfaction.

(vii) Monitoring (After Sales Service)

This is to assess how effective the marketing process has been. Did all the parents get the right information before choosing the school? Did they get adequate information during the child's educational career about education choices that had to be made? A key area could be to explore parental attitudes about things they would want to see remedied or changed. This can be sought by informal methods such as discussions with parents or local members of the community. A valuable formal method is to send follow-up questionnaires to past pupils and ex-parents. An example of this is provided by Thompson (1989).

ESTABLISHING A MARKETING CULTURE WITHIN A SCHOOL

The main thrust of this chapter has been that of taking a strategic view of marketing rather than adopting *ad hoc* responses to immediate marketing needs. It is clear that marketing should not be a 'bolt on' activity but an integral part of school management. To this end, it is vital that school managers create a culture in which all members of the school community help to define, design and implement a coherent strategy of relating the school to its clients.

CONCLUSION

The practical components of a marketing strategy have to balance the need to manage the image of the school and to be the vehicle by which accountability is made explicit. The role of the headteacher and senior management is therefore central in generating the values and principles to be marketed and in providing an example of marketing in practice.

This has fundamental implications for the nature of working relationships within the school which can then be extended to external clients. For example, the quality of internal communications is a vital component both in terms of what is expressed and how it is expressed. The marketing relationship demands constant checking that information is being provided in the most appropriate manner and that it is information which is needed. Equally the conduct of meetings says as much about values and perceptions as the actual contents of the agenda.

This relationship must be extended to all staff and therefore be a fundamental component of the school's accountability and permeate all working relationships. Unless staff have ownership of this concept of marketing then it is unlikely to be successful.

14

Evaluation in Schools

A great deal of evaluation goes on in schools every day, for an evaluative elements is hidden in almost any decision-making activity at whatever level—the individual teacher deciding upon the best approach to a particular group or topic, the head of department and colleagues choosing the *most suitable* courses for particular groups, or the headteacher managing responsibilities in the most appropriate manner. All of these examples would inevitably involve those concerned in a process of making evaluative judgments against more or less explicit criteria for chose, and of course parents and pupils are involved too. Obvious examples here are parental chose of school in the context of open enrolment here are parents and pupils are involved too. Obvious examples there are parental choice if school in the context of open enrolment under the 1988 Act, or the choice of option pathway at 14+ in the secondary sector. However, in many of these situation, the evaluative element is often very undefined and/or very subjective—it is often referred to as "formal evaluation." This should not, however, lead us to detract from the merit or power of this level of activity.

At the other extreme there is a range of activities which can be characterised as 'formal evaluation'. These examples may include formal inspections by HMI, or Local Authority Inspectors/Advisers reports to Governors, or more importantly, significant evaluation projects undertaken by staff within the school to investigate the effectiveness of a particular area of activity, either at the level of the whose school or at the level of a sub-unit within the school. For the individual teacher some forms of appraisal, too, may fit into this category. Formal evaluations are usually well documented in terms of the evidence collected and the conclusions drawn, whereas informal evaluations are not.

At various points along this informal/formal continuum a number of issues arise. Firstly, all evaluation is (or should be) concerned with doing things better, both now and in the future, although better can be described either in terms of effectiveness ('doing the right things' is the frequently used phrase), or in terms of efficiency ('doing things right'). We should make no bones about the relative significance of these two dimensions—of this, more later. There may also be further, related distinctions to draw between those evaluations where the major purpose is accountability rather than improvement *per se,* and between summative (output) and formative (process) styles of evaluation.

Secondly, we need to be careful about pushing too far the distinction between formal and informal evaluations. This is particularly the case when we consider the management of how we move from evaluation into the action or change stage. It may initially appear as strange that the 'weaker' end of the continuum (informal evaluation) is more successful in bridging this evaluation/action gap than is the 'stronger' end of a more formal evaluation. This is in part the case because there is a type of which represents a significant problem for managers of the process. The thinking would suggest the evaluation leads to an awareness of problems, that such awareness then guides remedial action and that, therefore, evaluation leads to improvement. Bollenand Hopkins (1987) report on this problem but our own experience also tells us that this is not always true — especially in relation to accountability-based evaluations. Sometimes, and perhaps quite often, we learn instead to live with the 'problem' rather than attempt to really solve it. We survive by 'managing the ambiguity' because the costs of doing otherwise are too great — another level of evaluation has intervened upon the first and over-ridden it, in a case an informal evaluation of the opportunity costs involved in a choice between solving the problem and living with it. In this sense, any attempt at formal evaluation contains within it the possibility of further layers of informal evaluations, which are never articulated but which can (often with great ease) over-ride the carefully documented and structured path of the formal programme. Those who would manage formal evaluation procedures forget this at their peril. Actually, of course, this means that if we draw to rigid a distinction between the formal and informal approaches then we inherently run the risk outlined above. Moreover, we also fail to learn the great lesson that can be drawn from the informal dimension—how to translate the evaluation into action.

There is no great secret here, just a ton of common sense. People undertake informal evaluations on issues which are important to them as individuals or groups—important in that they feel an issue or a problem in a real way—real in the sense that something has to be done about it in their working situation. Consequently, they are predisposed to action at the point at which they begin to evaluate—first the evidence and then the alternative course of action—in however 'ramshackle' a way. It is this prior commitment to action which should be the starting point too, for the more formal evaluations with which we are involved and with this chapter is mainly concerned.

The third feature of note at this stage is indeed more specifically concerned with the processes of formal evaluations, and it can be called the Cinderella Paradox. Of all the tasks facing managers and/on teachers in schools none has been more frequently (and formally) invited to the management ball in the last decade than evaluation—and none is so often obliged to leave early. After being saved from neglect or abuse, just at the point at which the real benefit of her attendance should become clear, time, energy or commitment runs out and her chance seems to be lost. This could be called the Cinderella phenomenon—the paradox element arises since this is so despite major efforts to the contrary.

The volume of literature which has been produced upon the subject of school evaluation and accountability, and the attempts by both central and local authorities to promote practice-led initiatives, have both been considerable. Centrally-led initiatives (as represented by *Better Schools* (1985), the work of the Assessment of Performance Unit or the GRIDS project) or local authority initiatives (for example the Sussex Accountability Project or the Oxfordshire School Report), have apparently had considerable impacts locally and for certain periods of time; but neither they, nor the flood of books, articles and LEA-generated guidelines seem to have created a self-sustaining process of formal evaluation in our schools. We need to ask why this is the case.

The answer to this Cinderella Paradox is important to those who would wish to develop such a self-sustaining process in the schools in which they work, and for which they are responsible as managers, for in that understanding lies the way forward. It is a situation which is broken down here into three parts, although they interact in a highly complex manner in the real world of education management. The following concentrates on the third of the elements as being that which is of underpinning importance but this should not lead to an underestimation of the value of exploring the first two elements more fully; and to that end a selective bibliography is provided for those who wish to pursue those avenues in greater detail. The three elements to be explored are:

(1) The nature of existing literature and practice

(2) Managing the process

(3) Evaluation design at school level.

THE NATURE OF EXISTING LITERATURE AND PRACTICE

There is a great deal of literature on the subject(s) of school evaluation and/or accountability and much of its is good in an isolated sense, but not in a comprehensive or integrated sense, although there are notable exceptions such as Hoyle's (1979) contribution. Seen as a whole the literature, whether from academic or practice led origins, is fragmented and non-cumulative. This can lead to a situation where it is sometimes actually confusing or contradictory.

In part this is due to the origins of the whole area of interest in the latter part of the 1970s when it was part of the knee-jerk reaction to the emerging consumerism being applied to education on a wide front, but which is usually symbolised by the

'Great Debate' established by Prime Minister Callaghan's Ruskin Speech of 1976. As these forces gathered momentum, they gave rise to an unfortunate emphasis upon the accountability function of evaluation, at the expense of the feedback or improvement function internal to the schools. This emphasis has conditioned the response of the profession to the whole process.

This early accoutability focus was well represented by the work of McCormick (1982) or Lacey and Lawton (1981) and there is a continuous thread of development from these concerns into the Education Act of 1986 and 1988. At its maximum this strand to the process resulted in the appearance, in the mind and late 1980s, of a number of publications which brought to the surface the concept of performance indicators, and did so in such a way as to relate them very strongly, if not exclusively, to the accountability context. Notable amongst these publications was the Audit Commission's (1986) *Towards Better management of Secondary Education,* the Coopers and Lybrand Report (1988) Local Management of Schools, and the Chartered Institute of Public Finance and Accountancy's (CIPFA 1988) *Performance Indicators in Schools.* But the time of the appearance of the last two in particular, the accountability context was also being heavily reinforced, and yet modified, by the emergence of the local management of schools concept and, within that, by the financial delegation aspects.

The CIPFA document in particular is interesting. It identified the following as those areas in which both quantitative and qualitative performance indicators should be explored:

1. Management of staff and the quality of teaching
2. Management of the quality of learning and of the curriculum
3. Pastoral management
4. Financial management
5. Liaison with other agencies and the community
6. Management of information

Although the report attempted to explain the nature of its proposals as a framework from which schools and/or LEAs should develop their own performance indicators, the climate of the time, and some elements of its presentation (those indicators identified as quantifiable and some of the values expressed in the selection of indicators) did little to move the debate away from the accountability focus.

In February of 1988 eight LEAs were involved in a DES pilot exercise and by the end of 1989 the results of the pilot were published as *School Indicators for Internal Management: An Aide Memoire* (DES), although this was put forward as only a first stage document for schools to consider. The categories used in the Aide Memoire are:

1. Basic school data
2. School context
3. Pupil achievement
4. Parental involvement
5. Pupil attitudes
6. Management

It is interesting to note that in comparison with the CIPFA document, the Aide Memoire is much more reflective of an earlier tradition of LEA-based checklist approaches to effectiveness. There is less emphasis upon quantification and more upon asking questions, and also an emphasis upon context and pupils which is significantly more professional and less managerial. (The word management appears in five of six CIPFA categories and only one of the six Aide Memoire categories.)

The spectre of an imposed accountability framework had apparently been abandoned, but it is worthwhile considering why this was the case. Perhaps the voice of the profession was being listened to, or perhaps the understanding of the logistics/costs of a fully blown system had grown—or perhaps other lines of though in the accountability tradition were emerging? One such line of thought may be seen in the context of local management of schools, when formuia funding is seen alongside open enrolment provision. That line of thought may suggest that, in a consumer or market-led system, quality control is a function of the market and there is simply no need to develop formalised, structured or bureaucratised approaches to accountability. In such a context the use of performance indicators could be left more open and more concerned with the internal management of schools, as those schools major identify which performance areas were significant to their major constituencies.

Whatever the case, in one way of another, the accountability phenomenon has exercised an important influence both on the literature and practice of evaluation in our schools. At the former level there has been a split between that literature and research with an accountability focus, and that which has concentrated more clearly upon school-based review for the purposes of internal development and improvement—and this split has not greatly aided schools in developing a self-sustaining approach to the whole area, either in the sense of developing the skills and knowledge base required, or in setting the climate in which they could develop.

This disarray in the literature and practice is in fact compounded even when looking within the improvement tradition itself. Compare, for example, the approaches taken by Shipman (1979) and Holt (1981) in two of the major contributions to the literature:

> This book is about ways of making schools more effective and about ways of ensuring that they are seen to be effective. It is not about the ends of education.... The concern here is with means not ends, on how to do it more effectively rather than what to do.
>
> *Shipman (1979)*

> There is no need to agonise too long over philosophical matters of aims. The need is for a set of working objectives that can focus evaluation. The objectives establish a tactical position that can enable the staff to get on with evaluation.
>
> *Shipman (1979)*

> The choice is between leaving evaluation to impressions that have no necessarily consistent or even detectable frame of reference, or organizing it so that the criteria of success and failure are spelled out. It is a choice between causal and systematic judgment.
>
> *Shipman (1979)*

> Above all, the disturbing things about the fashion for school 'self-audit' or self-evaluation is the assumption that a good school is one which uses the right mechanism or routines. The value judgments seem to take second place to the functionalism of schooling.
>
> *Holt (1981)*

> It (Shipman's view) is based on the fallacy that, in education, means can be divorced from ends. For values are implicit in every educational act, and there is no 'objectives' or 'systematic' way in which the quality of an act can be separated from the way it is performed.
>
> *Holt (1981)*

At issue here are fundamental differences concerning the location (input-process-output) of evaluation studies and the related differences in underlying concepts of effectiveness—these are issues which are explored in more detail in Section 3 following.

Much valuable work has, however, been undertaken within the improvement tradition, and it is possible to mention only a small selection of the available material. Notable contributions have been made from a number of sources. A wide range of the earlier LEA practice-led initiatives are reviewed by Clift (1982) in a brief but useful way, and Glatter (1986) outlines the background to school-based review in the framework of the international School Improvement Project. A particular example of the latter is the GRIDS project which will be familiar in outline to all readers but a useful review is provided by Macmahon, Holly and Steadman (1987). Bollen and Hopkins (1987) attempt to provide a mechanism or process for ensuring that the review-action gap is crossed in the context of school-based review. The brief publication from HMI, *Quality in Schools: Evaluation and Appraisal* (1985) and the DES *Better Schools* (1985) are also valuable, whilst evaluation in the context of the self-managing school is approached by Caldwell and Spinks (1988), amongst others too numerous to mention.

The problem remains, however, that these practice-led approaches, and the reporting to which they have given rise, are fragmented and non-cumulative as a whole, and may even be contradictory in win quite serious ways which do not help those in schools who would attempt to get to grips with the problems. The major division, that between the accountability and the improvement traditions, remains strong, whilst in the latter area itself, there is a major failure to establish a common currency of approach or practice. This is turn is related to the failure to examine underlying principles to the evaluation of effectiveness which alone could lead towards a more useful process of evaluation design by those in schools.

In a related area of study Reynolds and Reid (1988) have already indicated the need to move to second stage in the methods of schools effectiveness studies and part of their analysis is appropriate here:

> Much of the early work in the field has been highly atheoretical.... Much of the British work grew out of attempts to test the hypotheses of Jencks and Coleman and therefore tended to work within the same paradigm of traditional atheoretical empiricism as they....
>
> *Reynolds and Reid (1988)*

They go on to say:

> The problems caused by our atheoreticism, however, are now numerous. No piece of work is cumulative, either set against work from the past or against other work in the present...a work is not testable in theoretical terms...is unrelated to any current theoretical position except that of 'grubby empiricism'.
>
> *Reynolds and Reid (1988)*

Section 3 of this chapter will attempt to outline just one way in which theoretical approaches to effectiveness can be related to the process of evaluation design in schools. For now we turn to examine briefly the organisational and micropolitical issues surrounding evaluation.

MANAGING THE PROCESS

Some of the organisational and/or micropolitical factors involved in establishing more formal approaches to evaluation have already been touched upon (above). The danger of ignoring the power of informal agendas even within a formal process, the climate surrounding the different accountability/improvement approaches, the problems involved in ensuring that action follows evaluation and the possibility of wider micropolitical activities within evaluation are major issues for anyone involved in managing an evaluation process—and there are others. Few of these issues are simple in the sense that a straightforward solution is available. Indeed most of them are extremely complex in so far as they interlock, and in the sense that they are present *throughout* the evaluation indifferent ways. For example, building commitment to the process is not just something that has to be done before evaluation starts, but that commitment also has to be maintained throughout the process and then translated into a yet different form at the point of moving into the planning/action stage. The management of the process therefore is itself a dynamic task facing managers and one that requires the deployment of a wide range of skills—from resource management through motivation and staff development to the technical skills concerning evaluation *per se* and the whole spectrum of people management skills. Neglect of this area is the second of our reasons behind the Cinderella Paradox.

Before proceeding to a brief examination of some of these issues, there is a basic question of perspective to establish for the manager(s) involved, and this underlying 'mind-set' will undoubtedly condition responses to most of the questions to be raised here. At this point there is a close relationship to the major questions raised in chapter 1 about the location of management activities, in chapter 5 concerning staff development and chapter 6 on the management of change. The question is do we see evaluation within the school as a management responsibility to be fulfilled by those in overtly managerial roles or is it seen as something which is a professional duty of all staff? The role of the manager in relation to the second of these perspectives is clearly very different to what it would be in the former—much more concerned with the organisational and people processes of evaluation than with the technical issues or the substantive focus of any particular evaluation. It is suggested here that such a perspective takes on board the matters now to be raised in a holistic and genuine way, whilst the alternative, top-down managerial approach would rapidly involve managers in running the risk of crossing the line between management and manipulation in such a way as to diminish greatly the opportunity of a successful outcome—the destination revolves around the difference between the 'hardsell' and genuine 'ownership'. This area is neatly summed up by Holly (1987) in the context of self evaluation:

> Self-evaluation in the primary school is...internal as opposed to external evaluation; it is done by the members of staff—with appropriate support—for the members of staff...it is not a case of the work being done to or at these same participants.
>
> *Holly (1987)*

What then are the practical implications of this underlying approach to ownership and process as it unfolds through the various stages of evaluation design, data collection, judgment of evidence, reporting and then moving into the planning/action phase?

Although it would seem to be essential to approach evaluation from a negotiated perspective, one this is begun a rich arena for micropolitical activity is created. This negotiation would need to involve all of those concerned, and should be maintained throughout the process. For example, it would not only be necessary to negotiate the why, who and what elements of the basic design but also to look forward to the data collection stage, the judgmental period, the reporting stage and the planning/action processes that may arise. At any or all of these points, the people-rich environment gives rise to the possibility of destroying the trust which is essential, or of allowing/fostering micropolitical activity which is detrimental to the eventual outcome. Obvious examples which would destroy trust occur when the reporting stage is suddenly made available to an audience which was not included initially, or if un-negotiated methods of data collection are suddenly introduced into the middle of an on-going evaluation or, very powerfully, if the basic evaluation design is altered in some way—for example from within an internal/improvement paradigm to an accountability one.

The data collection stage is also extremely sensitive. It well behaves those who would obtain reliable data to negotiate access to it as fully as possible and, again, in an on-going way. It would be foolish in the extreme for senior staff to assume that they have *droit de seigneur* access to all the data required. Certainly the documented areas of data collection should be readily available, but the more judgmental or subjective areas of data are likely to be deeply hidden within groups or even held by individuals, who will only give access to that information in conditions where they feel that it is relevant and safe to do so. In this connection the methods of collecting data can be as sensitive as the data itself. In terms of the improvement of school practice, this is exactly the sort of information which is of paramount importance--much of the more readily available and objective documentation is likely to be more appropriate to descriptive rather than explorative evaluation designs.

Negotiation also needs to take place with regard to the identification of criteria for judgment within the evaluation. This is concerned with the phenomenon of the 'moving goal posts'. Again, if the criteria for 'success' are imposed or if they are suddenly shifted during the evaluation, then trust will be lost and the value of the exercise will be seriously compromised as people start to withdraw access to information or become selective in providing only that information which conforms positively to the criteria. The danger of reductionism of highly complex activities and consequently of de-skilling is ever present.

Reporting, and than moving forward into the planning—action stage if that is appropriate, also requires careful thought and wide agreement—perhaps with an initial agreement on likely approaches but always bearing in mind the possibility of renegotiation of these elements as the evaluation nears 'completion'. It is at this point that energies may be relaxing, and if this is so it may require extra attention, particularly to bridge the evaluation—action gap. Alternatively it may be the case that no action is required, and if that is the outcome of the evaluation then the fact should be acknowledged and congratulation offered to all concerned!

These various stages are not, of course, discrete and the relationships between the various elements also require a procative approach. For example the basic evaluation design will set parameters upon the other stages by indicating likely sources of data, methods of collection and criteria against which judgments can be made. These parameters should be made explicit to all concerned and subsequent re-negotiation should always respect those parameters too. Similarly, an awareness of the possibility of individuals or sub-groups within the body of those involved indulging in micropolitical activity should constantly be borne in mind. This is especially true of the evaluation is likely to have resources distribution implications for the future. Such strategies are possible at any point but are most likely to occur at the design stage when the broad outlines of the whole process are being forged—although *real* activists will maintain their efforts throughout, and some may even see a particular evaluation project as a micropolitical tool in a much wider campaign with which they are concerned.

For those who wish to pursue these process elements further, the literature is again rather fragmented and, at this point, quite limited, although recently more attention has been given to such issues.

The GRIDS documentation has much of an implicit nature to say about the process issues, whilst Hughes, Ribbins and Thomas (1985) develop a rather schematic approach to the relationships which can be identified within the situation. Day, Johnson and Whitaker (1985) consider questions of timing, and to some extent climate, alongside issues of the resources needed in both human and other terms for a successful evaluation to be carried out. This latter point is very important and suggests that a school should not be involved in too much formal evaluation at any particularly time. Questions concerning the human resources and skills (extended professionality?) required are dealt with by Holly and Hopkins (1988), and may of the other items identified elsewhere in this chapter contain much that is useful in terms of managing the process.

Finally, it is often suggested that any evaluation process should itself be reviewed and sometimes checklists are provided to facilitate this. It is interesting however the these checklists are usually provided in a way which sets the review as a *post hoc* exercise once the evaluation is completed. It would be much more helpful to review the process at the initiation and operating stages thus:

1. Is this the right time to be doing the evaluation?
2. how can the methods of evaluation be made explicit to all concerned?
3. Will the evaluation serve to inform decisions or judgments?
4. Who are the most appropriate people to carry out the evaluation? Are they available?
5. What information will be appropriate to the purpose of the evaluation? Where is the information and is access readily available?
6. What steps can be taken to allow for reliability and validity in the information gathered?
7. How much time will be required for each stage of the process?
8. Are the criteria by which judgment or decisions, may be made clearly stated and agreed?
9. Are there any possible side-effects or micropolitical issues in terms of the school as a whole, groups or individuals which may arise?
10. What is the audience for any report and what possible forms of reporting will be undertaken?
11. How will any further development resulting from the evaluation be managed?

This checklist may be useful in relation to the process issues out lines in this section, but it is far from comprehensive in relation to the wider aspects of an evaluation programme, and particularly so in relation to the underlying process of evaluation design. It is to that task that this chapter will not turn.

EDUCATION DESIGN

The 'atheoretical or 'grubby empiricist' basis to much of our thinking and practice about effectiveness (a concept) and evaluation (a process) was highlighted earlier—and this weakness underpins or compounds many of the issues raised in the previous section. In order to develop a self-sustaining programme of evaluation, much greater attention needs to be given to underlying views of effectiveness and to the task of building an evaluation design which is congruent with the effectiveness concept being employed. As a starting point we need to be clear about the relative significance of effectiveness and efficiency and to think through the relationship between firm.

Managers and teachers are rooted in particular schools and situations, and necessarily have a particularistic perspective which emphasis the uniqueness of that situation. Their requirement of effectiveness as a notion is that it should enable them better to understand, and then to improve, the performance of 'their' school in one or a number of ways. However, these schools are not static, they are changing in a number of ways and as these changes occur, so too does the concept of effectiveness required to monitor the new situation and yet further develop it. Effectiveness is therefore, to some degree, a shifting concept which reflect changing educational processes or priorities. Efficiency, on the other hand, is a much more static idea; always concerned with doing things in terms of the best possible use of resources—whatever those 'things' may be.

Efficiency without effectiveness is meaningless in the context of education (or anywhere else for that matter) but effectiveness without efficiency is at least a starting point for improvement. It is dangerous, of course, to push this thinking too far, because the latter situation is *only a starting point*—improved curriculum effectiveness is closely related to the way in which resources are used, and this clearly raises questions about the efficient use of those resources. The management of school-based finance could also be approached primarily from an efficiency perspective but if that were to be the case then much would indeed have been lost! Managers in schools should make no mistake then about the order of priority in the effectiveness/efficiency relationship—the latter is a subset of the former. Any evaluation design needs to be clear on this issue.

The evaluation design also needs to be clear about the location of evaluation in another sense—is it to be concerned with the evaluation of school outputs, or processes within the school, or even with using inputs as some way of judging (measuring?) success? This is often explained in terms of a simple systems theory view of organisation, with jargon attached as illustrated.

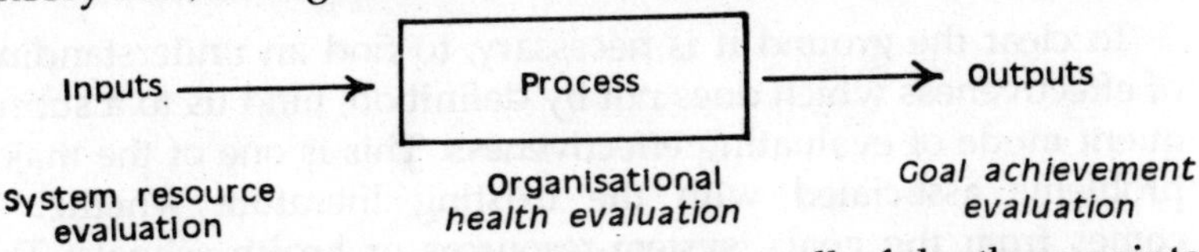

Evaluation can be carried out at any or all of the three points in the diagram. Consider for example these three statements:

(a) The school has attracted 25 per cent out-of-catchment enrolment.

(b) The staff really work as a term in the school.

(c) The school has achieved examination results 25 per cent better than the national average.

Each of these statement could be used in an evaluative sense and they represent input/process/output levels of evaluation respectively. Unfortunately, there is a tendency to select the location of the evaluation in this sense before a clear idea has been created about what it is that is actually being evaluated. The risk is then that the evaluation location (model) is not properly congruent with the area of effectiveness being investigated. We will return to this later, but for now it suggests to us that evaluation design is a two-part process—firstly, define the effectiveness concept you wish to explore and secondly selected the location (input/process/output or a combination) of the evaluation which will most usefully explore that concept. It remains to unpack these issues and to suggest ways in which the task can be approached. An important contribution has been offered in this area by Cameron (1980) from within the broad field of organisation and management studies. He suggests the idea of *frameworks for assessing effectiveness* as an alternative to the search for universalistic concepts of effectiveness. This undersold idea may provide us with a way of approaching the task of evaluation design outlines here. The structure of the remainder of this chapter will therefore be to examine Cameron's idea of *frameworks,* to relate this to existing major approaches to evaluation and to suggest that this does throw up practical management perspectives and tools for use at different levels in examining the effectiveness of schools.

Frameworks for Assessing Effectiveness

To clear the ground it is necessary, to find an understanding of effectiveness which does not by definition, bind us to a subsequent mode of evaluating effectiveness. This is one of the major problems associated with the existing literature whether it comes from the goals, system-resources or health schools. The most promising avenue is the notion of an *effectiveness construct* as utilised by Steers (1975) who tells us that:

> A construct is an abstract idea rather than a concrete phenomenon. It is based on the hypothesis that several variables will consistently covary or fit together to form a unified whole.
>
> *Steers (1975)*

Steers is, however, still looking for a 'united whole' or a generalisable construct and concludes that:

> until the construct can be explained...it will be difficult to make meaningful recommendations to managers about steps to improve effectiveness in their organisations.
>
> *Steers (1975)*

This does not mean that the idea is not useful—indeed it is very useful seen from the vantage point of one school. It is suggested that the effectiveness construct(s) for a school should be developed within at institution or at least with reference to it. The model suggested would have both static and dynamic characteristics—that is, some aspects of it could be expected to be present over long periods (say) academic dimensions, whilst other aspects would appear to serve particular functions but may then fade from view, perhaps to be replaced by other more pressing concerns, for example the evaluation of a change from horizontal to vertical pupil organisation.

Such a view of the effectiveness construct could also handle the two basic purposes of evaluation—accountability to stakeholders and feedback aimed at improvement. The accountability end of the evaluation would most clearly be related to the static part of the model whereas the improvement function would make most use of the dynamic characteristics. These relationships would not be absolute however since there would clearly be an important traffic between the two parts of the model. For the moment, the most important point is that we have developed a view of effectiveness that has dynamic properties and we are not, therefore, tied to any particular mode of evaluation—the manager(s) can provide detail of the construct(s) and they can be guided in this by Cameron's framework. Since universalistic approaches will not work we are left with a process of *selection* and the framework approach is really, at this state, little more than a guide to that selection.

Cameron gives us seven pointers. These are:

1. From Whose Perspective is Effectiveness Being Judged? One of the reasons why the universalistic criteria for school effectiveness have been so elusive is that different constituencies will have different criteria for judgment.

Whilst this remains a problems for theorists in their search for yet another 'holy grail', it is much less of a problem in the context of the individual institution where managers can make such an identification based largely upon the purpose of the evaluation exercise. This choice would not be permanent but would alter with time and changing requirements.

2. On What Domain of Activity is the Judgment Focused? All schools operate in a number of domains—a simple model for schools may be: academic, pastoral, organisational and disciplinary. However, this must not be seen as prescriptive, as the real decisions must be made at the institutional levels. A significant feature is that effectiveness in one domain may be in conflict with success in another. Is it perhaps better therefore to seek *optimisation* in all domains rather than *maximisation* in any one? Again, mdominant domains will change with time and perspective.

3. What Level of Analysis is Being Used? Effectiveness can be judged from a number of levels—the individual, the sub-system or the school as a whole. The choice here is clearly interdependent with 1 and 2 above and with 4 below.

4. What is the Purpose of the Evaluation? Although it may be true, as Hoyle (1979) suggests, that there are two basic answers to this question—accountability and feedback aimed at improvement—these terms cover a wide variety of different situations. To give just one example in the improvement area, the investigation may be constructed of academic performance in departments *x y* and *z*—or it may be aimed at making the decision as to which of these departments to close because of fundamental contraction. clearly, the effectiveness construct would be different in each of these cases.

5. What Time-frame is Being Employed? A relevant time-frame is required in order to validate any assessment since effects or outcomes may not be visible at all if the time-frame is wrong—for example it would be inappropriate to measure academic performance over a very short time-period whereas it may be appropriate to study certain organisational processes over just such a period.

6. What Type(s) of Data are to be Used? The choice here lies between objectives and subjective data—each with its advantages and disadvantages. The choice made will depend upon decisions about data availability but more powerfully upon other questions raised here about building the relevant effectiveness construct(s). Perhaps most importantly, the data employed must be acceptable to the operative perspective(s)—for example, many accountablility constituencies would only be satisfied by consideration of outputs.

7. What is the Referent Against Which Effectiveness is Judged? It is on this rubric that Cameron's work does not quite break free from existing theories of effectiveness, since one of the referents the suggests is:

> to compare organisational performance...against the stated goals of the organisation.

Cameron and Whetton (1983)

This clearly pre-determined the approach to the goal-achievement model at a stage when the manager has not yet fully defined his effectiveness construct. Therefore, in order to maintain flexibility at this stage, an alternative is suggested—based upon the educational audit of Dennison (1978). The audit would present three possible referent points for the evaluation— judgment in terms of either (a) an absolute standard; (b) comparison within or without the institution; and (c) the direction and extent of change. Clearly, one or all three could be utilised in the light of the effectiveness construct being established.

At this point it is necessary to state forcefully the position arrived at. Cameron's framework is not being used to select a particular approach to the evaluation of effectiveness (goals, system resource or health) but rather to guide the manager(s) to a position where a *relevant effectiveness construct* can be established. Cameron suggests that the questions above be considered 'in concert'. It is suggested here, however, that although the seven factors are inter-dependent, two of them act as controlling influences for the operation and therefore provide the starting point for the practical task of creating the effectiveness construct. These two are clearly number one, the effectiveness perspective, and number four, the purpose of the evaluation. It is suggested therefore that domain focus, level of analysis, timeframe, type(s) of data employed and referent(s) employed will be functions of perspective and purpose if the construct is to have validity and utility. This can be expressed diagrammatically for ease of presentation as shown in Figure 14.1.

Working through this model allows us to create an effectiveness construct which is rooted in a particular situation and which is focused on a specific task. It remains to evaluate the construct.

Evaluating the Construct

Broadly speaking there are three alternative approached available. They are discussed here in the order in which they are most commonly utilised in schools: the goal-achievement model, the systems-resource model and the organisational health model. There is sometimes a suggestion that a fourth

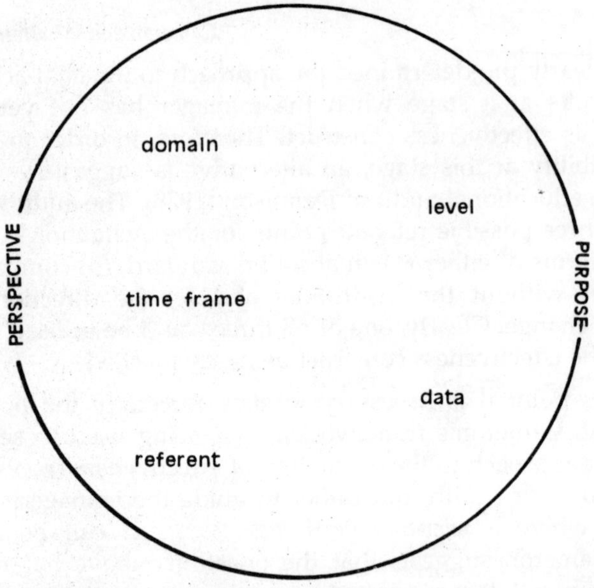

Fig. 14.1 Elements of an Effectiveness Construct.

model exists—the participant satisfaction model which defines effectiveness as the extent to which all of the organisation strategic constituencies are at least minimally satisfied— this however seems to be derivative of the goals model and will not be treated separately.

Each of the three models has advantages and disadvantages and choice should be made in relation to the relevant effectiveness construct, not as an a *priori* decision. What then are the salient characteristics of the three approaches and what do these characteristics indicate about the utility of each?

The Goal-Achievement Model

Perhaps the major attraction of the 'goal approach' is its conceptual simplicity or its conceptual attractiveness to those managers working in schools. Effectiveness is defined in terms of the extent to which goals are achieved. Teachers have a long experience in curriculum areas of either the setting of objectives or of working towards objectives laid down by others (perhaps by examination bodies, universities or now, the 1988 Act), and which they broadly accept as valid. This process has also been greatly developed over the last decade. Interestingly, they are involved too, either implicitly or (increasingly) explicitly, in an evaluation of their success levels relative to these goals. The alone is a powerful incentive to adopt a goal-based approach within those constructs or parts of constructs where it can be utilised.

Furthermore, the same advantages are multiplies greatly when consideration is given to acceptability of the evaluation to other constituencies, particularly non-expert or lay constituencies existing out-side the school. The evaluation can be presented in a form that is readily intelligible and which can be understood by such constituencies. The systems-resources approach and the organisational health view both have serious problems in this area of acceptability—even to those well within the boundaries of the profession.

Much of the criticism of the goal approach revolved around the whole series of problems associated with defining educational objectives. Lengthy review of these arguments is not possible here but a way forward is provided by Steers' (1975) notion or *operant* goals. Briefly, this suggests that attention should not be on goals prescribed (by senior management?) or derived (from functional theory) but rather on goals actively and actually pursued by the school (or a part of it).

This approach to the idea of goals is not tied to the search for universal meanings for effectiveness and managers at different points in the institution would see much less difficulty in defining their goals than would theorists. That they could not in every situation do this does not mean that the method should be abandoned in total. If the effectiveness construct, or a part of it, is amenable to a goal approach, there are strong reasons (above) for adopting it.

The Systems-Resource Approach

The systems-resource method of evaluating effectiveness centres upon a school's ability to acquire needed resources from its external environment. The view holds that successful schools are able to attract extra or better quality resources—and this can be measured. Price (1972) makes three major criticisms of the model from a technical perspective, but again these need not detain us here for they are essentially criticisms aimed at the model's (in) ability to provide a universal framework. From a school management perspective, other problems are evident, perhaps the most important being the 'complexity' of the concept and its level of acceptability of different constituencies. A proper use of systems-resources requires at least some understanding and (perhaps) 'belief' in the general area of systems theory; and this is very unlikely even with professional constituencies.

Another issue arises with 'focus' of the systems-resource approach which (as stated in the literature) forces attention onto the boundary relations of the school with its environment and, furthermore, suggests that the school is in competition with other for resources. The open enrolment and local management aspects of the 1988 Act lend reality to this situation as never before.

If a (or the) major element of the effectiveness construct was designed to explore and evaluate the relationship between the school and its environment then the systems-resource approach would be applicable, within the constraints of acceptability already referred to.

This does not mean however that this would be the only situation in which systems-resource would have validity—an example at a different level will illustrate this. If the construct was aimed at exploring different levels of achievement between departments or functions of a school, then the approach could be very powerful indeed if the sub-units concerned were themselves treated as systems within an overall super-system. If it could be shown that there was a relationship between the perceived success levels of (say) the departments and their abilities to attract resources from the super-system then the evaluation method would become a very powerful tool for managerial activity as a method of tackling the 'problem'. Thus, evaluation would lead to activity in a way that the goal approach would not seem to be capable of, and this is a considerable merit.

The Organisational Health Approach

The organisational health approach is also related to open-systems theory and therefore shares some of the problems of systems-resource with regard to acceptability, but not to the same degree. A cogent statement of the model is provided by Miles (1969). Successful schools are said to exhibit smooth or healthy organisational processes, with a lack of strain or conflict. At least some of the dimensions of 'health' suggested (if not all) fit every easily into the liberal democratic cultures of the west and the approach can to some extent be 'acceptable' to non-expert or non-professional constituencies. The absence of internal strain, individuals highly integrated into the system, smooth internal functioning, trust and benevolence are all *positive* features when seen from a liberal culture and it is (too) easy to make a jump from such 'cosy' views to claims of effectiveness. Indeed the very opposite may be the case.

The danger of confusing efficiency with effectiveness is perhaps greatest in the organisational health model. There are also methodological difficulties inherent in this approach. Miles suggests that one of the features of a healthy organisation is goal focus.

> In a healthy organisation, the goal (or more usually goals) of the system would be reasonably clear to the system members and reasonably well accepted by them.
>
> *Miles (1969)*

At this aggregated level of whole school goals criticisms about the problematic nature of goals would be valid. But perhaps the major difficulty of this model is the wide-ranging characteristics it attempts to bring into the framework and the necessarily judgmental nature of many of them. This is also, in the context of the relevant effectiveness construct, its major strength for it alone can provide the holistic perspective to effectiveness which is of crucial importance at the whole school level and which can also have a direct bearing upon the performance of individual members of staff. Emphasis would therefore be placed upon those dimensions of the model which are 'people-based' and which are capable of affecting the relationships between individuals and the schools as a whole.

Each of the major approaches to evaluation thus has its own advantages and disadvantages in the evaluation process and selection can be made with reference to the effectiveness construct under consideration. The goals approach has strength in terms of acceptability at all levels but would seem to have particular strength at those levels where goals are well defined. Thus, the smaller the unit under analysis the greater its validity—i.e. at the levels of individuals or sub-units such as departments and pastoral 'teams'. It is at the level where school-wide goals are under consideration that definitional problems comes into play.

The systems-resource method would be of little utility in relation to individuals but may be of considerable use at the sub-unit level. If relationships between sub-units were being studied then a powerful perspective could be created by a system-resource viewpoint. This would also be the case if the focus of attention was the relationship between sub-units and the super-system of which they formed part. Also if the focus was concerned with the relationship between the super-system (school) and its environment, the system-resource approach may be appropriate, in which situation the controlling factor would be the constituency of the evaluation. If the report was a managerial tool designed for internal 'consumption' then acceptability may be positive, but if in addition the report had to satisfy environmental constituencies it would certainly need major overhaul in terms of presentation in order to give it acceptability.

The organisational health perspective is most useful in its approach to the relationships between individuals and the organisation since it alone provides the holistic perspective which is needed even to attempt an exploration of such a complex series of webs. It is a tool likely to be useful to those most concerned with personnel management because of its emphasis on factors such as power equalisation, communication adequacy, goal acceptability, cohesiveness, autonomy and morale. This would suggest its utility for whole school issues.

If an effectiveness construct is carefully put together *at the appropriate level* and then evaluated appropriately in the terms outlined here, the results of the evaluation should possess both acceptability and utility.

CONCLUSION

This brief application of the frameworks approach is of course very partial—it gives only some examples of possible features in the creation and evaluation of a consruct. The fine detail could only be determined by the teachers (managers) in question working in the context of a real situation. Similarly, although it would seem that a goal-based approach to the evaluation of effectiveness would be the dominating mode of activity, for reasons given earlier, it would not be the only one—for example the health approach would have much to offer in a construct focused on the personnel domain.

The keynote of this chapter builds upon the philosophy of chapter 1—that to some degree all teachers are managers and that they must be involved in the evaluation of effectiveness at all levels within the school. Only in this way can a series of relevant effectiveness constructs be created and only in this way can *collective* professional autonomy be preserved and even enhanced. With the present state of the art it is unrealistic to attempt to utilise universalistic approaches to evaluation in the school context—and in the context of a pluralist society this will always be the case. The framework view offers the opportunity of tailor-made constructs as an alternative to the 'blunt instruments currently on offer—and it may help to initiative that self-generating approach to formal evaluation with which this chapter has been concerned.

15

Teaching and Human Resource Development

Now that we have laid the foundation for understanding philosophical analysis with its historical and methodological background, it should not be too difficult to follow an analysis of basic concepts of education. We will begin with three of the most important concepts: *teaching, learning, educating,* along with such satellite concepts as *training, conditioning, instruction,* and *indoctrinating*. Covered in a later chapter will be the concepts central to proposals made to teachers on how they should go about their task: *behavioral outcomes, relevance, readiness, and learning to learn*. We will then consider concepts that come out of curriculum discussions. Another important area of examination will be the place of *values* in education. A final chapter will analyze the concept of *democracy* and its bearing on education. All of this is merely a sampling, an important sampling, for as R.S. Peters has pointed out, there are enough concepts in education awaiting analytic clarification to keep philosophers busy for the next half-century.

WHAT IS A CONCEPT?

Since the word "concept" is used so frequently, it is important to understood what is meant by it. A concept, such as *teaching*, for example, is an abstraction from the interrelated body of propositions in which it naturally occurs. By looking closely at the way this concept is used in its natural setting, we can discover its logical powers, the way it work linguistically, and separate it out from concepts that are similar in some ways, but distinct enough to be regarded as significantly different. *Counseling* or *preaching*, for instance, are in many ways like *teaching*, but their logical performance is different enough to be distinguished from it. Conversely, other concepts, like *instructing*, are closely related to *teaching*. These relationships can be diagrammed or mapped, somewhat like relatives in a family tree.

Thomas Green tell us that "a concept is a rule." "When someone learns a concept," he writes, "without exception, what he has learned is a rule, a rule of language, or more generally, a rule of behavior." When we learn the meaning of *teach*, we have learned the rule or rules that guide the correct usage of the world. This does not mean that we, or perhaps anyone, can state the rule. Rules of speech are often very complicated. When we analyze our usage, however, we rely upon our implicit understanding of such rules, and progressively bring to light some of the logical dimensions of the terms.

Paul Komisar and Thomas Nelson suggest that a "conceptual analysis of teaching should culminate (simply) in a definition of the term teaching." This way of saying it distinguishes conceptual analysis from the attempt to say what teaching *ought* to be , or from proposing some special program of teaching as the model for teaching as such. These later efforts are useful in their own way, but they are not conceptual analysis. Komisar and Nelson point out, "Unfortunately, in most educational jargon a concept of something (for example, readiness or education) includes not only a statement of the meaning of the term (readiness, education), but also bits of facts, anecdotes (sometimes called 'theories'), and even value judgments regarding the actual phenomena."

It would be a mistake to suppose that the logical boundaries of the concept of *teaching* can be clearly asked. The rules that govern its use are numerous and sometimes ambiguous, but this does not prevent our being able to mark out with considerable clarity some of the main features of the term so as to distinguish it from terms that are quite different. Also it does not prevent us from seeing the relationship of *teaching* to *telling* or *indoctrinating*. For example, when the edges of a red patch in a painting are blurred, we are not prevented from seeing the red patch in relation to its surroundings, and distinguishing it decisively from a neighboring blue patch.

Now let us begin the mapping of what we mean by *teaching*.

THE TEACHING CONTINUUM

Thomas F. Green, in his essay "A Topology go the Teaching Concept," diagrams teaching and its satellite notions in the following way. By keeping this diagram in mind, it will be easier to place these notions in logical relationship to one another

Behavior, Conduct		Knowledge, Beliefs	
Intimidation	Training	Insrtructing	Propagandizing
Physical Threat	Conditioning	Indoctrinating	Lying

The Region of Intelligence

Teaching aims, on the one hand, at changes in behavior and conduct, or, on the other hand, at the acquisition of new knowledge or beliefs. *Training* is clearly an effort to change behavior, while *instructing* aims at the acquisition of knowledge or beliefs. The fact that *training* often includes instruction, and that instruction may be supportive of some aspect of a training program, should not obscure the logical difference between these two aspects of the teaching concept. *Conditioning* belongs on the behavior side of the diagram, to the left of *training*, because it appeals less to intelligence than to training. When we come to *intimidation* or *physical threat*, we have moved outside of the region of intelligence, although such methods are sometimes used to affect changes in behavior. We shall see why intimidation and physical threat lie outside the boundaries of *teaching as such*.

On the right side of the diagram, *indoctrinating* is a kind of *instructing*, but it appeals less (as we shall see) to intelligence, and therefore is to the right of *instructing*, moving to the edge of the region of intelligence. *Propagandizing* and *lying* are beyond appeals to intelligence, and therefore, like physical threat, are outside the pie of *teaching*. Other related concepts can be put on the diagram as we proceed.

Unlike swimming, or playing tennis, you cannot tell from simply watching a person's behavior whether or not he is teaching. The teacher may be talking or silent, sitting, standing on his head, moving, or resting. Thus, teaching is not a specific set of activities. To know whether a person is teaching, we have to judge his behavior by a relevant standard or criterion. I shall argue that the proper criterion of whether a person's activities are *teaching*, depends upon whether he is intentionally trying to bring about in another person some kind of understanding, coupled with a disposition to use that understanding in appropriate ways.

On the other hand, no one can teach without doing *something*. "What were you doing?" "I was teaching." "Yes, I know, but what specifically were you doing?" "I was just teaching, that is all." "But were you lecturing?" "NO, as a matter of fact I was listening to a recitation." To teach, then, means to do something, but that something must satisfy the above criterion.

Let us turn our illustrative conversation around. "What were you doing?" "I was leading a discussion." "Oh, you were teaching." "No, it was a group counseling session." No doubt, teachers sometimes counsel, but in this they are not necessarily teaching. How does counseling differ from teaching, since many of the activities of counselors are similar to those of teachers? They differ from one another by the criterion of their success. A counselor's aim is different from that of a teacher. This aim or standard defines his behavior, just as the criterion of educating defines the activity of the teacher.

The teacher does many things: keeps order, sends sick children to the school nurse, counsels an upset child, turns up the heat, or opens a window. Our problem can be put schematically:

Doctoring (medical) is to medical care
And counseling is to psychological therapy
As teaching is to X

Our question is, "What is X?" Peters answers this question as follows: "If we look at such a process from the teacher's point of view he is intentionally trying to get learning processes going by exhibiting, drawing attention to, emphasizing, or explicating some fraction of what has to be learnt or putting the learner in a position where his experience is likely to become structured along desirable lines."

The teacher is not teaching when he opens the window, polices students, or supervises the school lunchroom. If the room is disorderly, too hot, or the children hungry then learning is unlikely to go on. These activities sustain teaching, but they are not themselves teaching.

TEACHING IS TRIADIC

Teaching involves three elements: a teacher, a subject matter, and a student. "What were you doing this afternoon?" "I was teaching." "What were you teaching?" "Oh, nothing at all, just teaching." This does not make sense. To teach means to teach something, a subject matter.

"You say you were teaching." "Yes." "Whom were you teaching?" "No one, just teaching by myself." "You mean you were teaching yourself?" "No, I wasn't teaching anyone, not even myself." This does not make sense either.

One of the ways to clarify the concept of *teaching* is to agree on a standard example, what philosophers all a "paradigm case." The following incident from one of Plato's dialogues is a good candidate for such a paradigm. In the *Meno,* Socrates illustrates one of his favorite doctrines by teaching one of Meno's slaves a concept in geometry. Socrates does not *tell* the slave about the Pythagorean theorem concerning the square of the hypotenuse. Socrates asks him questions, beginning with things he already knows, such as that a square has four equal lines, and so on. Gradually, he works up to the more complex notion of triangles with squares built along their sides, until the slave is able to draw the conclusion that the square of the hypotenuse of a right angle is equal in area to the sum of the square of the other two sides. It is hard to imagine someone questioning whether this is teaching or not.

This is a logical model of *teaching*. The elements are all here: A teacher who understands enough to lead the inquiry, a subject matter, and a potential learner.

TEACHING AS A "TASK" WORD

Suppose Socrates had failed in his instruction, would we say that, he had not been teaching? I think not. Teaching intends to bring about learning, but sometimes it does not. If the teacher does not intend to bring about learning, he is not teaching. If he intends learning, he can still claim to have been teaching even though he fails. One way of making this point is to say that teaching is a *task* word rather than an *achievement* word. Communication, for instance is an *achievement word*. You cannot *communicate* without getting some message through to another person. *Fishing*, on the other hand, like teaching, is a *task* word. A man may fish without catching anything. However, as James Gribble points out, "if no one had ever caught fish by dangling baited line into the water it would not be called fishing. Verbs only develop a *task*" sense if an activity is sometimes successful." This suggests that with any specific activity that claims to be *teaching* being it is necessary to establish that there is some chance of learning being generated. *This leaves the status is some chance of learning being generated*. This leaves the status of any specific so-called *teaching* method open to inquiry.

The claim that some form of activity is properly designated a *teaching method* is also subject to other criteria than potential success. Learning can, no doubt, be brought about through threats and intimidation, but this would not normally be called *teaching*. The reason is that *teaching* in its paradigmatic sense belongs to the sphere of intelligence, and these methods make little or no appeal to the understanding or intellect of the learner. If we saw someone beating a child, we might agree that the child was learning something, but we would hardly credit the beating as *teaching*. Here again, the lines are not clear. Threats and rewards are sometimes used in teaching. It is only in extreme forms that we would categorically refuse to count them as teaching. These boundaries become clearer when we examine some related concepts.

TRAINING

Compare the Socratic model with the following: You teach your dog to jump through a hoop, or your parrot to say, "Thank you." The three standard elements are again present: a teacher, a subject matter, and a potential learner, but the element of understanding is missing. Despite the fact that it would be correct to speak of "teaching your dog tricks," ordinary speech still recognizes a difference. We would not, for instance, say that your dog or parrot were "well educated." We would say that they are "well trained." If you *taught* computer to play chess, we would not say that the computer was "trained," much less "educated" to play chess. Nor would we say that the computer "understood" chess.

Ordinary language often makes no distinction between training and teaching. "I taught him to swim," and "I trained him to swim," our speech makes the distinctions that are useful for clarifying the full meaning of *teaching* as distinct from *training*.

Even in complex subject matters like medicine, law, or education, we speak of *training*: medical *training*, legal *training*, or teacher *training*. The expression "medical education" or "legal education" are not quite right. When we use these latter expressions we imply something more than training. When we talk about the "education of doctors" or "the education of teachers," we mean something more than the *training* of doctors or teachers. We are concerned with their nonprofessional backgrounds. One of the issues in the education of teachers lies precisely in the difference between narrow professional *training* and a broad *education*. One would not say, "My education is in medicine/law/the ministry/teaching." We would say, "My training is in medicine, etc." This is true also of learning other subject matter: history, literature, or languages. You would not say, "My education is in history." You would say, "My training is in history."

Throughout the preceding examples, the notion of *education* is broader than that of *training*. In a later chapter, we shall see in more detail what the concept of *education* involves. For the present, it is enough to indicate that it is closely related to certain central notions of *teaching*. Education involves, as does the paradigmatic sense of *teaching*, the notion of understanding rather than the mere acquisition of specific skills or limited bodies of knowledge.

It would be wrong to deny that *training* is a kind of teaching. It lies within the range of the meaning of *teaching*, but moves slightly out of the central focus. The *trainer* is a teacher, but not quite a model of the *teacher*. When we are training, we are engaged in teaching, but all teaching is not training. The concepts are related, but not identical. One concept cannot be directly substituted for the other.

This can be seen by comparing the trainer of animals with the trainer of swimmers. the trainer of animals does not, of course, give reason to his subjects. The trainer of swimmers very likely does. A human subject may improve his performance in a skill if he understands relevant instructions. In this sense, the trainer of animals is further away from the central meaning of *teaching* than the trainer of human beings. This distinction shows up in an expression often used by teachers of the mentally handicapped: "Trainable but not educable." As Green says, "Training resembles teaching insofar as it is aimed at actions which display intelligence." To quote him more fully: "In proportion as training is aimed at a greater and greater display of intelligence, it more and more clearly resembles teaching, and one of the clues as to how closely training approaches teaching is the degree to which it involves explanations, reasons, argument, and weighing evidence. It is because training sometimes approaches this point, that we can in many cases substitute the word 'teaching' for the word 'training' without any change in meaning."

CONDITIONING

Conditioning lies on the border line between teaching and non-teaching. The classical example of conditioning is, of course, Pavlov's dogs learning to salivate when the bell rings. Like training, conditioning aims at changing behavior. But can it count as a species of *teaching?* The following considerations will help decide the matter. We say that Pavlov "conditioned" his dogs to salivate. It would be odd to say that he "trained" them to do so. Even in animal training, there seems to be a presumption that the animal cooperates with some degree of intelligence. We speak, in fact, of an animal than can learn complicated tricks as an "intelligent" animal. Surely, no one would say this of Pavlov's dogs. No intelligence of even the most subhuman variety is required for this type of behavioral change, even when it takes place in a human being.

It is possible, for example, to condition a person's pupilary reflex to respond to verbal commands, such as "contract". Even the subject himself may eventually give the command to contract his own pupils, but no intelligence is involved. The subject has no conscious control over his pupilary reactions and cannot improve the situation by trying harder or in some more skilled way. The pupilary reaction is induced in exactly the same way that salivation was induced in Pavlov's dogs.

No doubt, in most training, even in complex behavior like speech, there is an element of conditioning or reinforcement. The concept of *practice* involves some such elements. Though, in the later case, there is a norm observing activity on the part of the learner that transcends the purely reflex activity of the body. As the practicer advances in his skill he discriminates wrong from right modes of *practicing*. A pianist, for instance, will repeat certain passages in order to imprint, so to speak, the muscular reactions that are needed to perform the passages correctly. Hence, when the time for performance arrives, he need not think about this part of his playing. It has become automatic.

We will return to this psychological topic at several points in the remaining chapters. It is an important current topic in education. There is a great deal of uncritical acceptance by educators of techniques offered by psychologists who operate within the context of conditioning theories. Their suitability for teachers should be examined carefully.

If *conditioning* lies at the border of permissible meanings of *teach*, it would seem that mere physical threat and intimidation lie outside the pale. Torture, for instance, would undoubtedly, change human behavior, but it could hardly qualify as a species of teaching. Suppose, as William James speculated, your optic nerve were successfully grafted into the auditory centers of the brain so that you could "see" sounds. Would it be correct to say that you had been *taught* to see sounds or that you had *learned* to see them? Surgery, then, belongs outside of both *teaching* and *learning*.

KNOWING AND BELIEVING

The teaching continuum diagram is divided between those activities intended to change behavior (on the left), and those intended to bring about a grasp of some new knowledge or some change in beliefs (on the right). How shall we view this division?Instructing or indoctrinating are concerned with such matters as *true* and *false*, correct and faulty *reasoning, evidence*, and so on. Training and conditioning, on the other hand, do not involve such questions. There is no problem of *truth* in inducing pupilary contraction; the issue is one of success or failure.

If we come to *know* or to *believe* something, we suppose it to be *true*. There are many ways in which we may be said to *know* or to *believe* something, and these are relevant to teaching, especially when we wish to distinguish, say, the kind of believing that results from *indoctrination*, and that which is aimed at *instructing*, or in the most fundamental sense of *teaching*.

The logic of belief systems is, therefore, highly relevant to certain elements in the concept of teaching. Green points out the contrast between "holding beliefs evidentially and non-evidentially." A belief held evidentially is one that is subject to change through rational criticism. Many beliefs are not of this character. Some beliefs, such as those held by virtue of their function within the psychology of the individual, are not held evidentially. Beliefs of this sort form a psychological system, but not necessarily a logical system. Within the psychological system, some beliefs are more fundamental than others, but they are functionally central rather than logically primitive. If attacked, they will no doubt be defended by so-called *reasons*, but these will, upon inspection, prove to be rationalization. Moreover, when the alleged *reasons* for a psychologically central belief are refuted, the belief is not abandoned; the believer simply retrenches with fresh rationalizations. Even contradictions among such beliefs may not move the believer because he has developed mechanisms for keeping these clusters of beliefs isolated from others. Thus, a firm believer in *democracy* may also remain racially prejudiced despite the inconsistencies which may appear among the elements in his belief. The inconsistencies are themselves masked by rationalization or protected by the simple device of not thinking of the two incompatible items at the same time.

These observations have an important bearing on the meaning of *teaching*. The intention of teaching is rationally or evidentially held beliefs. The person instructing, for instance, is subject to questions concerning the reasonable grounds of the beliefs he is seeking to convey.

This raises several questions. One is the status of *indoctrination* as a mode of teaching. Another is the relationship between knowing and doing, or understanding and performing. Let us consider the latter issue first. To do this, we will have to examine several related concepts, such as *telling* and *drilling*.

UNDERSTANDING AND PERFORMING TELLING AND DRILLING

Komisar argues for a distinction between the teacher intending that the student *understand* something and intending that he *learn* something. Imagine, he suggests, that we "go through the proof of some theorem (*T*) in such a way as to get an auditor to recognize it as proof of *T*." To accomplish that, he writes, "we would not so much expose the reasoning...as drill the students in the steps seriatim." I doubt that he can make this distinction stick.

Would we say that the student had *learned* the theorem if he could parrot the proof without understanding? He would certainly have learned something, namely to parrot certain words. Would that count as having learned the theorem? Or, conversely, would we say that he had not learned anything about the proof if he understood but could not repeat it? No doubt, the student who could repeat the proof with understanding would have learned in a more significant sense than in either of the other cases. In this case, the teacher would have succeeded in his intention more fully. There is a meaning of *learning* in the sense of rote repetition as well as in the sense of *coming to understand. Coming to understand* coupled with the capacity to express that understanding in relevant ways more adequately states the intention of the act of teaching than either of these elements.

It may clarify the distinctions we are making to note another teaching word, *telling*. "I told him about X" is not quite the same as "I instructed him in X." "I demonstrated X to him" lies somewhere between the two concepts. telling is certainly a part of teaching, but it is not enough. Telling a pupil that 6 X 7 = 42 is not really *teaching* him that this is so. It is only when the teacher aims at the pupil's understanding, why is the product of 6 X 7, that he can be said to have been *taught* this subject matter. Komisar would say that the student had not *learned* unless he could somehow do the sum himself after forgetting the way in which it was explained, even if he had really understood the explanation of it at the time. Certainly, being able to do the sum one's self is a reasonable addition to mere understanding, but it does not preclude saying that understanding alone is a kind of learning in its own right. To say that *drill* would have been used if learning had been the goal is to fail to see that *drill* without understanding is as defective, if not more defective, as a teaching procedure than rational demonstration without drill. The drilled student would, no doubt, be able to perform the drilled behavior, but he would not know what he was doing and would not, therefore, be able to perform similar assignments because he would not see the formal likenesses. On the other hand, the student who once understood would, in most cases, be able to recover that understanding and practice to become skilled, not only in this particular problem, but in others of the same order.

Referring again to the continuum of the teaching chart, we should notice that *drilling* belongs with instructing as a mean of inculcating knowledge or changing beliefs. Yet it has strong affinities to training and conditioning on the side of the chart dealing with changes in behavior. *Drill* can be properly viewed as a kind of training (or *practicing*) that aims at an ability to perform verbally. There is no question of its required use by the educator. It is especially appropriate in the audio-lingual method of teaching languages, in memorizing basic information like the multiplication table, and so on. Here understanding is at a minimum or may even be virtually absent. In saturation language courses of the audio-lingual variety, any reference to dictionaries, written symbols, grammar, or the logical structures of languages is held to have a negative influence on the rate of learning. What is demanded is the instantaneous imitated response in the new language—even when the speaker does not have the slightest notion of what he is saying.

Drill is of the essence in such instruction, and no one would deny that instructors in such sessions were teaching. Their pupils often become proficient in a very short time. The drill, however, would fail in its purpose if the pupils remained in the parrot stage of the course. Gradually, as the verbal responses become habitual, the student finds himself *thinking* in the new language. He associates meanings and understands concepts as in his native tongue. A person who could merely rattle off correct responses to stock questions in French exercises would not have learned French unless he came to understand the meaning of the stock questions and answers. The instructor awaits the time when his student can converse about matters that have not been presented for drill. The test of his mastery comes in this wider context where lack of understanding would reveal a fatal deficiency. The reason that the original stock phrases become pregnant with meaning is that they are used over the over again in relevant contexts. The student is doing more than drilling. He is observing situations in which the words are appropriate and responding to them intelligently.

Thus, there is a lattice of logical connections among such concepts as *telling, instructing, explaining*, and *drilling* as forms of teaching aimed at, but not requiring, *learning*. Not "requiring," because, as we have seen, *teach* is a *task* word, not an achievement word.

INDOCTRINATING

Thus far we have seen that a number of concepts like telling, instructing, demonstrating, and drilling belong to that side of the teaching continuum concerned with inculcating new knowledge or changing beliefs. What is the status of *indoctrinating?* Is it teaching? Our answer is that it belongs to the teaching continuum, but only at its edge, and, as in the case of *conditioning,* with reservations. This shows again how fuzzy some of the boundaries are among the various parts of the territory we call *teaching*. Indoctrination can be viewed as a form of *telling,* accompanied by a special rationale. Green puts it well when he says that "the intent of indoctrination is to lead people to hold beliefs as through they were arrived at by inquiry, and yet to hold them independently of any subsequent inquiry and therefore secure against the threat of change by the later introduction of conflicting reasons or conflicting evidence." The views held as a result of indoctrination are thus held nonevidentially.

The paradigm of *indoctrination* that naturally comes to mind is a priest teaching the catechism. In its narrowest sense, this may be mere *telling* and *drilling* to assure that the pupil can recite the proper answers to the catechetical questions whether he understands them or not. This is, no doubt, a caricature of catechism classes. In actual practice, the meaning of the catechism is usually more or less explained, and, depending upon the sophistication of the priest, reasons are offered on behalf of the standard answers. If one were to hear the instruction, he might even consider it an instance of teaching in the paradigmatic sense of attempting to bring about an understanding of evidential beliefs.

White in his essay on indoctrination identifies the factor that distinguishes what is going on here from teaching in the paradigmatic sense, namely, that the priest aims at "fixing the pupil's beliefs so that they are unshakable."

It is well to sort out the essential nature of indoctrination from its theological context for two reasons. First, in modern education, scarcely anyone supposes that it is the task of public school teachers to teach religious doctrines in this way. The modern concern over indoctrination is, therefore, over something broader than the subject matter of religious doctrines. The second reason is that almost any subject matter can be the content of indoctrination. Child-centered theorists of education, for instance, regard all traditional methods of teaching as indoctrination. Indoctrination is then any method of instruction that aims at "fixing the pupil's" beliefs so that they are unshakable. This could apply as well to a nontheological subject, such as patriotism or morality.

Are teaching and indoctrination compatible? If teaching must carry with it a rationale that is capable of being understood by the pupil, then indoctrination would seem to lie outside the pale of teaching. Some will complain that indoctrinators very often give reasons for their views. No doubt, but we have seen that there is a difference. The reasons that are given in teaching are always, in a theoretical sense, contradictable. Teaching implies an unfinished inquiry into the logic or meaning of a subject matter, and the unfinished nature of the inquiry means that the beliefs are at no stage strictly "unshakable." In principle, they are subject to expansion, revision, or even contradiction. Of course, it would be absurd to suppose that one might change his fundamental principles every other day. Some beliefs exhibit a quasi-permanent status. The difference in principle is nonetheless important, and a student who would *come to understand* must realize the tentative and challengeable character of all his learning if he is to escape being the subject of indoctrination.

I suspect that merely knowing that one was being indoctrinated would set a limit to its success. If one were to say to a student, "I am now going to indoctrinate you," he would be in a good position to question the whole scheme, and, no doubt, would do so. Similarly, the person who said, "I hold the views to which I have been indoctrinated to be true," would already imply that he had other reasons for holding them. If he did not have some additional reasons, he would be like the person who says, "I hold these proven views to be unproven." Or, "I hold these false views to be true." Or, "I hold these uncertain and doubtful views to be unquestionable.". All these sound odd because they *are* old.

It may be well and good to say that teaching logically excludes indoctrination, but the story is more complicated. White confesses that he first faced up to this question when he considered how much of his own field of political science appeared to be vulnerable to the accusation of indoctrination. It is relatively easy to avoid indoctrination in areas where rational accounts of subject matter are available, and where public verification leads to a consensus of informed investigators. However, in the realms of religion, political beliefs, and morals, where deep differences exist between men of equal intelligence and goodwill, the problem is complex.

White believes that in these realms indoctrinate is inevitable. Teachers, he thinks, will inevitably indoctrinate where they cannot determine an issue with reason. Hare, for instance, believes that moral judgments cannot be rationally justified since they are based upon what he calls "decisions of principle." It would then seem that morality would have to be indoctrinated or left out of the educational enterprise. Since, as we shall see, education itself is based upon moral assumption—doing something good for people—a flaw is thereby introduced into the very foundation of education itself. Is there a way out of this difficulty?

Without disputing Hare's characterization of morals at this point, let us expand his principle. There is a contingent or decisional element in all human knowledge in the sense that it rests upon ultimate assumptions that are not themselves rationally provable. Science, for instance, could not proceed without the assumption of some order in nature that is within our comprehension if we investigate further. This assumption of comprehensible order is a kind of scientific *faith* if you will, but *unproven* does not mean arbitrary or whimsical. It is hard to imagine human existence without some such assumption. Its denial would subvert not only science but common sense as well. Democracy is also based upon unprovable assumptions about the powers of men to govern themselves, and the foolishness of allowing any single group of men to have unlimited power over their fellows. This kind of assumption is not provable, but it is vindicated in experience. The same argument would be used by a Christian, Jew, or Buddhist who has also made a decision of principle about his style of life.

The point is that since human knowledge has this contingent and decisional character, there is no escape from indoctrination by eliminating every scrap of subject matter from education that cannot be grounded empirically in the consensus of inquirers. The solution to our problem would rather seem to lie in another direction, namely, to teach students the contingent character of human knowledge and evaluation as soon as they are able to grasp such a concept. Faiths, whether political, religious, social, or moral, will find their place in the educational process, but students must be initiated into an understanding of the grounds upon which these are so diversely held.

No doubt, this requires a rare kind of detachment on the part of an educator, rare, but not impossible. No doubt, the believer in democracy will tend to indoctrinate rather than to teach, but a full-fledged teaching enterprise will include the detachment that leads students into a full understanding of the kind of human commitment a democratic faith really is.

According to this view, indoctrination belongs to the sphere of teaching even if on the margins and with fuzzy lines of demarcation between legitimate and illegitimate forms of indoctrination.

ENABLING BELIEFS

Green makes another proposal that suggests the same outcome. He points out that among the class of nonevidential beliefs there is a subclass that can be rationally justified in a nonevidential way. He calls these "enabling beliefs." An example of such an enabling belief is a conviction of the value of truth. The value of truth cannot be empirically proven, partly because any empirical argument on its behalf would have to assume its truth. Is the teacher who instructs his pupils in the value of truth indoctrinating? Yes. He wants his pupils to have an unshakable conviction on the subject. Is he justified in this? Yes, says Green, because this belief is not a belief in any particular truth, but a belief that enables men to come to any truth at all. "A deep conviction concerning the value of truth," he writes, "is in this sense rationally defensible because without it there can be no rational defense of any belief whatsoever." Green's further comments on this point:

> It is not, therefore, the aim of teaching to eliminate all passionate convictions. The aim, on the contrary, is to seek every possible assurance that our passionate convictions, our enabling beliefs, are also rationally or evidentially held. Such enabling beliefs may

> be open for examination, capable of refinement and elaboration, but under no conditions can they be exchanged for others. Their abandonment cannot be warranted on the basis of evidence or reasons, because they are precisely those beliefs without which we could not seriously entertain the evidence.

I think that the words "evidential held" are a slip of the pen. It is well to keep the motion of "evidential belief" for those beliefs that require empirical evidence. I would say that enabling beliefs are "rationally held, but not "evidentially held."

Are there other beliefs that qualify in this way? None, I suspect that fit the Cartesian turn so neatly as belief in the value of truth. There are other candidates, such as belief in goodwill, or justice, and probably belief in some order of better or worse among values. The denial of any of these would preclude most of the inquiries and decisions that are essential not only to education, but to any form of civilized human existence.

Indoctrination, thus hedged with these several qualifications, would seem to belong legitimately to the teaching continuum.

At this stage, the major outlines of the territory we call *teaching* should be coming into focus. More details will be added as we turn to a related subject,the concept of *learning*.

16

Learning and Human Resource Development

Analyzing the concept of *learning* poses difficulties that did not appear in the study of the *teaching* concept. There is no paradigm of *learning* as there was for teaching, and therefore no comparable way of logically relating various kinds of teaching. This makes the definition of learning—the discovery of the *necessary* and *sufficient criteria* for something to count as *learning*—more difficult.

This is not to say that we do not know how to use the word in ordinary language. In ordinary usages, the strands of meaning that make up the cord we call "learning" are more frayed than in the case of teaching.

It is widely presumed that the concept of *learning* has attained clarity among psychologist. Let us begin with this claim. In challenging it, we will discover that we will also be examining another claim, namely, that psychologist possess, or are about to possess, the key to the business of learning.

THE PSYCHOLOGICAL DEFINITION OF LEARNING

Psychologists say a great deal about the "psychologist of learning." On the face of it, this would suggest that educators would do well to turn to them for empirically grounded suggestions both for a definition of learning and how to do their job. There are good reasons for bringing both of these views into questions. Consider first the problem of definition.

According to most psychologists, *learning* is the relatively permanent modification of behavior as the result of experience. Experiments in learning generally deal with the methods by which such behavioral modifications may be brought about. Is all learning of this sort? I think not. In the first place, learning may take place without the modification of behavior. In some cases, the modification of behavior is at most a probable evidence that learning has taken place. Consider an example in the previous chapter. An instructor goes through a proof in geometry so that the student understands that proof. Suppose that a few minutes later the student cannot duplicate the proof. Would we say that he had not learned anything? Or suppose that he could duplicate the proof, but never bothered to do so. Would we say he had not learned *nothing?* All we could say was that we had no behavioral evidence that he had learned something.

On the other hand, suppose that he did duplicate the proof. Would that be evidence that he had *learned* the *proof* in the fundamental sense of having "understood" it? Not at all. He may have a facile memory so that he can duplicate the proof without understanding. In this case, his behavior cannot stand as the sole meaning of learning. To repeat: He might behave in the required way without having learned in the most significant sense of the instructor's intention (namely to "understand" the proof), and he might not be inclined to [or be able to] duplicate the proof, and still have learned something significant.

The significance of this example becomes more apparent if we expand it to ask, "What is the behavioral equivalent of understanding mathematics?" Doing mathematical operations? Yes, but specifically which mathematical operations? All of them? That is absurd. Just those that one understands (has learned)? How could we reasonably exhaust the class of understood mathematical operations for any given person? Typical operations, then? How do we know we have touched on every kind of mathematical operation the person has learned? Suppose we have a mathematical genius. He may perform operations no one has ever performed. The point should be clear: There is no behavioral *equivalent* for the state of having come to *understand mathematics*. The best we could hope for would be some kind of behavior as *evidence* of understanding.

The linguistic theorist Naom Chomsky points out that when a child has *learned* a *language* at even the most elementary level, the number of possible meaningful sentences that he could understand in that language is of orders of magnitude greater than the number of seconds remaining in his life. The *behavioral equivalent* of having *learned a language* is then empirically impossible to arrange even in principle.

The relationship of learning to behavior, then, turns out to be equivocal. This becomes even clearer when we note that behavior may change significantly without any learning. A person's behavior may alter significantly simply because he *decides* to do something he already knows how to do. Suppose, suggests one critic, a bank cashier *decides* to become an embezzler. His behavior will change significantly, but not due to learning. Or, again, suppose a person accidentally sprains his ankle. This is certainly *an experience*, and his behavior changes from walking to limping, but he has not *learned* this new behavior. The formula "either inherited or learned" would seem to be inadequate in the light of such instances.

Since this is an important issue in educational theory, let us consider the psychological point of view further. Hardie claims that all learning is one of two types. Type one is a case of learning to give old responses to new stimuli. The classical instance is Pavlov's dogs learning to salivate at the sound of a bell. Type two is the reinforcement of a selected item of behavior by rewarding that behavior every time it occurs so that, in the future, it will occur with a high degree of regularity. An example of this later type is the hungry pigeon that peeks at random until it accidentally touches a button that releases food. The reward leads again to the desired behavior which is again rewarded. As the number of reinforcements increases undesired response become fewer and the desired response becomes fixed. The pigeon has *learned* to peck the button when it is hungry. Thus, Hardie says, "learning is the building, more or less permanently, of new associations; and the associations must be either between a response (already tied to one stimulus) and a new stimulus or between a response (untied), and a stimulus that had not been associated together before." Hardie commends this account because, as he says, "A description of both types of learning can be given without any reference to internal, unobservable, mental processes.

In Hardie's arguments it is not hard to detect opinions strongly reminiscent of the empiricist criterion of meaning that reigned during the logical-empiricist phase of the history of analysis. This is what Peters calls the Hobbes-Hull-Skinner thesis. Hull is the celebrated psychologist who systematically formulated the theory of learning embodied in Hardie's type one. Skinner is famous for his formulation of type two, the reinforcement theory of learning. The seventeenth-century philosopher Hobbes is the most celebrated modern exponent of materialism. He contended for a world view in which everything is merely matter in motion.

Peters' characterization thus places this learning theory as a species of materialist metaphysics, a reversion to a mode of thought rejected by analysts. I suggested earlier that analytic thinkers, belonging as they do to the empirical tradition, sometimes show a softness toward materialism from time to time despite their how estimate of metaphysical theories. Peters' objections to this learning theory are analytical. Of course, no thinking can go on if the nervous system is not in order, but this in no sense means that we can learn about thought from inspecting the body. Peters comments as follows: "…. We cannot begin to describe what we mean by performances such as remembering, perceiving, and knowing in such terms. For how can we get notions like being right about the past or having good evidence for what we say by studying the movements of the body or brain? We have to understand human conventions and human language and the criteria in terms of which actions and statements are assessed."

Peters distinguishes between *happenings* and *actions*. *Happenings*, such as an eye blink, occur, but actions, such as winking, are something we do. Learning the former is not the same as learning to perform the latter. As he says, "human goings-on are not all of a piece" and there "cannot therefore be any one type of explanation for them, any one type of learning."

Another difficulty with the behaviorist's theory of learning lies in the ambiguity of the notion of a *stimulus*. To say that a person blinks his eye due to the stimulus of a puff of air against the eyeball is clear enough, but what is the *stimulus* for a wink? A wink is a social act set in a situation that cannot be explained by reference to mere physical stimuli. Events that evoke a wink must have a meaning. This meaning is inseparable from the way a person views the world in which he lives. You cannot understand the wink until you understand the actor's understandings, valuings, and perceptions. Also, you cannot do this without entering a symbolic realm that has no strict behavioral (physical) or observable counterpart.

Green clarified this distinction between a *happening* and an *action*. Where happenings are under consideration, we can be said to have acquired a disposition to act "in *conformity* to rule," whereas in the case of *actions*, we have acquired a disposition to act "in *obedience* to rule." A rat that has learned to run a maze correctly can be said to have acquired a disposition to behave "in conformity to rule." There is, after all, a correct way to run the maze, but the rate could not be said to have behaved in this manner by having *considered* the rule. "To learn to obey a rule," writes Green, "is not simply to acquire a disposition to act in a certain way, but a disposition to act in that way *because* it is a correct way." Since a great deal of human learning is of this sort, it is false that all learning falls within the categories of conditioned-operant learning as claimed by Hardie and many psychologists. Furthermore, it follows from this inadequacy of behaviorist psychology that while some human behavior may be *explained* by discovering likely *causes*, other human activity can only be understood by finding *reasons*.

One possible objection to this distinction comes from psychologists of the Freudian persuasion. If we accept the apparently reasonable proposition that all behavior is motivated, we open the door to the psychologist who deals in subconscious or unconscious motivation. His claim is that all so-called *rational* behavior is essentially nonrationally motivated, and that the alleged *reasons* for the activity are merely rationalizations. The agent, then, is really not an agent at all, he is the pawn of unconscious forces. I am not sure how the Freudian and Skinnerian psychologists get their respective theories to form a consistent system, but together they would seem to give a fairly good argument against what I have been calling rational activity. Can anything decisive be said against this argument? I think it can.

Suppose A gives what he thinks to be a genuine *reason* (as distinct from a causal *explanation*) for some activity. B remarks that he knows why A holds this view, namely, for nonrational psychological causes unknown to A. C comes along and points out that B holds this view not because of the *reasons* he sets forth, but because of nonrational psychological causes in his own psyche. D comes along, and so forth. Surely, if there is anything at all to the notion that sometimes men hold their views for nonrational *causes* other than their public announced *reasons*, this can be maintained only if some other men (psychologists, perhaps) hold their views of such behavior for genuine reasons. If no one has rational grounds for his opinions, then no one can validly assert as *true* that anyone else is holding his views for nonrational causes. If anyone can have rational opinions, then others, beside psychologists, may also hold them. In short, the universalization of the doctrine of nonrationality is self-contradictory.

A more linguistic argument can be given for this same position. The notion of *rationalization* presupposes the notion of *rational*. A rationalization is a pseudoreason that has only the form of reason. No one could rationalize unless he understood to some degree what it was to reason, for in rationalizing, we all want to appear reasonable. This desire to *appear* if not *be* reasonable makes sense only if there is some meaning to being rational.

Furthermore, if we are to take ordinary language as the standard for our reflection, we cannot relegate the multitude of discussions about reasons (in science, morality, or practical affairs) to the limbo of nonsense. This distinction clearly exists in ordinary talk, and it is not the product of some philosophical theory, it is simply there. To reject it is to opt for a revisionist metaphysic of the Hobbesian variety. It is hard to see how this view could be the considered product of analytic reasoning. Consider, finally, the anomaly of the philosopher who reasons that all reasons are rationalizations.

This discussion of psychology illustrates how many facets there are to the simple question of finding out what we mean by *learning*. The upshot of our inquiry thus far is that the behavioristic approach is inadequate. Behavior, it turns out, is neither *sufficient* nor *necessary* for something to count as *learning*. This does not mean that the *psychology of learning* is not about learning. No one could question this. Rats indeed *learn* to run mazes. This is not, as Hardie seems to suggest, a paradigm of *learning* the way Socrates instructing Meno's slave is a paradigm of *teaching*.

Lacking such a paradigm, we may not be able to state clearly what *learning* is, but we can still look at linguistic usage to make some interesting and useful distinctions.

OTHER APPROACHES TO THE DEFINITION OF "LEARNING"

One proposal to facilitate the making of useful discussions in the learning concept is to sort out learning, by the thing learned. The trick is to substitute "learning X" for "learning." Thus, the proposal goes, learning to run a maze is a different kind of learning than learning a language. This lead is valuable because we certainly must note important differences among such things as learning to run mazes, learning to speak a language, learning to value something, learning that something is true, learning to believe in something, and so on. It is doubtful that this helps us with the concept of learning as such. Learning X, whatever X may be, is always simply a case of learning. None of these *learnings* turns out to be more or less central to learning than any others. Simply considering them as *learning* does not cut the *learning* pie in a logical way. Most of these distinctions, as Green has argued, turn out to be distinctions in teaching. Thus indoctrination (a method of teaching) may be a way of bringing about someone's learning (for example) that "X is true when X is false." This illuminates more clearly what we mean by such learning than when the reference to the teaching process is omitted.

A more promising suggestion is to direct our attention not to the subject matter learned, but to the *mode* of learning. In the section that follows, we will examine several important modes. However, again, I find myself in agreement with Green: these distinctions turn out to be differences that stem from the logic of the teaching concept rather than from the learning concept. The reasons for this will become more apparent as these various modes of learning are examined. Before leaving our present topic, however, let us note briefly some educational applications of our analysis to this point.

SOME CONCLUSIONS ABOUT THE PSYCHOLOGY OF LEARNING AND EDUCATION

The first conclusion from this analysis is that psychological studies of learning may not necessarily be of interest to teachers. The psychologist may discover all sorts of ways to induce learning that could not count as *teaching*. Jestingly, I once suggested to a student that she could learn something the way the rats learn to run mazes. Her reply was, "I don't want to get that hungry." Very hungry rats learn to run mazes more quickly than well-fed ones. Would keeping students very hungry and rewarding them with bits of food as they responded in desired ways count as teaching method?

Or, more drastically, perhaps rats learn to run mazes more efficiently when they are subjected to electric shocks at appropriate times. Would we say that wiring students' desks counted as a teaching method? The psychologist might reply that our reluctance to use such methods is due simply to our present moral values. If we were less squeamish, we might become better teachers. Green points out that a change in our ethics would not change the logic of the teaching concept. The distinctions that were made between *indoctrination* and *instruction* or between *conditioning* and *training* would hold regardless of a teacher's ethics. The notion of *teaching* is ethically neutral, and our analysis of these distinctions is a logical, not an ethical matter.

This doubt about the applicability of psychology to education goes against the grain of most publications on the psychology of learning. Edward Best, in his essay on "The Suppressed Premise in Educational Psychology," points out that in many such publications a suppressed moral "should" is presupposed. Authors assume without argument that given a successful experiment in psychology, the new procedure should be used by educators. My point is that the logic of the intermediate moral exhortation must be spelled out carefully before we know whether or not the psychological material is useful to teachers.

When, for example, Hull and others discovered that *need reduction* functions in learning situations with rats, some writers immediately suggested that teachers use the *needs* of their students as counters in the teaching game by *reducing* these needs as rewards (and therefore motivation) for learning. I am not arguing that this is bad. What I want to point out is that this proposal poses a host of educational questions that are not even hinted at by the educational psychologists. Here are some of them: What do we mean by *human needs?* Which *needs* should be *reduced?* How are such human needs as the need for status, friendship, knowledge, and so on, best *reduced* for sound educational purposes?

This should be sufficient to warn the educator who is tempted to believe that his task may be made immediately easier by applying psychological materials directly to educational situations.

MODES OF LEARNING: KNOWING HOW AND KNOWING THAT

Ryle, in his essay on "Knowing How and Knowing That," says that "... when a person is said to understand something in the sense of 'shrewd' or 'silly,' 'prudent' or 'imprudent,' the description imputes to him, not the knowledge, or ignorance, of this or that truth, but the ability, or inability, to do certain sorts of things." "In ordinary life," he says, "as well as in the special business of teaching... we are much more concerned with people's competences than with their cognitive repertoires, with the operations than with the truths that they learned." Here Ryle opens a new range of meanings for analyzing the concept of learning. To learn in the sense of understanding certainly means to know some facts. But it means more than that. It means the ability to perform certain kinds of acts in accordance with the norms that define the correct performance of those acts. To understand chess is to play well, not simply to state the rules of the game.

This point is important, but it is possible to overrate it. It is true that a good chess player does not rehearse the rules of chess to himself as he plays, but he may rehearse certain strategies. He could not be said to understand chess as fully as someone who could tell us the rules or spell out his strategies. Nor do I think that we would properly say that a computer that plays a good game of chess "understands chess." I suspect that when we say that the machine has "learned" to play chess, we are using the word "learned" metaphorically. By the conventions of our language organisms *learn*, but inanimate objects do not. If a nail is bent and then straightened, it will tend to bend at the same place when strain is placed upon it. Would we say that the nail *learned* to bend in that particular way? We *might* say this of a plant that was bent in certain ways by the gardener, but here the word *learned* would seem odd. On the other, hand, we would say that a dog *learned* to hold its tail in a certain way if it was held in that position repeatedly. As we go down the scale of intelligence and awareness from human beings to animals to plants to stones, the term *learned* becomes increasingly inappropriate.

At the human level, some modicum of memory seems to be required for something to have been *learned*. We would not say that the nail "remembered" where it was bent. *Remembering* refers to the past in a special way, such as getting things correct. We would not say that I "remembered" something that happened yesterday if that event had not occurred. Nor would simple mechanical repetition count as *remembering* similar past events. For human learning at least, some element of remembering seems to be involved. To perform some activity correctly means more than the ability to repeat it in accordance with a rule for that performance. It means to refer the present performance to the past in such a way that it is done *because* the person recalls that this is the way it should be done. The computer that plays chess does not remember anything. The machine cannot make any reference whatsoever to the past. Its behavior and structure are strictly present tense.

It is true, as Ryle points out, that the intelligent man does not always rehearse the reasons for his proper action. This does not means that his memory is not involved in his performance. In hard cases, he may indeed rehearse his reasons for a given action. Even in this type of case, however, Ryle is correct in pointing out that general reflections never add up to understanding without the test of appropriate action. On this he says, "Knowing how to apply maxims cannot be reduced to, or derived from, the acceptance of (general)... maxims."

Human learning then includes both knowing *that* and knowing *how*. Yet, it certainly includes more. A child could not be said to understand (to have learned) that one should keep quiet while others are talking if he was in the habit of interrupting. He might, in a factual sense, know *that* it was not proper. He might also know *how* to remain silent by simply stopping. Until he performed what he knew, until he was *disposed* to remain quiet at appropriate times, he could not be said to have really learned.

Ryle makes another point in this connection. "To perform intelligently," he writes, "is to do one thing and not two things...." Nor is it to do three things: "Being quiet while others speak," shows itself in being appropriately quiet, and when this is fully understood the child simply does it at the right time. He does not rehearse mentally some facts or principles, then invoke his *disposition* to act in this way, and then, at last, quiet down. These things are all of one piece. This does not prevent our discovering by analysis that his activity includes all three things. The reasons are clear: The child may indeed be able (1) to rehearse the rule about being quiet (without being quiet), (2) to show that he can be quiet when he wants to (without being quiet at the proper time), and (3) to demonstrate his disposition to behave in this way by being quiet appropriately. Only the full range of these *knowing* is what we mean by the child understanding that he should be quiet while others speak.

It could also be said that he did not understand what he was doing unless he had some grasp of the meaning of respect for other people, and the conditions for intelligible discourse. Being quiet while others speak is a good rule only in certain settings. To be able to discern the proper setting for invoking the disposition to remain silent is part of understanding the rule. If, for instance, he remained silent during a football game because other people were shouting, we should regard this as odd. Also, in some conversations, if he did not occasionally interrupt to show he understood, his silence might well be misunderstood. Good conversation is not a dialogue of set speeches.

The point of this analysis is that knowing *that* and knowing *how* are closely related in human learning. Also, something more is involved: a disposition to behave in accordance with both knowledge and the rules of activity.

LEARNING DISPOSITIONS

This notion of a *disposition* deserves more attention. Ryle seems to treat a *disposition* as though it were similar to the property of a physical object. To say that the child has the disposition to remain quiet while others are talking, according to Ryle, would be like saying that glass is brittle, that is, it will, under certain conditions, fly into small fragments. Is this, adequate account? I think not.

Intelligent, honest, cheerful, and *proud* are disposition words. Ryle is correct in saying that they imply specific behavior under certain conditions. An *intelligent* persons, given a puzzle, will set to work in such a way as to solve it. So far, *intelligent* would seem to be like *brittle*, but there are some important differences. To learn to be intelligent does not mean to learn a set of automatic responses to set situations, not even to a very large number of set situations. To be intelligent means to understand a whole range of rules of reasons that are relevant in complex ways to uncountable numbers of potential situations. It means to be aware of a standard.

Moreover, it means to value that standard. A person is not intelligent merely because he has the ability to act in reasonable ways. He must also prize rationality. He must want to act reasonably. Without such a positive evaluation of reasonable ways of behaving he will not invoke his ability to be rational. To say that glass has a *disposition* to shatter would be to say that somehow it *wants* to shatter under the appropriate conditions. Learning to be intelligent, then, is to learn a disposition, and learning a disposition is a complex mixture of knowing *that*, knowing *how*, and valuing in certain ways. Valuing is the link between capacity and inclination. Valuing itself deserves more attention, but we must leave this matter until a later chapter where it can be explored more extensively.

LEARNING WHY

Another mode of human understanding is the ability to answer the question *why*. To know facts, to have appropriate skills, even to possess a disposition to perform in certain ways is not a complete account of human learning if one cannot answer *why* questions. *Why* is a complex concept. "Why did the pipes freeze?" might be answered by pointing out that the temperature dropped, or that they were not properly insulated. Another answer might be, "I forgot to drain the system." The later explanation refers to human activity, not to physical laws. Questions like "Why do you regard that as the moral thing to do?" Or, "Why did that happen?"require different Or, "Why does he behave like that" require different kinds of answers appropriate to the logos of that subject matter. Even the person who behaves irrationally has some method in his madness. The search for this *why* lies at the base of psychotherapy, and it is surprising how often the answer turns out to be more like answering the *why* of rational behavior (giving reasons) than answering the *why* to purely physical events (giving causal explanations).

It is important to underscore the point that there is no one answer to *why*. Failure to realize it is the source of many confusions. "Why do you prefer that painting to this one?" is a question that normally calls for a different kind of answer than the question "Why do you like your steak well done?" The latter question might be answered by pointing out that work in a slaughterhouse had taken away one's taste for rare meat, or that when one was a child this was the kind of food one learned to like. Explanations of this kind are often sought to questions about preferences in art, but they are beside the point. A preference for one painting rather than another is generally not a question of personal history, but of knowledge about art. There is nothing odd about being conditioned to like certain foods, but taste in music is not purely a matter of conditioning. In fact, a person who would understand art often must overcome his early conditioning in order to be open to the work itself, to allow the logos of art to determine his judgments. He must learn the *why* that is appropriate to judgments about art.

OTHER SENSES OF LEARN

There are many other modes of learning that deserve analysis. For instance, it is valuable to distinguish the sense of "learning that X is true" from "learning to believe that X is true." As Komisar says, to say "He learned the secrets of the Chancellory" means that he really knew what those secrets were. The notion of *true* is decisive for this kind of learning. On the other hand, to say "He believes that the secrets of the Chancellory are such and such" does not imply that these are indeed the secrets of the Chancellory.

Another kind of learning mentioned by Komisar is "learning to be," as in learning to be a friend. This he correctly calls "learning in the commital sense." There are reasons for questioning the appropriateness of calling the behavior that follows from commitment or decision a result of learning. We may, however, ask an important educational question: Is it possible to teach commitment or decision? Later, we shall examine a variety of teaching proposals, such as: to teach human beings how to relate, how to learn, how to be creative, and so on. Whether or not these can be taught will depend in part upon what we mean by such proposals, and whether that meaning is consonant with what we have learned about teaching.

Later still we have samples analyses of two major concepts in the constellation of education: *teaching* and *learning*. It is time that we turned to the concept of *education* itself.

17

Values for Human Resource Development

An initial difficulty awaits the analytic philosopher who raises the question of values in education. The opinion prevails, not without reason, that critical philosophy tends more to undermine values than to establish them. This opinion finds support in the history of empiricism from Hume to the present. As we saw in the first chapter, the immediate predecessor of ordinary language analysis was logical-empiricism, a view that received popular expression in Ayer's *Language Truth and Logic.* There Ayer relegated value statements, along with metaphysical and religious talk, to the region of subjective feeling. such a view is not auspicious for anyone looking for guidance in sorting out their values, for it says in effect that there is no rationale whatsoever to valuing unless it be sociological or psychoanalytic. As Jawaharlal Nehru once said, "I am strongly attracted to an ethical view of life, but I would find it hard to justify logically." In this opinion, he mirrors the views of empirical philosophers like Bertrand Russell. yet these men would have undoubtedly agreed that no issue is more urgent in present society and education than the status of morality and values.

No major decisions about education can be made without some judgment about what ought to be done. Educators are challenged from the left and right, by the poor, by the blacks and others minorities, and by the young themselves. Traditional values no longer seem adequate and no criteria for making new choices seem compelling. This educational perplexity is a mirror of our bewildered society struggling through a period of serious threats to its very existence.

It, in a day of such conflicting counsel, philosophy can speak only of and about the science, but can say nothing to this perplexity, its usefulness to educators is, to say the least, pitifully limited. In this chapter, I hope to show that recent developments in the analytic tradition are not only congenial to value discussions, but that they have begun to illuminate the rational search for valid criteria. I do not want to exaggerate this claim, nor to suggest anything final about it. Warnock, in his book on *Contemporary Moral Philosophy,* concludes by saying that "This is a subject in which there is still almost everything to be done." Analysis is in a phase of serious investigation of moral questions and the upshot is more a matter of intelligent conjecture than rational assurance. The conjecture is based upon a prediction that as moral language is subjected to clarifying analysis a new respect will be gained for the inherent rationality of evaluation and practical decision making.

VALUE PRESUPPOSITIONS IN EDUCATION

Every human activity presupposes values that are essential to that activity. Science, for instance, presupposes the worth of knowing those things that science discovers. If you deny the proposition that these things are worth knowing, there would be no sense in doing scientific work. Similarly, education presupposes certain principles and values that must be accepted if one is to take education seriously. These principles and values fall into two groups: Those that are inherent to discussion about the school and its curriculum, and those that are inherent to teaching and learning.

Establishing schools, for instance, presupposes that education is doing some kind of good to somebody, benefiting both the young and the society as a whole. Whatever our rationale for these values, this kind of activity makes no sense whatsoever without presupposing this benefit.

The school shares with all social agencies the presumption that their existence is justified by their human effects. They are shot through with values assumptions. The curriculum, in particular, presupposes that it is knowledge most worth having. This is true whether we are talking about skills, humane learning, or science.

This may seem obvious, but it is a very important observation. It follows that if there is no rational foundation to moral deliberations, comparable in some way to the rationale of our scientific deliberations, then the whole enterprise of deciding about social policies is vain, or at least arbitrary. If it is arbitrary, the only final arbiter must turn out to be sheer unprinciple force. In Plato's *Republic,* Thrasymachus argued in exactly this way. What men call "justice," he said, is simply the rule of the strong in their own interest. Socrates countered by pointing out that strong rulers, lacking some kind of principles about values, would not know their real interests and would, therefore, not know what rules to promulgate and enforce.

The point is that sheer power may enable men to enforce their own policies, but it does not illuminate what policies they would really prefer if they knew that was the best for them. Practical deliberation, in short, is impossible without presupposing some rational order of evaluation. Thrasymachus assumed that men already knew what they wanted, and that what they wanted was in their best interests. The history of personal or social decisions un-illuminated by reason is a melancholy record of disillusion.

The second area in which education presupposes values is in the activity of teaching. Teaching, as we have come to view it, assumes that understanding itself is a value of high order. The philosopher John Stuart Mill asked: Which is better, Socrate unsatisfied or a fool satisfied? If we settle for the latter, there would be no reason to teach. Unless knowing is better than being ignorant, why teach? Mill thought that any man who had tasted knowledge and compared it with his former ignorance would naturally prefer to know. The value of understanding certifies itself. There are other values of this kind, truth, beauty, and friendship, for instance. When they are experienced and understood, they are prized above falsehood, ugliness, and loneliness. The fool, said Mill, cannot appreciate such an argument because he is ignorant.

There are other values presupposed in teaching beside the worth of knowing as such. For instance, without freedom there can be no teaching, and if freedom is not prized, teaching becomes impossible. Here are some others; mutual personal respect of teacher and learner, the value of intellectual or physical discipline, and the worth of the subject matter taught. The absence of any of these would preclude the activity of teaching. When, for instance, we teach a youngster to concentrate or to organize his ideas we teach him a value as well as a procedure: the value of a focused and ordered mind. When we teach him to analyse, we presuppose the value of criticism. Writing, speaking,and reading presuppose the value of communications with his fellow in the human community.

So much for the values inherent in the immediate circle of educational activities. Here larger questions remain to be considered. What about moral education? What personal and social values should be taught to the young beyond those inherent in educational activity as such? What rational justification can be given for decision about such questions? This brings us to the larger questions of moral philosophy?

A NEW MORAL PHILOSOPHY

In his essay entitled "Toward a Philosophy of Moral Education," Frankena notes that despite the interest of the recent past in "character education" and "moral spiritual values in education," no really, significant philosophical work on moral education has appeared since the works of Dewey and Durkheim. Fortunately, a generation of analytic philosophers has arisen, of whom Frankena is one, who have ventured beyond the limitations of the earlier skepticism of logical positivism, men like Wisdom, Toulmin, Hampshire, Nowell- Smith, Baier, Aiken, Edward, Melden, and Rawls. These writers, among many others, have tried to clarify the rationale of moral activity. Many of the arguments in this chapter depend upon their work.

Analytic literature on moral philosophy tends to consider separately two different, though related, questions. The first has to do with ethics, with what Baier calls "the moral point of view." The second has to do with values. The logical problems related to these two issues are somewhat different as we shall see.

THE MORAL POINT OF VIEW

Let us examine what is involved in taking a moral point of view. Moral questions arise when there is a conflict of interests among people. If I ask the moral questions. "What should I do?" what I am asking for is valid rules that would settle interest disputes in a reasonable way. There are several things that characterize moral situations. There is first this conflict of interests between two or more people. Unless other people are involved decisions do not involve moral questions, though they may involve values questions. Alone on his island, Robinson Crusoe had value decisions to make, but he had no moral problems until Friday came onto the scene. Before Friday arrived, he had no need of principles to mediate claims between him and anyone else, but he still had to decide how he was going to spend his time—smoking, and drinking coconut beer, meditating like a monk, or cultivating new skills, and so on.

A second feature of moral situations is that judgments must be impersonal. If Crusoe decides to do something to or for his man Friday, it is genuinely moral decision only if he can agree that Friday should do the same to him if their situations were reversed. If he said, "I have just made a moral decision to do X which is only in my interest, but contrary to Friday's interest," a third partly could properly ask, "Would you approve of Friday's making the same kind of decision if your situations were reversed?" If he said, "No," then the proper rejoinder would be, "Then why call it a *moral* decision?"

A third characteristic of moral judgments is universality. Suppose we ask Crusoe, "If two other people in this same situation were to ask your advice on what ought to be done, would you advice one of them in your present situation to do to the other what you intend to do to Friday?" If he said "No," then we would know that he did not understand the meaning of giving moral advice. A *moral decision must be universal in its application.* That is, advice is not moral that advises differently in situations that are in all relevant particulars the same. If may not allow irrelevant differences among people or situations to affect such judgments, Skin color, for instance, is in most cases an irrelevant consideration. If color is pleaded as a reason for a given decision, it is required to show why the color makes some real differences.

Suppose we ask, "But why should I be moral?" Two answers have been suggested to this question. The first is that almost everyone appeals to morality on his own behalf whenever he feels that he has been cheated or dealt with unfairly. He makes his claim as a person in the court of human interest. Once he makes such a claim he has already submitted his interests to the adjudication of moral reflection. He cannot remain rational and ask for moral consideration only when *his* interests have been violated.

The second reason for being moral is suggested by Baier. He says, "We should be moral because being moral is following rules designed to overrule reasons of self-interest whenever it is is in the interest of everyone alike that such rules should be generally follows." Baier's argument is, of course, not a moral argument. Nor should it be, since our question is why we should consider moral arguments in the first place. Baier's appeal is to prudence, not morality. However strong this argument might be, in most cases, it is still possible to reject its conclusion in particular cases without contradiction. Suppose a person had good reason to believe that he could violate moral rules secretly in his own interest, while appearing to everyone to be abiding by those rules. He could then congratulate himself that the effect of his behaviour will be exactly the same as if he had acted morally. If he could steal, for example, without anyone knowing of the theft, then he could benefit from his act without publicly approving of theft. however, he would have to believe that very few members of his society would follow his example, and if they did, he would have to condemn their behavior as immoral.

The only consideration that could prevent this type of evasion would be if the prized personal integrity above prudence.

But the worth of personal integrity cannot be rationally established on the grounds we have considered thus far. This brings us to a further question, whether there is any rational way to establish ideas or priorities among values—among them the value of being moral for its own sake.

So, far then, we have been that morality has its own rationale. Once, the moral point of view of adopted, certain conclusions follow. The only reason given for adopting the moral point of view is one of prudence. Practically speaking, it is of course a very powerful consideration. In a society which sought out wrongdoers so efficiently that violation's of moral rules were promptly punished, this prudential consideration could be a very persuasive one. This was essentially Hobbe's argument for a strong state.

It is time now to examine whether there are valid rational arguments in support of value preferences or ideals. There are good reasons of economy why this question should be avoided if possible. Formal ethical theory is limited to the logic of *sharing* in whatever human beings are interested. It does not attempt to prescribe that in which they ought to be interested. If you try to answer the latter question by saying they should be interested in values that, say, would accrue to the *welfare of human beings,* a great many difficult questions arise. Any such prescription would have to presuppose, among other things, some knowledge of the true nature of being human. It would have to say, for instance, that no human being ought to value the extermination of a race of human beings, that his interest is somehow contrary to the best possibilities of men. Now, this is not far from common sense when it is not under the pressures of war or oppression.

Most of our moral expressions presuppose it. It, however, presuppose that there must be open to inquiry the possibility of giving some rationally defensible ideal description of what a human being ought to be, or what kind of values he would choose if he knew what he was doing.

What follows is nothing like a complete answer to this question, nor is there space to indicate the inquires that are being made into this matter, but it suggests a start on the question.

IS MORALITY PURELY FORMAL

We have seen that the "moral point of view" is a purely formal argument. Morality dictates impartiality, fairness, and universality in the sharing of things thought to be valuable, but it does not give any grounds for deciding which things should be shared in this way. Hare asks us to consider the case of a Nazi officials at a Jewish extermination camp being asked,. "Suppose you discovered that you are a Jew, would you still think what you are doing is right?" If he answered, "Yes, I would still believe that Jews should be be exterminated," then he would have fulfilled the demands of the moral point of view. He would have shown a willingness to be impartial, fair, and universal in his judgment by not making himself an exception. No doubt, very few Nazis would have made this reply, but the fact that it is theoretically possible shows that a purely formal theory or morality has a serious limitation.

Warnock complains of the present status of moral philosophy in this same vein. He asks whether there is not more to the moral point of view than purely formal considerations. In the preceding example, would we say in any ordinary sense that the Nazi official was taking a defensible *moral* position? Is there not, asks Warnock, in moral feeling a sense that somehow what is called for is something that could be called concern for the welfare of human beings is general? This, according to him, is one of those areas yet to be adequately analysed.

Another element in moral sensibility that is not adequately clarified by a purely formal theory of morality is the feeling of what Kant called "unconditioned" or "categorical" obligation. The question might be put as follows: Why does a reasonable man feel the *compulsion* of moral demands? Kant thought that reason alone compelled him. It is a moot question whether the power of a reasoned argument is the same as the categorical obligation of a moral command. Why, for instance, does a person fell very strongly about keeping his promises, so strongly, in fact, if he intends to break them,he offers extensive reasons for doing so. Why is the burden of proof felt so strongly by the promise-breaker? A psychologist might argue that the compulsion is irrational, and he might be right. But in common speech, we certainly distinguish very clearly between the compulsions of the instance and the compunctions of the sane. Moral compunction would seem to be one aspect of mental health. This, too, is a feature of moral language yet to be adequately analyzed. The following discussion may help illuminate part of this question, though not decisively.

THE LOGIC OF VALUES

Let us see whether adequate reasons can be given for preferring one set of interests to another. In the first place, it is clear that *many disputes over values can be settled by empirical means.* That is, the rules of scientific evidence can be used to decide some moral questions. This is true in three classes of value disputes.

(1) Where the value in dispute is a *means* to another value already agreed upon. If, for instance, there is a difference of opinion about the worth of a certain course of action (X) that is alleged to lead to an agreeable result (Y), it is often possible to decide empirically whether, infact, this sort of action has in the past led to such results as Y and whether in the future it is likely to do so.

(2) Empirical methods are also frequently, if not always, decisive in settling disputes over the evaluation of a given situation. In a court trial over an alleged case of negligence, for instance, the court cannot decide whether this is truth an instance of negligence until the facts have been fully explored. The defendant believes that the relevant facts will show him not to be negligent. The prosecution has beliefs to the contrary. The argument is largely a search for the facts—an empirical matter. Of course, in such an argument nonempirical questions will be raised, such as points of law and even philosophical considerations, such as, "Is a person who has just had a heart attack *negligent* when his car then strikes another?" Given agreement on such matters, the judgment of negligence hinges on the facts themselves. This does not mean that every reasonable man would agree that, given that facts, it is without doubt a case of negligence, for *negligence* is not one of the empirical facts. Any person who

disputed there judgment would no doubt search for other facts in support of his difference of opinion.

The point of these remarks is that differences in judgments of value are often not really disputes over values, but over facts, and since we have reliable methods for reaching public agreement on facts, many value disputes can be settled in this way.

One classic instance where an appeal to facts changed the legal and moral evaluation of a social practice is the Supreme Court decision in 1954, on racially "separate but equal" schooling. For sociological reasons, the court found that "separate" in practice always meant "unequal," even where comparable facilities and funding were present. The implication of laws opposed to race mixing in the schools, they held, automatically created a climate inimical to equal educational opportunity. This decision is still disputed, but the dispute has now largely shifted to factual considerations. In this arena, the chances of eventual public agreement are higher than where the dispute is over a difference in value judgments.

To repeat the logic of this argument: Two situations that are exactly alike in every relevant respect must be valued in the same way. Value is not one of the facts of the situation, but the facts of the situation are relevant to a decision about its value. In such cases, it is not correct to say that evaluations are purely subjective.

(3) The third area in which facts are sometimes useful in settling value disputes is when an empirical examination of means-values shows that their cost is greater than the end-value sought. It might be desirable, and even possible, to use means X to attain value Y, but if X turns out in some way to cost more than Y is worth, then reasonable men will decide against X. The United States could have "won" the Vietnam war, for instance, by killing everyone in North Vietnam, but even supposing this did not lead to a larger war, the moral enormity of paying this price does not seem worth such "victory." Or, to use a domestic example, we could no doubt reduce highway mortality to near zero if we enforced a ten mile per hour traffic speed with a death

penalty. In this case the price of the means-value seems too high even though the end-value is highly desirable.

CONSISTENCY IN VALUING

Rationality can be also seen presiding over decisions about value in a second important way, namely, in the application of the rule of consistency. If you can show a reasonable man that his evaluations are inconsistent with one another, he usually will acknowledge that he must modify them in some way to overcome the criticism. The adult with the fourth martini in his hand lecturing the young of drug abuse is not presenting a very impressive argument. The logic of the situation is evident to the young if not to adults. To be consistent without giving up the martini, the argument would have to be changed from "don't drugs" to "use my drug rather than yours."

If education is the cultivation of reason in the student so that he is more capable of understanding himself and his environment, then it would seem that exploring discrepancies like this in our private and public life is a plausible educational acvitity. Lynd's study of the typical American "Middletown" shows that there is plenty of grist for this mill. Here are a few of the value contradictions to which he calls attention: (1) Individualism is a prime value, and "survival of the fittest" is a law of nature that made Americans great. But, people ought tobe charitable, helpful to one another, loyal to the group, and work for common purposes. (2) Democracy is the ultimate form of living together because all men are created free and equal. But, you cannot trust popular votes and some people are "more equal" than others. (3) The family is our basic and most sacred institution. But, business is our most important institution and other institutions must conform to its needs. (4) America is really a "Christian nation." But, a man must make as much money as possible, and religion should stay out of economics and politics. (5) America believes in progress. But, the old tried fundamentals are best. people who desire change are suspected of being the dupes of foreign radicals.

Neither a society nor a person enjoys having such contradictions pointed out, but it is fatuous to suppose that rationally cultivated mind can overlook such tasks. This philosophical consideration is supported by the sociological fact that societies tend in varying degrees to be *systems* of values articulated through its various institutions. If the tensions among its values is too great, the society itself is in peril.

RULES FOR DECISION AMONG VALUES

A third way in which rationality presides over the activity of valuing lies in the way in which certain rules have emerged from the practice of reflective evaluation. These rules have been a part of values studies since Bentham and have been elaborated by his successors. For instance, a fruitful or fertile value is better than a sterile one. Other things being equal, a reasonable man will always choose a value that leads on to other values over one that is sterile of future satisfactions. The classical virtues, such as temperance and rationality, are fruitful in this way. Another rule is that a durable value, one that lasts a long time, is preferable to a short-run value. For much the same reason, a more intense and/or extensive value is preferable to a tepid or a narrowly applicable one.

To be sure, these rules are not always easy to apply in practice, and they do not constitute (as Bentham thought) a simple calculus of values, but in general they are often relevant considerations in any value dispute. What I mean by saying that they cannot be put into a simple calculus is illustrated by the fact that there is, for instance, no rule for preferring intensity to duration.

THE FINAL TEST IDEALS AND VALUES

It would be wrong to assume that if the preceding assertions about reason in evaluation were true, values could be established by straigtforward arguments alone. There is no way to make a value conclusions the inevitable result of a logical argument. When we desire to "prove" to someone else that an ideal or a value is authentic or valid for him. we may make many of the foregoing moves and still fall short of a demonstration. The final decision will have to be made by the person himself when he "sees" that you are right.

Take, for instance, the effort to demonstrate that a given painting is beautiful. If the person you are persuading does not see that it is beautiful, there are a number of things you can do. You can talk about its design, its agreeable composition, its symbolic significance, and so on, but the painting must somehow "show" itself to the viewer, establish its own value in his eyes. In this case, arguments are a complex kind of showing, first from this angle, then from that, but the conclusion must be "seen."

In the same way, an ideal, such as a democratic society, incorruptible personal integrity, or the values of becoming a knowledgeable person, and so on, cannot be logically drive home to anyone. However, these ideals and values can be displayed so carefully and so fully compared with their alternatives that it is reasonable to believe that most men, given time and attention, would come to approve them.

A LOGIC OF MAKING VALUE DECISIONS

Many of the foregoing observations about the role of reasons in moral and value judgment find their natural context in practical decision making. *Scientific* decisions are made by a happy combination of logic and sense observations. Such decisions have a high standing in our judgment because they tend toward public agreement. Can anything comparable be said about practical decision making? Before scientific logic was known and widely accepted, men made factual judgment that were as much disputed as present day value judgments. Perhaps (we should recognize that it represents a kind of faith judgment), if we explored the area of the practical deliberation with the same dedication that we have brought to cognitive deliberation, we could bring about a morel general agreement on major value choices. At the very least, we would be clearer about what is really at dispute. Coming to know and coming to value are not the same thing, but they have analogous structures.

This change in the focus of inquiry from the logic of values to the logic of practical decisions (valuing) promises a possible solution to some of the logical puzzles of past discussion. Aristotle long ago insisted upon the distinction between theoretical reason oriented to *knowing something* and practical reason oriented to *deciding what to do* about something.

The difference is important. Aristotle searched for the highest good (summum bonus), and in modern times. Moore explored the meaning of *good* itself, but this is to treat values as objects of theoretical reason. It is when we turn to practical reason, to the business of deciding and evaluating, that we discover the context in which values appear. *Value* in this context becomes a classification word for modes of valuing rather than a substantive noun for some *thing* in the world. To search for the properties of this alleged *thing* has not been as helpful as philosophers hoped. It turns out, as we have seen from the discussion of the *Taxonomy,* that there may be a logic to deciding, just as there is a logic to knowing. It is in this context of asking. "What must I do?" rather than asking "What can I know?" that the logic of evaluation is made most clear.

DECISION MAKING

Here is one analysis of what goes on in making a decision. Much of it is a development of Dewey's "Five Steps of Thought," and shows at once some of the parallels between knowing and deciding.

1. The first stage in decision making is a problematic situation. If this is a *knowing* situation, as in a scientific puzzle, the pattern is a cognitive one. If it is *practical* situation, then it calls for moral and value directives. It is *problematic* because there are no ready to hand solutions. The first thing to clarify is the problem itself. Why is it felt as a problem? What is unsatisfactory? What values are threatened or desired that are no present? Why are customary solutions unsatisfactory? Such clarification also needs analytic reasoning to resolve questions concerning the meaning of the concepts involved.

2. The second stage requires two moves: a factual one and an evaluative one. We must answer such questions as these: (a) What needs to be known in order to solve the problem? How can I find out? What biases are at work in making these factual inquires? How do things look from different perspective? (b) What principles are relevant? Are they consistent with one another? Can we agree on them? What values are at stake? What kind of priority can we give to them? Are they consistent with one another? Are compromises possible?
3. The third stage of decision consists in formulating possible solutions. Here a new set of questions is asked: How do the respective proposals satisfy the various interests that are at stake? Are they fair? Are there other solutions that would be more value inclusive and fairer? Other questions similar to those asked in stage two are also relevant: What are the likely *factual* consequences of each alternative? What ideals, principles, and values are stage in each of the proposals? Who will be hurt and who helped by them? Lastly,. what wider significance would such a solution have beyond the immediate context of the problem at hand?
4. Finally, the decision itself. Decision is not like the conclusion of a formal argument. What would count as a reasonable decision follow from the deliberation, but it is not conclusive. Reasonable men might differ, but there is a range beyond which they would not differ. The conclusion does indeed follow from the argument; it is not just a whimsical addition to it. The reasons for this are apparent. First, the whole process is very complex and requires problematic arrangements of values, differences among relevant ideals, and orders of priority in principles. In the nature of the case, this kind of thing is not as neat as mathematics. Second, practical deliberation prophesies a probable future not a certain one. There is bound to be an element of risk in such a prophesy.

Thus, *deciding* is not the same as concluding. To conclude that such and such is a wise course is not the same as deciding to follow it.

Decision making, then, has a logos, a rationale that can be taught. Teaching this logos is not the same as passing judgment on particular issues, nor is it the same as deciding to act in particular ways.

With all its defects, it can be safely said that the habit of reflection on decision making is likely to lead, in the long run, to more satisfactory results than other alternatives available to us. Also, it is the one method that can hope to make the grounds for decisions publicly known and debated.

THE LOGIC OF LEARNING VALUES

So far in this chapter two things have been noted: First, education presupposes values. Second, value talk and decision making have a rationale that qualifies them as something that can be taught. These conclusions are somewhat novel in the setting of modern empiricism though they are gaining support from the current analyses of moral and value language. Henry David Aiken, urging the importance of this element in education writes that "the concept of knowledge has been so badly misanalysed and misconceived in our western philosophical tradition that it might almost be better to say that the business of the learner is more with feeling or volition or sensibility than with something called 'cognition'." I agree with the sense of his remark, but it must be added that as long as *feeling* and *volition* are looked upon as merely arbitrary personal matters, devoid of any rationale, an emphasis upon them could be a way of embracing a simple irrationalism. The burden of this chapter so far as been to show that feeling and volition have a a rationale even if it is not the rationale of scientific cognition.

Only if this is the case can we talk about evaluation. I contend that values sensibility is not essentially more subjective than cognitive learning. Nicholas Rescher, in his *Introduction to Value Theory,* shows some interesting parallels.

Cognitive	*Evaluative*
Belief	Valuing or desire
Correctness of belief	Correctness of valuing or desire
Believes to be true	Valued or desired
Actually true	Valuable or desirable

One thing noteworthy about this chart is that the concepts of *valuable* and *desirable* are not the same as simply *desired*. There may be such a thing as wrong desire just as there is such a thing as incorrect belief. Some thinkers go astray at this point by repeating Mill's famous fallacy of equating *desirable* with *being desired*. There is no contradiction in saying that you desire something undesirable. Or, conversely, you may not desire to learn, for instance, but it may be desirable that you do so. Authentic values, then, are in part the fruit of reflection.

A final critical word. Both Rescher and Bloom assume an atomic beginning to value learning, leading to more wholistic appreciation at a later stage. However, there is a counterhypothesis that should also be explored, the hypothesis that no value is ever notices or acted on that does not *at the very fast* belong, in some dim way at least, to one's overall perception of life—his *implicit* "philosophy of life." I suspect that value learning goes both ways. The child inherits culturally some perspective on life from his earliest years.

He brings this to school with him. he may change this perspective as he learns, but it remains as an active element in his learning experience. This is the reason why a ghetto child, for example, often finds the values of middle-class society difficult to understand or even boring and uninteresting. His world is different even at the age of six. The teacher who wants to breakthrough this barrier must understand the world-orientation of his pupil, and present values to him that make some sense in terms of his implict world view. What I am saying is that the learning of evaluation may move from whole to part just as much as from part to whole.

This counterhypothesis does not impair the conclusion we have already reached, namely, that there is a rationale in value-learning. Whether it is from part to whole or from whole to part, or both together, the same conclusion follows: Learning to value is not a random affair, it has a rationale of its own, a rationale that places it within the proper sphere of learning as an activity of understanding.

ARE MORAL CHOICES AND DECISIONS ABOUT VALUES RELATIVE?

The person who expects philosophical analysis to offer a logic of moral judgment and evaluation that leads to certainty and a set of absolute will feel disappointed at the tentativeness of our conclusion. We have, indeed, arrived at a kind of relativism. Is such a conclusion of value to educators? I believe it is.

This relativism is not the same as scepticism. It does not say that one choices is as good as another or that some values are not better than others. Within limits, there are the kinds of choices reasonable men would make. Moreover, the longing for an absolutism that haunts this inquiry, is after all, a will-o'- the-wisp. In the past, there have been, to be sure, systems of absolute rules and value prescriptions. In practice, however, two things have occurred. Either these absolutes were amended to allow exceptions, or they were simply ignored. The commandment against killing, for instance, was amended to exclude criminals or foreign enemies. Killing in self-defense, for instance, was allowed, and so on.

Perhaps more practically, there is no set of absolutes that may be used as the basis of instruction in public schools. If such a doctrinaire ethic were offered simply as a set of divine imperative without rational content, then they could not, on our premises, even be out rational content, then they could not, on our premises, even be *taught,* they would have to be indoctrinated. The law furthermore prohibits the domination of the public school curriculum by any dogmatically guaranteed moral teaching. In any case, the great majority of today's citizens simply will not accept any such dogmatic moral code. Even those who remain faithful to the churches in which these codes had their origins are asking for reasons.

Finally, it can be pointed out that thought rational deliberation is relative, there are many principles and values that have a great deal of stability. Like the "enabling beliefs" that we described earlier such values as truth or goodwill are so fruitful in so many situations, and so flexible in their aplication to any conceivable new situation, that their chances of being repudiated by further inquiry are slim indeed. As Rescher says, "it is unlikely to the point of inconceivability that many of our historic social and personal values—'justice,' 'intelligence,' 'kindness,' to give just three examples—could ever, under any realistically foreseeable circumstances, lie open to valid negative criticism."

WHAT ABOUT RELIGION AND WORLD-VIEWS

A special problem for public education arises from the close relationship that world-view have to evaluation. Hare, in his work *The Language of Morals,* writes that "if pressed to justify a decision completely, we have to give a complete specification of the way of life of which it is a part." Though this complete specification is impossible to give in practice, he says, "the nearest attempts are those given by the great religions...."

A man's *religion* is his most general life-orientation, his steady estimate about what is real and valuable. In this sense, philosophical naturalism is as much a *religion* as Roman Catholicism. American law does not permit the public schools to support the establishment of any religion whatsoever. Therefore, it cannot be the trustee of any one world-view. Does this final barrier prevent the teaching of values in the schools? In answer several distinction need to be made.

First, the schools cannot represent any single world-view of either secular or official *religion.* There is no dispute about that, and even if it were not against the law, in pluralistic democracy, there would be no fair way to determine what the official view should be.

Though the schools cannot teach such world-views, they can teach *about* them. Public education may reasonably offer the student an appreciation of the various live options that human beings face in the modern world. Fortunately, a new teacher need not espouse a world-view to understand and appreciate it. Teaching *about* world-view should include a comparison of difference and similarities. It is important for student who will be choosing one or another of such life-style to have some appreciation for the decision of others. In a democracy, this is the only way they will be able to work together for the common welfare without mutual suspicion and destructive conflict.

The effect of a national dialogue on such matters could also have a salutory effect on the organizations that represent these respective faiths. The mere fact of entering a dialogue of reason and imaginative sharing should incline rival faiths to develop a more adequate and publicly agreeable account of their own faith.

Finally, it may be noted that though values have their final synthesis in some world view, they are also often rooted in the common life with its common interests and problems so that agreement can often be reached at this level even when there are differences at a *higher* level. At present, for example, a substantial segment of Roman Catholic thought supports the basic premises of American democracy in agreement with the thought of both Protestants and Deweyan naturalists. Even group postulates its own metaphysical support for a common value, and that can only mean a wider consensus on an important public concern.

A FINAL WORD ABOUT VALUES IN EDUCATION

Looking back over the argument of this chapter, it occurs to me that I have been eager to make a case for the rationality of evaluation that despite many cavils I have not made enough of the complexities involved.

Social phenomena as a whole may be viewed as a kind of pyramid, of which the economy and socio-economic relationships form the base. At its apex, are a world view and its value system (reflected in the prevailing education system) which gave, or try to give, a meaning to the whole range of human experience. This value system may be a derivative of the world view put forward by influential social philosophers of the country and the period, or may be just a conglomerate of adhocisms devised by the dominant or ruling class. Further, when a society is basically heterogeneous, it is reflected in different sets of value system being bundled together in social thought or in education.

The terrain of evaluation is very complex, and philosophers have differed with one another about how it should be mapped. Some have emphasized moral values, others have argued that rules derive from such utilitarian principles as the greatest good of the greatest number. There is no single kind of argument to be used in a given case, but it is interesting that each of these philosophical points of view serve no illuminate some aspect of the good life. Stoicism, for instance, clarifies the kinds of principles that are our best resort when we are faced with circumstances that cannot be changed but must be endured with dignity. Pragmatism, on the other hand, illuminates procedures that are reasonable when problems can be resolved. Idealism often holds up values that are obscured bỳ utilitarians, and utilitarians demonstrate the power of many common and pedestrian values to bring about agreement in moral disputes. The merit of ordinary language analysis is that it can use the insights of these various schools as they are embodied in our linguistic usage. It keeps us from opting for implausible claims that outrage the wisdom embodied in our common speech and create a forum for the various trends of moral discussion.

The pluralistic nature of moral reflection strongly suggests the truth of Wittgenstein's remarks about a common family of meanings related in diverse ways rather than any single theory structured like geometry. At the present stage of philosophy, the rationale of moral decision making could very well commend itself to the educator.

The point is that there is a logic which defines simplification into a single set of rules or principles, but which can operate in practice to make choosing more rational. New observations and experiences will no doubt bring forth fresh principles or a vision of new values, allowing previous decisions to be amended and made more adequate. Adequacy, in this context, is tested in the satisfactoriness of human life itself, in human enrichment and enlargement.

Since man's experience grows—and men grow with it—this enlargement is natural if not inevitable. it is not merely a random or whimsical affair. We can, without too much wisdom, see the difference between growth and deterioration in the choices that men make. Human maturity takes many forms, but most of them are recognizably superior to immaturity, though they may not all be equally meritorious. Inquiry into which forms of maturity are most fully human does not imply uncertainty about the value of maturity as such, and the dialogue among reasonable men about the various ideals of human existence should serve only to enlarger and elevate them.

There is no reason, despite our contemporary perplexities, for giving in to skepticism or a moral nihilism which is usually a prelude to a despairing reliance on some dogmatic or narrow morality. If educators can bring themselves to deal with moral matters, calling upon other disciplines to support them in that task, there is at least prospect that new generations of students disciplined in the rationale of evaluation might add a new dimension to the common life.

18

Democracy and Human Resource Development

To talk about analytic philosophy in education without dealing with the concept of *democracy,* insofar as it has a bearing on educational concepts, would be to ignore one of our deepest national concerns. America has big commitments to both democracy and education, and we have yet to see clearly how these commitments relate to one another. It would be a mistake, however, to suppose that philosophy in the analytic vein can function as advocate for programs or wise advisor on vexing problems. Its role must be more modest: that of a logical conscience continually seeking the clarification of meanings, exposing presuppositions, or showing the relationships between ideas.

WHAT IS "DEMOCRACY"

An analytic answer to this question can neither begin nor end with abstract definitions of democracy. A good example of the analysis for which we are looking is to be found in Peters' *Ethics and Education*. Peters argues that defining democracy simply as "rule of the people" is too vague and has little substantive meaning outside of some actual social system. A better approach, he suggests, is to examine the recent history of existing Anglo-American democracies and note their presuppostions. These systems came into being primarily as the result of a determination by the people of England and America not to be subject to arbitrary political authority. Peters says of the American Constitution, for example, that it is "one of the greatest monuments to rationality in the history of man," that it "represents an elaborate attempt to provide effective government within a system of checks and balances that were meant to safeguard the rights of individuals and of minorities against the possible tyranny of both the executive and the popular assembly." In this, the Constitution is a descendent of the Magna Carta and other English institutions.

The presuppositions of the institutions that emerged out of these historical developments could be said to constitute the constellation of meanings that we call "democracy" in the Anglo Saxon tradition. What are some of these presuppostions? (1) The first is that authority is conditional. (2) A second presuppostion follows from this conditional acceptance of authority: a commitment to rational discussion in the process of making political decisions. Rational discussion in this context means something like what we have called the process of moral deliberation.

(3) It follows from the nature of such decision making that it cannot be assimilated to a mere polling of personal interests. If democracy were merely government by the wishes of a majority, some kind of computerized polling of interests could conceivably tabulate it better than the voting procedures presently used by democratic societies. However, a rule of majority wishes would be as arbitrary in its way as the will of an absolute sovereign. What is implied in Anglo-American democracy is something else: public *deliberation* on policy with a considered *judgment* as the conclusion. Such judgments, says Peters, cannot be spun out of the purely abstract concept of "the rule of the people."

(4) These procedures of *advise* and *consent* presuppose another condition, namely, some safeguards for the public expression of opinion, a freedom of the spoken and written word and voluntary assembly. If there were no such freedom, it would be vain to talk of consultation.

(5) Decision by consultation presupposes, moreover, some further procedures for public accountability. A democratic gov-

ernment must be kept constantly responsive to the process of consultation and judgment. That is to say, in principle, the government must be subject to change in an orderly manner. Democracy institutionalizes the process of governmental change so that the costly process of revolution may become unnecessary. This presupposes (6) that the people understand the nature of their government well enough so that there is a minimal consensus on procedural principles. Without agreement on fairness, respect for persons, the importance of considering everyone's interests, however bizarre, co-operation with other citizens, even those with which one disagrees and the appeal to reason, public discussions would degenerate into propaganda and abuse. Perhaps, *understanding* is not an adequate term for this. One might almost say that we are talking about a popular *disposition* to participate in democratic processes in accordance with its rules.

These are then the presuppositions imminent in Anglo-American democratic institutions as they have developed concretely. Because this *democracy* emerged historically, it would appear likely that these procedures may not be imitated easily by peoples who have not had similar historical experiences. They are rational for people with a specific history, but they are not considered rightly as abstract ideals.

FURTHER PRESUPPOSITIONS OF DEMOCRACY

The foregoing discussion begins with the concrete historical institutions of Anglo-Saxon countries. It cannot be denied, however, that discussion of *democracy* in a wider sense have been going on since Plato. They raise some general philosophical questions that deserve some attention, particularly since they are part of current popular views on the subject.

The first concerns a doubt that human beings are capable of self-government. Plato's contempt for democracy as a "great beast" is still shared by many. Is the ideal of self-government unrealistic? We have seen that it is probably unrealistic without some propitious form of historical experience, but the wider question is one concerning human nature itself. Does democracy presuppose that men are more ideal than they actually are? Some of its defenders have made themselves vulnerable to this charge, but an accurate account of what self- government presupposes is somewhat more sober.

Self-government does not presuppose ideal men. It presupposes that no men are good enough to be trusted with unchecked power over other men. It denies there could be a group of men who could qualify in wisdom and goodness as Plato's philosopher kings. This is a presupposition of limits to general human wisdom and benevolence. It agrees with the axiom that power corrupts and absolute power corrupts absolutely.

Anglo-Saxon institutions, built upon the strategy of the separation of powers, and a continuous series of checks and balances, takes this weakness into account. It requires for every great power a countervailing power that will keep it from becoming tyrannical. This general proposition does not tell us what actual powers men ought to have, but only that they may not be trusted too far. It does not solve the practical problem that can emerge when the powers of a society are so counter balanced that necessary action cannot be taken, or taken in time. Reasonable principles do not absolve men from the work of forging viable institutions that ex-emplify those principles.

There is a counterproposition that is also part of the democratic creed, namely, that men are wise enough and good enough to make collective judgments about their welfare. There is no proof of this. It is simply a presupposition of this form of social life. If it is not true, however, the minimum degree of mutual trust, forebearance, and reasoned cooperation necessary for social existence will fail to materialize. Again, fortuitous social history may make this more likely at one time than at another. The minimum consensus may not be possible at certain junctures of history. These periods will inevitably run the risk of the unchecked misuse of power. It may be presumed that one of the tasks properly assigned to the schools of a democracy is the education of citizens with at least minimum qualifications for administering its major institutions.

Democracy, then, does not presuppose a utopian view of human nature. It presupposes that men are neither angels nor devils, but that they are capable at times of approximating both. Men can approximate moral rectitude and objective rationality in making judgments about the conflicts of human interests, but none of them is so free from the limitations of his own perspective that he can see everywhere equally. The possession of unchecked power reduces a person's need to consider the interests of others and therefore, to that degree, the likelihood of attaining impartiality in vision and judgment. Democracy is thus a theory of social organization that claims to approximate the nature of men as they actually are. It may strain their virtues, but it does not depend upon their perfectibility.

Democracy also presupposes some rationale to evaluation, some difference between desires and the desirable, between wishes and wisdom. Reliable values are not, as we contended in the last chapter, matters of mere subjective prejudice. They are capable of improvement if not perfection by rational determination. Philosophers who argue that democracy presupposes that there are no rational standards of moral or value deliberation are, I think, mistaken. This claim rests upon the argument that where there are no such standards, there is no reason to impose a system of values on anyone who does not agree with it. So far so good, but if there are no rational procedures for settling claims between conflicting groups, to what arbiter may men turn. If not to persuasive deliberation, it appears that arbitrary power becomes the only alternative. A society with no faith in deliberation could, at best, attain some kind of uneasy compromise depending upon the power of a given group to impose its will on the final determination. Such a society would become an arena of a power struggle unmitigated by any rational considerations except self-interest. Hans Reichenbach, who has argued for this view, might reply that, unfortunately, this is the way it is. This argument underestimates the case that can be made for reason in matters of morals and values. Reichenbach's view is a natural product of the positivism of the thirties and suffers from the limitations of that philosophical position.

This leads us into one of the difficulties inherent in any view of democracy that equates the voice of the people with the voice of God or the voice of truth. In cognitive matters, we know that this is not true. Legislatures or referendums cannot determine matters of fact, they can only register the prejudiced decision of majorities, but neither can majorities automatically determine warrantable judgments of value. Only rational deliberations can hope to reach such judgments. This means that whereas decisions will have to be made in some way responsive to agreements to which we have referred or democracy turns into the "Great Beast" of popular and ignorant opinion which Plato so rightly feared. Such a democracy may execute a Socrates or order the cremation of a racial minority. America is even now torn between a majority prejudice against her black citizens and her traditional institutions of democratic impartiality. Only if the majority of citizens is educated in the meaning implicit in her traditional institutions can this issue have any chance of a favorable outcome.

EDUCATION IN A DEMOCRACY

What would characterize a democratic educational system? Two things immediately suggest themselves: Education universally distributed and democratically organized. Neither of these was apparent to our immediate predecessors who fostered an education for the elite, governed by the elite. The elite in this case is the upper middle class who conceived of education in their own terms.

At the present time, these two democratic claims in education have come to the fore, not without dispute. The basic claim appears to be unanswerable. Any educational system that calls itself democratic may not exclude any minority from its benefits. Nor would we call it democratic if those involved in the system did not have some share in the decisions about how the system functions. Advise and consent must prevail in education as in politics.

Furthermore, almost as obvious is the fact that, as Peters says, "Without education an individual in a modern industrial society is unlikely to be able to proceed very far in developing the particular aspect of a worthwhile form of life to which he is suited; also an education system acts selectively in equipping citizens with skills and knowledge that are essential to the community's viability and development." On the one hand, if the individual is to be given the opportunity to fulfill his own life, he must have access to the education he needs. On the other, society cannot function without skilled and knowledgeable citizens. This latter notion includes the fact that we noted a moment ago: Democracy is not viable as a social system without citizens who understand its institutions and values and who are disposed to abide by the principles implicit in them. One of the larger tasks of education in a democracy is thus the creation of the rational consensus on what Maritain calls the "democratic charter." This does not mean, as Maritain points out, that everyone has to agree on a philosophy justifying these principles.

I have said "rational" consensus because education could not create this agreement by indoctrination or conditioning without ceasing to be an educational enterprise. It can reach for consensus only by bringing students to understand the principles and values involved and showing the inherent rationality of such a view of our common life. This consonance between the concepts of *teaching* and *educating*, as we have come to view them, and the *democratic charter* has been noted by Scheffler. He points out that although every culture has to renew itself through some kind of collective effort or die, it is not the case that it will necessarily do so through *teaching* in the standard sense. "To favor the widest diffusion of teaching as a mode and as a model of cultural renewal," Scheffler writes, "is, in, fact, a significant social option of a fundamental kind, involving the widest possible extension of reasoned criticism to the culture itself."

Democracy implies the possibility of large-scale change through public deliberation, a deliberation that cannot, in the nature of the case, be merely a head-count of personal interests. To quote Scheffler again: "To support the widest diffusion of teaching as a model of cultural renewal is, in effect, to support something that poses a threat to culture whose basic social norms are institutionally protected from criticism." We have already noted that such a concept of education is not consistent with the kind of societies that emerged under Hitler and Stalin. This is a logical point. Cultural renewal through education, in our sense, presupposes something like an open democratic society, and, conversely, a democratic society presupposes the education of its citizens in the rationality of deliberation that is at the heart of *teaching*.

AUTHORITY

The problem of authority arises in education at three levels: (1) Where should authority over the whole system be vested? (2) What kind of authority can be justified in the local school? (3) What is the authority of the teacher?

The answer to the first question is clear: In the people. If an educational system is to be democratic, it must be responsive to their needs and desires. However, we meet the same problem that the American founding fathers faced with the Congress. If governmental policy was to represent considered judgment, not merely the momentary wish of a majority, then rational deliberation must somehow intervene between the act of consulting interests and determining policy. The same can be said of the people's control of education. Direct popular participation in educational decisions has not been altogether salutary in American communities. It has often taken the form of popular pressure against experimental or controversial programs. Often the result has been counter educational.

Two things are required: a forum where educational policies may be debated in a rational way and a corp of responsible educators who will carry out educational policy in the light of that debate. Forming such institutions is not a philosophical affair. The following principle would seem to commend itself: Educational policy decisions should be placed neither too near the local school nor too far away. If it is too near, then the school is subject to the whim of every pressure group. If it is too far, then the popular interest will not be a significant component in the decisions. The present dogma that the local community should have control over the local school deserves critical reevaluation in the light of this principle. A school whose curriculum is merely the whim of local pressure groups is unlikely to be an educational institution. If there is no consultation with the local community, it will not be a democratic school system. What is needed is an arrangement that assures maximum consultation coupled with a maximum of rational deliberation before educational decisions are made.

AUTHORITY IN THE LOCAL SCHOOL

The second question, regarding the control of the local school itself, is also a proper concern for an educational system that calls itself democratic. The local school is not democratic if all the decisions about the conduct of teachers and students are made by a powerful principal. This is a surprisingly widespread practice. Where this is the case, the life of a school takes on the complexion of a prison run by an authoritarian warden. To be sure, a principal must be responsible for directing the institution, but he need not have the authority of a dictator. Students and teachers alike should be regularly consulted on the rules that control their miniature society. The consultation must be real. If debate is held only to discover that the principal has made the decision in advance, the result will be cynicism and rebellion on the part of both teachers and students.

A democratically run school would allow students considerable latitude in making the rules that control their behavior. Surely, teachers can be trusted to agree on the rules that should prevail concerning their own behavior while on the premises. If these freedoms are not observed, for what kind of democracy are the students being prepared? It is also a fact that the climate of such an authoritarian institution will very likely be restive and unfriendly, a climate not conducive to learning. The student will, furthermore, come to associate learning with an oppressive atmosphere from which he longs to escape. Compulsory attendance will have already contributed its bit to this feeling, almost like a jail sentence, and must be consciously offset by the strategy of democratic participation and freedom. The teacher in turn will dislike playing the role of policeman and lose his zest for teaching. What must happen in teaching cannot be compelled in either the teacher or the learner. The more the atmosphere is one of congenial cooperation and agreement, the better the chance of exciting teaching and of awakening the student's understanding.

Again, philosophy cannot propose the means to this happy possibility. All that analysis can do is to clarify the issues at stake. The solutions will always be relative to the kinds of teachers, administrators, and students in the school, coupled with the type of community in which it is set.

THE AUTHORITY OF THE TEACHER

There is no question but that the teacher must exercise authority of some kind. Leaving aside the question of his responsibility for order in his own classroom, let us examine his authority as a teaching agent. He should, of course, know more than his students about the subject he is teaching. His authority here is derived from his professional mastery of the knowledge relevant to that subject. One would expect from this a certain deference on the part of the student to the teacher, but the teacher's authority is a derived authority. It does not follow from the mere fact that the teacher is the teacher and the student is the student. It derives from the warranted findings in the subject being taught. This means that whenever the teacher decides some matter by virtue of his being an authority, the student has the right to ask why the decision was made in this way. A *teacher* must be able to give reasons. If he stifles questions, he conveys a false impression of his role and teachers a wrong-headed obedience on the part of the student. In today's environment, this response may very likely lead the student to reject the teacher's authority in toto, unless he has been trained to render unquestioning and obedient responses to commands. This could hardly be said to prepare a student for participation in a democracy, to say nothing of preparing him in the subject matter being taught.

I have urged that teaching lead the learner to understand and to respect his own powers of understanding. The needs of democracy underscore this even more. Therefore, a teacher must open the opportunity for students to question him and allow debate on why he says the things he does. Sometimes a teacher does not know the answer to a given question and thinks that if he admits as much, he will undermine his authority. The opposite is the case. Ignorance may be an invitation to group inquiry. It gives him the chance to say that he will re-examine what he has said. He need not apologize for not being omniscient. He may cite authorities to support what he has taught and yet admit that even this does not settle the question with finality. In *teaching*, there is no finality, though there is usually evidence that will satisfy a reasonable questioner.

Sometimes even after standard authorities are examined, the question is still not settled completely. This is an occasion to make the student aware that the answers are not complete, and that the student himself may add to the store of human learning if he is willing to prepare himself for the task. Education does not mean to find all the answers, but to discover how men come by answers that seem warrantable to them. Any given knowledge claim is not infallible, it is a rationally assured claim that is infinitely better than the opinion of the ignorant. This temper of mind is itself good training for democracy for it creates an open mind at the same time that it teaches practical commitment. We cannot but commit ourselves to what we now believe to be warrantable knowledge, but we can still be open to further questions and the possibility upon some later occasion to change our commitments.

The hope of a *teacher* is to produce a student capable of critical thought. We need not concern ourselves further with this notion as we have discussed the question of the meaning of *critical thinking* in several places. There is, however, a related question that needs clarification, namely, the teaching of controversial subjects.

TEACHING CONTROVERSIAL SUBJECTS

At first sight the teaching of controversy would seem to upset the necessary democratic consensus. If we look deeper, we discover that democratic consensus is not the same as agreement on specific policies or programs. The consensus that supports a democratic society is agreement on the democratic charter, the charter that calls for freedom, deliberation, fairness, and so on. That consensus is quite consistent with—and even productive of—controversy. It is in controversy that the charter is tested and made evident.

In a democratic society, the student may not be indoctrinated into agreement. A student must understand the charter and agree to disagree with others in the spirit of that charter. This opens a whole range of disagreements on social programs, political parties, and even religions, but in a fruitful way. It proceeds by rules that give men some hope of living with their disagreements and of resolving many of them.

Nor is this utopian. If the school sticks with the consensus of the community at the level of politics and program, it will, in the long run, nourish irrational outbreaks of strife in the life of the community itself. Only if the citizens understand the spirit of democratic disagreement—a disagreement that challenges every way in which things might be done—can irrational strife be minimized. The idea of democracy as aversion to irrational authority carries with it the commitment to controversy. Almost everything we have proclaimed as central to the educational enterprise supports the alliance of education and a society of intellectual openness, continual re-examination, and rational deliberation. This is in everyman's interest though he may not know it.

Democracy implies that no one man or faction sees everything there is to see. Conservatives remind us of the richness of the past, and liberals remind us of the danger of resting complacently in the present. Dialogue among men of different perspectives is the very life of a democratic society. One obligation of the school is to make this clear to generations of future citizens. As soon as the conservative brands the liberal as a subversive radical, or the liberal abuses the conservative as a fascist reactionary, then the charter of democracy begins to give way to something entirely different.

EQUALITY AND QUALITY IN EDUCATION

Another problem facing the democratic educator is how to reconcile equality with quality in education. In his book *Excellence*, John Gardner asks, "Can we be equal and excellent too?" He places in opposition two aphorisms acceptable to our culture: "All shall equal be." "Let the best man win." He cites Merle Curti on the Jacksonian era when equalitarianism reached absurd heights: "The democratic faith further held that no special group might mediate between the common man and truth, even though trained competence might make the difference between life and death. Thus in the West, even licensing of physicians was lax because not to be lax was apt to be thought undemocratic." The problem lies at the heart of the democratic charter: on the one hand, equality and the commonweal, on the other hand, the person and his achievement. Actually, they are both needed. Without achievement on the part of individuals, without allowing the talented to rise and exercise their excellence, society itself would be deprived of the riches that come from those talents, but this is bought at the price of equality. Carried too far, a society is in danger of becoming elitist rather than democratic. A solution, if a dialectical tension can be called that, lies in moderating both the notion of equality and the notion of competitive achievement. "In its moderate forms," writes Gardener, "equalitarianism prohibits ruthlessness in the strong, protects the weak from wanton injury and defines certain areas of equality which must not be transgressed, but does not seek altogether to eliminate individual differences or their consequences." The common man understands this in sports, but the hard task is to make it applicable to economic competition, politics, and in the other areas of social life.

The historical alternative to *achieved* status has always been *hereditary* status. The latter is in contradiction to democracy. Achieved status means a mobility upward for talent wherever it appears. In its raw form, it became, in nineteenth- century America, a crude social Darwinism. The point seems to be that a democracy dare not lose either achievement through performance or equality.

The problem of achieved status and the competition of ability lies chiefly in the fact that everyone in each generation does not start from the same place. In education, the culturally disadvantaged child generally cannot compete with his more advantaged colleagues regardless of his innate talents or capacities. Early in the game, he may become disheartened and drop out of the race altogether. Special classes for the disadvantaged may not seem like equality, but they are based manifestly on erasing an inequality that is present at the earliest stages of education. If society itself were not plagued by inequalities of income, housing, and so on, the school might not be faced with the problem. If education is to be democratic, it must try to make up, in its own sphere, what has been faulted elsewhere. If it succeeds in any measure, the educator will have helped in part, at least, to remedy the larger social inequity and contributed to the democratization of his society.

The same principle holds true for higher levels of education. An educational system that excludes students from college and university because of financial need cannot call itself democratic. The problem of admitting students who are culturally disadvantaged up through their high school years is a harder one to solve. Here again, a democratic system is committed by its nature to attempt to mitigate this unjust consequence by special provisions until groups formerly excluded from the system can function within it more competitively.

In conclusion, we may observe that not only is a democratic view of society consistent with what we have come to understand by education, but that a democracy may be the only kind of society in which the full meaning of education can become manifest.

19

Concluding Remarks

THE MODELS COMPARED

THE perspectives discussed in the previous chapters represent different ways of looking at educational institutions. They are windows which afford a view of life in schools or colleges. Each portrayal offers valuable insights into the nature of management in education but none provides a complete picture. The five approaches are all valid analyses but their relevance depends on the situation and the type of institution concerned. In certain circumstances one model may appear to be applicable while another perspective may seem more appropriate in a different setting. There is no single approach capable of presenting a total framework for our understanding of educational institutions, as Baldridge *et al*. (1978) demonstrate:

> [...] the search for an all-encompassing model is simplistic, for no one model can delineate the intricacies of decision processes in complex organisations such as universities and colleges [...] there is a pleasant parsimony about having a single model that summarises a complicated world for us. This is not bad except when we allow our models to blind us to important features of the organisation.

The five models differ along crucial dimensions but taken together they provide a comprehensive appraisal of the nature of management in educational institutions. We have chosen to emphasize four main aspects of organizations and it is useful to reconsider these elements in comparing the five perspectives.

There are significant differences in the assumptions made about the *goals* of educational organizations. Formal models over that objectives are set at the institutional level. It is thought that goals are determined by senior staff and the support of other teachers is taken for granted. The activities of schools and colleges are then evaluated in the light of these official purposes.

Democratic models suggest that members of an organization agree on its goals. These approaches have a harmony bias in that they assume that it is always possible for staff to reach agreement based on common values. Unlike formal perspectives the objectives are not imposed from above but emerge from a participative process.

Political models differ from both the formal and democratic models in stressing the goals of subunits or departments rather than institutional objectives. Moreover there is conflict as groups seek to promote their purposes. Goals are unstable as subunits engage in negotiation and alliances form and break down.

Subjective models emphasize the goals of individuals rather than institutional or group purposes. The concept of organizational objectives is supplanted by the view that individuals have personal aims. Schools and colleges are regarded as the subjective creations of the people within them and the only reality is their individual perceptions of the organization. Goals attributed to organizations are thought to be the purposes of the most powerful individuals within them.

Ambiguity models claim that goals are problematic. While other perspectives assume that objectives are clear at institutional, group or individual levels the ambiguity approach suggests that goals are opaque. Objectives are also regarded as an unreliable guide to behaviour. In this view it is mistaken to regard policies or events as a corollary of the goals of the institution.

The notion of organizational *structure* takes on different meanings within the various perspectives. Formal and democratic models regard structures as objective realities. Individuals hold defined positions in the organization and working relationships are assumed to be strongly influenced by these official positions. Formal models treat structures as hierarchical with decisions being passed down from the leader. Democratic models present structures as lateral with all members taking part in the decision process.

Political models portray structure as one of the unstable and conflictual elements of the institution. The design of the structure is thought to reflect the interests to be served by the organization. The elements within the structure may become the settings for conflict between interest groups anxious to promote their policy objectives.

Subjective models regard organizational structure as a product of the relationships of individuals rather than a fixed entity which constrains the behaviour of its participants. The interaction of members of the organization is reflected in the structure which is valid only as long as it accurately represents those relationships.

Ambiguity models assume that organizational structure is one of the problematic aspects of institutions. Structure is ambiguous because of the uncertain relationships between loosely coupled subunits. The relevance of structure may be further compromised by the fluid participation of members in committees and other forums.

Relations with external groups are an increasingly important consideration for educational institutions if they are to survive and prosper. These links with the *environment* are portrayed in very different ways by the various perspectives. Some of the formal approaches tend to regard schools and colleges as 'closed systems' relatively impervious to outside influences. Other formal theories typify educational organizations as 'open systems', responding to the needs of their communities and building a positive image to attract new clients.

Democratic models tend to be inadequate in explaining relationships with the environment. Policy is thought to be determined within a participatory framework making it difficult to locate responsibility for decisions. Heads may be held accountable for outcomes which do not enjoy their personal support, leading to confusion among external groups and stress for the leader. Democratic approaches gloss over this difficulty by the unrealistic assumption that heads are always in agreement with decisions and are thus expected to be in a good position to explain them to outside bodies.

Political models tend to portray relationships with the environment as unstable. External bodies are regarded as interest groups participating in the complex bargaining process which is thought to be characteristic of decision-making in education. Internal and external groups may form alliances to press for the adoption of certain policies. Interaction with the environment is seen as a key aspect of an essentially political decision process.

In subjective models the environment is treated primarily as a source of the meanings placed on events by people within the organization. Individuals are thought to interpret situations in different ways and these variations are attributed to differences in the backgrounds of, and external influences upon, participants.

Ambiguity models regard the environment as a source of uncertainty which contributes to the unpredictability of organizations. The signals from outside groups are often unclear and contradictory, adding to the confusion inside schools and colleges. Interpretation of messages from a turbulent environment may be difficult thus further emphasizing the ambiguity of the decision process.

The styles of *leadership* inevitably reflect the particular features of the diverse models of management. Within formal perspectives it is thought that the official leader has a key role in decision-making, determining goals and formulating policy. Heads and principals are located at the apex of a hierarchy and they are acknowledged as the leaders both inside and outside the institution. It is assumed that the leader possesses much of the organization's power.

In democratic models policies are thought to emerge from a complex process of discussion at committees and other settings, both formal and informal. Influence is distributed widely within the institution and the leader is one participant in a collegial style of decision-making. Heads are assumed to have the prime responsibility for the promotion of consensus among their fellow professionals. A hierarchical approach is regarded as inappropriate for participative organizations.

Political models assume that leaders are active participants in the process of bargaining and negotiation which characterizes decision-making in organizations. Heads and principals have significant resources of power which they are able to deploy in support of their interests and objectives. Leaders may also mediate between groups in order to develop acceptable policy outcomes.

Subjective models de-emphasize the concept of leadership preferring to stress the personal attributes of individuals rather than their official positions in the organization. Leaders are assumed to have their own values and objectives which necessarily influence their interpretation of events. Heads and principals may be able to exert control over colleagues by enunciating institutional policies in line with their own personal interests and requiring the compliance of staff with these interpretations.

Ambiguity models stress the uncertainty facing leaders and the difficulties associated with the management of unpredictability.

There are two schools of thought about the most appropriate leadership strategies for conditions of ambiguity. One mode is to engage in various tactical machinations in an approach similar to those adopted by political leaders. The alternative stance is to adopt an unobtrusive style with an emphasis on personnel and structural issues. Here the leader sets the framework for decision-making but avoids direct involvement in the policy- making process.

The five perspectives differ significantly in the ways in which they treat goals, structure, environment and leadership. There are also notable variations in respect of other aspects of institutional management. The major features of the five models are identified in Table 19.1.

Table 19.1

Comparison of Five Models of Management

Elements of Management	*Formal*	*Democratic*	*Political*	*Subjective*	*Ambiguity*
Level at which goals are determined	Institutional	Institutional	Subunit	Individual	Unclear
Process by which goals are determined	Set by leaders	Agreement	Conflict	Problematic May be imposed by leaders	Unpredictable
Relationship between goals and decisions	Decisions based on goals	Decisions based on agreed goals	Decisions based on goals of dominant coalitions	Individual behaviour based on personal objectives	Decision unrelated to goals
Nature of decision process	Rational	Collegial	Political	Personal	Garbage can
Nature of structure	Objective reality Hierarchical	Objective reality Lateral	Setting for subunit conflict	Constructed through human interaction	Problematic
Links with environment	May be 'closed' or 'open' Head accountable	Accountability blurred by shared decision making	Unstable External bodies portrayed as interest groups	Source of individual meanings	Source of uncertainty
Style of leadership	Head establishes goals and initiates policy	Head seeks to promote consensus	Head is both participant and mediator	Problematic May be perceived as a form of control	May be tactical or unobtrusive

APPLYING THE MODELS TO SCHOOLS AND COLLEGES

The five perspectives represent conceptually distinct approaches to the management of educational institutions. However, it is rare for a single model to capture the reality of management in any particular school or college. Rather aspects of several perspectives are present in different proportions of each institution. The validity of the various models depends on five overlapping considerations:

1. The *size* of the institution is a key influence on the nature of management structure and process. A small two teacher primary school necessarily operates very differently from a large multi-department polytechnic. The two primary teachers are likely to determine policy by informal agreement while the head is acknowledged as the official leader by external groups and individuals. It may be appropriate to regard the management of such schools as comprising elements of both the democratic and formal models.

In large and complex institutions such as polytechnics and colleges there are numerous decision points leading to the development of alternative power centres. Staff may owe their first loyalty to their discipline and their department. These sub-units compete for the resources they require to advance their objectives in a process encapsulated by the political model. In certain circumstances the situation may be so fluid that the ambiguity perspective may appear to be appropriate.

2. The nature of the *organizational structure* may have a significant impact on the ways in which schools and colleges are managed. Heads who establish participative machinery may be motivated by a desire to involve professional colleagues in decision-making. The intention then is to create a democratic framework for policy formulation. However, the introduction of committees and working parties also provides a focus for political behaviour. Interest groups seek representation on these bodies and engage in bargaining and alliance building. The democratic and political dimensions are both enhanced by the introduction of a participative structure while the formal per-

spective necessarily has a reduced validity in these circumstances.

3. The nature of the managemnt process depends on the amount of *time* which participants are able and willing to devote to the wider organizational and managerial aspects of their work. In the primary sector teachers have full-time classroom responsibilities and only the head is available to deal with management issues during the school day. This fact suggests that the formal model is likely to apply to most primary schools. In secondary schools, and particularly in post school institutions, staff have periods of nonteaching time which they may be able to devote to committee work or to other managerial activities. The existence of this 'free' time is an important precondition for the development of democratic and political approaches.

The validity of democratic models may be circumscribed by the reluctance of staff to participate in decision-making. Where teachers opt out of committees and working parties they may be signalling their indifference to a participative approach. This tends to reduce the appropriateness of democratic perspectives and may also limit the applicability of political models. Where individuals ascribe different meanings to structural devices like committees, the subjective approach may appear to be particularly relevant.

4. The *availability of resources* is likely to play a part in determining the relevance of the various models. In periods of expansion it may be possible to adopt a rational approach to the distribution of resources or to rely on a collegial stance. When resources are limited departments face the possibility of cutbacks in staff levels or reductions in capitation or equipment. Such threats to the viability of academic units are likely to lead to these groups seeking to defend their interests. Committees and working parties may begin to resemble political arenas as subunits seek to retain existing resource levels. Davies and Morgan (1983) chart the shift from formal and democratic approaches to a political perspective as resources dwindle:

> As long as powerful individuals and groups received what they perceived to be reasonable shares of expanding resources, the

> core organisational coalitions were maintained in relative harmony [...] As resources to meet the policy commitments and funding demands of competing organizational groups have diminished, institutional administrators have experienced an increased level of conflict.

5. The nature and rate of *change in the environment* are additional considerations which impinge on the process of management inside schools and colleges. In periods of stability institutions may be able to adopt formal or democratic approaches to the internal operation of educational institutions. When the environment is turbulent and unpredictable the ambiguity model may be particularly appropriate. Doubts over levels of funding and the size of pupil or student intakes are major sources of instability in the 1980s leading to confusion within institutions.

It may be possible to conclude that small schools are correctly typified as formal or democratic organizations, especially in periods of stability. Equally, large, multipurpose colleges undergoing rapid change may be explained best by political or ambiguity models. The large number of schools lying between these two extremes are likely to possess features of all five models which vary in significance from time to time and from one activity to another. Adherents of the subjective model would add that much depends on the perceptions of individual staff and pupils.

> Each set of models shades into the next because each model is necessarily partial [...] What is important will vary from one situation to the next, and from one observer or participant to another[...] Usefulness is not an objective criterion; it depends on the attitudes, values, beliefs, skills and experiences of the user. (Cuthbert, 1984).

ATTEMPTS AT SYNTHESIS

Each of the five models presented in this volume offers valid insights into the nature of management in schools and colleges. Yet all the perspectives are limited in that they do not give a complete picture of educational institutions. Rather they turn the spotlight on particular aspects of the organization and consequently leave other features in the shade. Some writers argue that it is possible to obtain a comprehensive appraisal of organizations by using elements from some or all of the models. Ellstrom (1983) makes the case for such a synthesis:

> [...] each model emphasises certain variables, while others are de-emphasised or ignored. Consequently, each model can be expected to give only partial understanding of the organisational reality. [...] it might be possible to obtain a more comprehensive understanding of organisations by integrating the [...] models into an overarching framework.
>
> A basic assumption [...] is the idea of complementarity [...] That is, the models are viewed as compatible, rather than as mutually exclusive alternatives.

Enderud (1980) and Davies and Morgan (1983) have developed integrative models incorporating ambiguity, political, collegial and formal perspectives. These syntheses are based on the assumption that policy formation proceeds through four distinct phases which all require adequate time if the decision is to be successful. Attempts by leaders to omit certain stages or to hurry issues through the process may lead to subsequent breakdown or create the necessity for a loopback to earlier phases.

The models posit an initial period of high ambiguity as problems, solutions and participants interact at appropriate choice opportunities. This anarchic phase serves to identify the issues and acts as a preliminary sifting mechanism. If conducted properly it should lead to an initial coupling of problems with potential solutions.

The output of the ambiguous period is regarded as the input to the political phase. This stage is characterized by bargaining and negotiations and usually involves relatively few participants in small, closed committees. The outcome is likely to be a broad measure of agreement on possible solutions.

In the third collegial phase the participants committed to the proposed solution attempt to persuade less active members to accept the compromise reached during the political stage. The solutions are tested against criteria of acceptability and feasibility and may result in minor changes. Eventually this process should lead to agreed policy outcomes and a degree of commitment to the decision.

The final phase is the formal or bureaucratic stage during which agreed policy may be subject to modification in the light of administrative considerations. The outcome of this period is a policy which is both legitimate and operationally satisfactory. The Davies and Morgan (1983) version of the model is shown as Figure 19.1.

Enderud (1980) emphasizes that the significance of each phase varies according to the different perceptions of participants as well as the nature of the issue:

> With its four phases, the model [...] reflects a mix of different realities in [...] decision making—an anarchistic, a political, a collegial and a bureaucratic reality—which may all be part of any one joint decision process. This composite picture will be one of the reasons why different participants often can interpret the same decision as largely anarchic, political, collegial or bureaucratic, according to the phase which is most visible to them, because of their own participation or for other reasons.

Although Enderud acknowledges that the individual interpretations of participants may influence the visibility of the models the subjective perspective is not featured explicitly in the syntheses discussed by him or by Davies and Morgan (1983). Theodossin (1983), however, does link the phenomenological approach to the formal or systems model using an analytical continuum. He argues that a systems perspective is the most appropriate way of explaining national developments while individual and subunit activities may be understood best by utilizing the individual meanings of participants:

> Asked to account for and to explain national movements (e.g. secondary school comprehensivisation, the reorganisation of teacher training), we are more likely to find that a systems perspective is an appropriate form of conceptual organisation: to think in terms of thousands of private biographies of the participating individuals is clearly to concern oneself of with more detail than one can

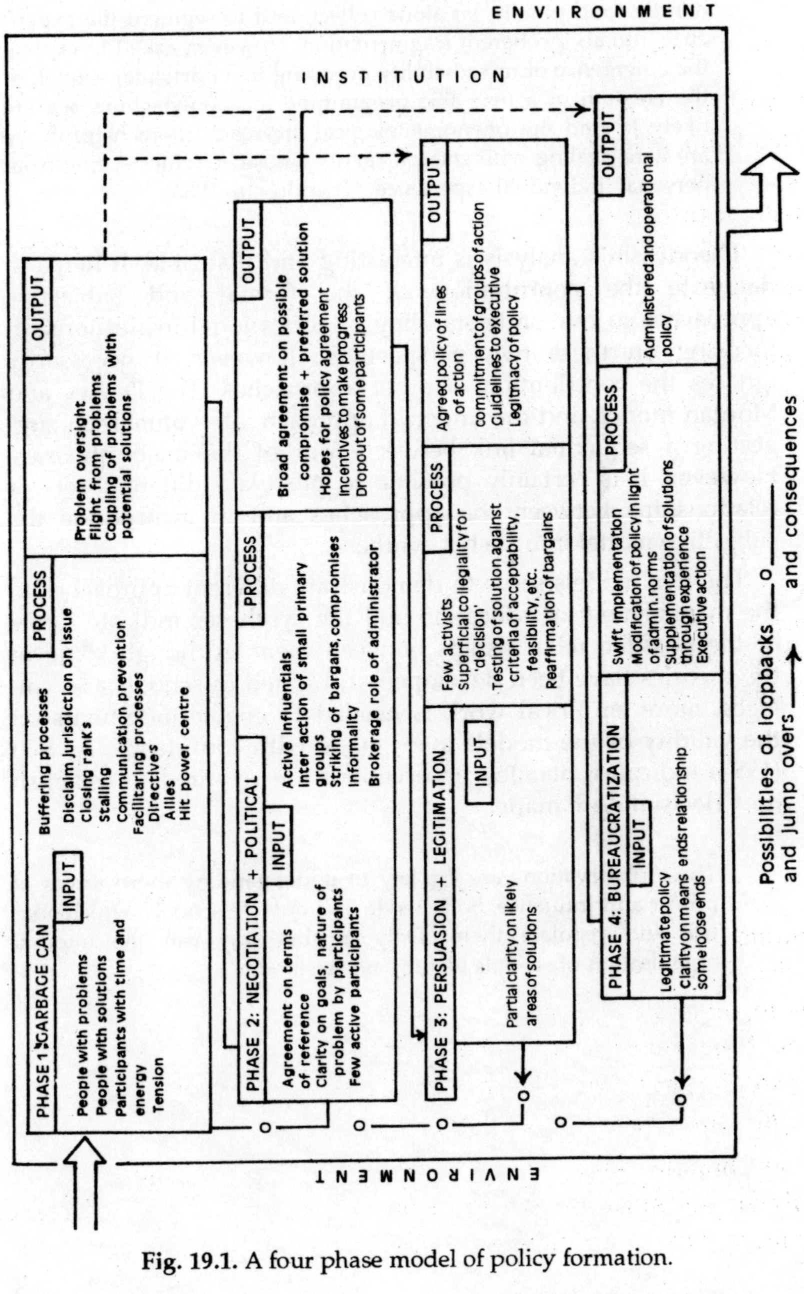

Fig. 19.1. A four phase model of policy formation.

> handle conceptually, let alone collect, and to segment the experience into an incoherent fragmentation. However, asked to explain the emergence of mixed-ability grouping in a particular school, or the creation of a new BSc programme in a polytechnic, we are likely to find the phenomenological approach more helpful: we are here dealing with change agents whose activities spring from personal, individual experience. (Theodossin, 1983).

Theodossin's analysis is interesting and plausible. It helps to delineate the contribution of the formal and subjective approaches to our understanding of educational institutions. In focusing on these two perspectives, however, it necessarily ignores the contribution of other approaches. The Davies and Morgan model, and the Enderud approach, are valuable in suggesting a sequential link between four of the major theories. However, it is certainly possible to postulate different sets of relationships between the approaches and to incorporate the subjective model into such a synthesis.

The five models serve to demonstrate different approaches to the management of education and the syntheses indicate a few of the possible relationships between them. Although some of the theories have been developed and tested in schools and colleges, more empirical work is needed to enable judgments on the validity of the models to be made with confidence. As Bell (1984) indicates, detailed observations are required to establish how decisions are made:

> These observations are the key to understanding those forces of power and influence, both inside and outside schools, which control and regulate them. Only in this way can the internal organisation of schools be fully understood.